Trauma-Informed Care

Trauma-Informed Care

A Casebook

Cognella Casebook Series for the Human Services

Jerry L. Johnson and George Grant, Jr.

Grand Valley State University

SAN DIEGO

Bassim Hamadeh, CEO and Publisher
Amy Smith, Senior Project Editor
Alia Bales, Production Editor
Jess Estrella, Senior Graphic Designer
Stephanie Kohl, Licensing Coordinator
Natalie Piccotti, Director of Marketing
Kassie Graves, Vice President of Editorial
Jamie Giganti, Director of Academic Publishing

3970 Sorrento Valley Blvd., Ste. 500, San Diego, CA 92121

To my wonderful parents, Lee and Joanne Johnson, who continue to encourage and support me in my endeavors ... you are the best parents a man could have.

—Jerry L. Johnson

I want to thank my sisters, Alice D. Denton and Alyson D. Grant, for their wisdom, guidance, and love.

—George Grant, Jr.

BRIEF CONTENTS

DETAILED CONTENTS

PREFACE

WELCOME TO OUR new Casebook Series for the Human Services. This series of books is designed to improve professional clinical practice education across the human services. As the editors, we are thrilled by our partnership with Cognella to make these books available to educators and students across the human services spectrum.

This text, *Trauma-Informed Care: A Casebook*, will enhance the clinical preparation of students and practitioners across the helping professions, who are either presently working with this population or interested in doing so in the future.

As graduate and undergraduate social work educators, we (Johnson and Grant) understand the struggle to find quality clinical practice materials that translate well into a classroom setting. In the past, we used case materials from our practice careers. Then, in the early 2000s, we edited and published the Allyn and Bacon Casebook Series. The original Casebook Series covered eight different practice areas (substance abuse, mental health, domestic violence, sexual abuse, adoption, foster care, community practice, and medical social work).

Although we were happy with the first series, we wanted to improve its quality and usefulness in the classroom, while updating the topics to more closely match current trends. Over the years, we sought and received extensive feedback from readers and faculty adopters about the strengths and weaknesses of the previous series. Most important, we asked specific questions about each case's ease of use in the classroom.

In preparing the new series, we relied heavily on this feedback, resulting in the book you are reading, and forthcoming Casebooks in the series. We believe the new Casebook Series for the Human Services, as evidenced by this text, published by our friends at Cognella, achieves our goal of enhanced learning opportunities and ease of classroom use.

Our goal is always to give students the chance to study, assess, and analyze how experienced practitioners think about practice, struggle to resolve practice dilemmas, and make clinical decisions to meet the needs of their clients. We believe the structure of our cases, written in narrative voice and story format, allows readers access to the minds of experienced practitioners in a way that will improve engagement, assessment, diagnosis, and treatment-planning skills, but more important, enhance the way students think about their clients and practice.

Overall, we intend for the Casebook Series for the Human Services to provide a learning experience that:

1. Provides readers an overview of our previously published Advanced Multiple Systems (AMS) approach to practice (Johnson & Grant, 2005). This practice perspective describes an approach to practice as either a simple guide to working the cases in the Casebooks and for later in their practice careers.

    More important, we define AMS through a series of Guiding Practice Principles, developed by the editors over the course of long careers, study, and experience. Our Guiding Practice Principles offer a way for practitioners to think about and act in practice settings to help guide successful engagement, leading to a positive helping experience for clients and professionals.

2. Offers personal and intimate glimpses into the thinking and actions of experienced practitioners as they work with diverse clients across different practice settings. In working through each case, students have the chance to demonstrate their understanding of the clinical and social issues presented, while learning to use high-level "assessment thinking" through the various questions and exercises included to help make sense of each case.

3. Provides multiple opportunities to develop comprehensive clinical assessments, diagnoses, treatment plans and emergency plans for a variety of presenting problems from a diverse client group. These exercises also provide excellent opportunities for large and small group discussions to enhance the learning experience.

4. Offers students an up-to-date critical review of best practices for the practice area focused on in each book. The final chapter of each book will guide readers through the professional literature and evidence-based research to provide an extensive review of current practice trends in the field of study.

As former practitioners, we chose the cases to be featured carefully. Each case making "the cut" focuses on the process (thinking, planning, and decision-making) of clinical practice and not necessarily on techniques or outcomes. We chose cases based on one simple criterion: it provided the best possible opportunity for excellence in practice education. We asked authors to "teach practice" by considering cases that were interesting and difficult, regardless of outcome, and to let the readers into their internal thought processes as their case progressed.

In addition, each case focuses on client engagement and cultural responsiveness as important aspects of the practice process. As we like to remind our social work students, there are two words in the title of the profession: "social" and "work." For the "work" to occur, students must learn to master the "social"—primarily, client engagement and relationship building in a culturally inviting and responsive manner.

As you will learn in Chapter 1, clinical practice is relationship based and, from our perspective, relies more on the processes involved in relationship building and client engagement than on technical intervention skills. Successful practice is often rooted more in the ability of practitioners to develop open and trusting relationships with client(s) than on their ability to employ specific methods of intervention.

Yet, this critically important element of practice is often ignored, or only mentioned in passing as a "given." Our experience with students, employees, and practitioner/trainees over nearly four decades suggests that it is wrong to assume that students and/or practitioners have competent engagement or relationship-building skills. Developing a professional relationship based in trust and openness, where clients feel safe to dialogue about the most intimate, and sometimes most embarrassing, events in their lives, is the primary responsibility of the practitioner. Hence, each case presentation tries to provide a sense of this difficult and often elusive process, along with ways each author managed the emerging client relationship.

TARGET AUDIENCE

We believe this series is applicable and useful for education and training programs from community college to advanced undergraduate and graduate programs in the helping professions. We also know of many social agencies that provide our previous texts to new employees for review and practice. Hence, the Casebooks are appropriate in social work; counseling psychology; counseling; mental health; psychology; and specialty disciplines, such as marriage and family therapy, substance abuse, and mental health degree or certificate programs. Any educational or training program designed to prepare students to work with clients in a helping capacity may find the Casebooks useful as a learning tool.

STRUCTURE OF CASES

The cases in this book have two different formats. In Chapters 2, 3, and 4, the cases are presented as in-depth narratives. Written as stories, the authors provide an inside look into actual therapy sessions as they build rapport, develop client engagement, and make decisions about how best to gather personal information leading to an accurate assessment, diagnosis, and treatment plan. These stories often include client–practitioner dialogue to help readers peer inside a confidential therapy session, and periodically explore practice literature to explain certain dilemmas as they arise in the case.

The narrative case studies are designed to maximize critical thinking, the use of professional literature, evidenced-based practice knowledge, and classroom discussion in the learning process. At various points throughout each case, the editors include a series of thought-provoking and/or action-based questions to guide and enhance the learning process. We want readers to collect evidence on different sides of an issue, evaluate that evidence, and then develop a professional position that they can defend in writing and/or discussion with other students in the classroom or seminar setting.

Chapters 5 and 6 use a different case study format. In these cases, the authors completed intake and assessment interviews and compiled the client information on a standard comprehensive assessment form, minus clinical conclusions, meaning, or summaries. Those sections of the assessment form are left blank. Readers are asked to read and understand the client information and complete each section of the assessment that requires "assessment thinking," that is, to develop their own clinical conclusions, meaning, and summaries, as required. At the end of each case, readers can develop a comprehensive narrative assessment based on the client's information, an accurate clinical diagnoses, an appropriate treatment plan, and an emergency/safety plan. Moreover, readers are asked to determine the client's stage of change (see Chapter 1) for each clinical diagnosis. These cases make for excellent in-class exercises, teaching both clinical decision-making and professional assessment writing.

We hope that you find the cases and our formats as instructive and helpful in your courses, as we have in ours. We have field tested these two formats in our courses, finding that students respond well to the length, depth, and rigor of the case presentations.

ORGANIZATION OF THIS TEXT

We organized this book on practice with trauma-informed care to maximize its utility in any course. Chapter 1 provides an overview of our Advanced Multiple Systems (AMS) practice approach, focusing on a series of Guiding Practice Principles gleaned from the editors' nearly 80 years of combined professional experience. The AMS is one potential organizing tool for students to use while reading and evaluating the cases.

The Guiding Practice Principles provide important ways of thinking and approaching clients in all practice settings to help the engagement, assessment, and treatment process. These principles are not connected to theory, method, or practice setting/role. Like a professional code of ethics, the Guiding Practice Principles offer critical elements for effective clinical and relationship decisions.

In Chapter 2, Dianne Green-Smith tells the powerful narrative story of several therapy sessions with Mr. Chuckie, a 77-year-old African American male who suffered the trauma of Hurricane Katrina and its aftermath. Over the course of this chapter, Green-Smith dives deeply into the mostly unpublicized events and human effects this major environmental, governmental, economic, and human tragedy had on its victims. This chapter also focuses on the struggles professional practitioners often experience when working with clients presenting with significant trauma.

In Chapter 3, Ash Herald presents the troubling case focusing on Jordan, an adolescent female who identifies as male who experiences significant personal, family, and social issues on his way to embracing his desired gender identity. This case demonstrates how communities, including family, peers, religious institutions, and especially schools, assist in supporting the psychological and physical trauma experienced by adolescents attempting to find their way in life, especially when that path involves gender identity issues.

In Chapter 4, Elizabeth Sharda provides a look into the life and world of Lauren, an adolescent girl forced into the foster care system, and into a foster care placement that may not be suitable for her situation. Sharda examines how Lauren copes as she attempts to escape her life of parental issues and trauma, in the context of trying to find a place where she can heal.

In Chapter 5, Melissa Villarreal presents the case of Gary Greenwell, a successful local salesman and involved community member, who reveals how he lived through a childhood filled with trauma, rape at the hands of his father and friends, and loss. In this case, Villarreal provides insight into the client's struggle to live a normal life as a husband and father while concealing the secrets of a horrific childhood for more than 30 years.

In Chapter 6, Salvador Lopez-Arias offers the case of Suzie Burnett. Suzie is a lesbian woman in a long-term committed relationship who suffers with problems on the job because of her gender identity and desire to surgically transition from female to male. Her gender identity creates a hostile work environment. This leads to an employer-mandated assessment where Suzie reveals a life of trauma, substance use, and social disruption.

In the final chapter, Jerry L. Johnson and Glen Brookhouse provide a comprehensive review of best practice methods in the field of trauma and trauma-informed care. The authors present the current literature and research/evaluation results to determine best practices.

ACKNOWLEDGMENTS

We would like to thank the contributors to this text for their hard work, experience, and willingness to share their work with our audience. We would also like to thank Amy Smith, Laura Pasquale, and all the professionals at Cognella for being great to work with, for their faith in the Casebook Series, and in our ability to manage multiple manuscripts at once. Additionally, we want to thank our students over the years for serving as "guinea pigs" as we refined our case formats for publication. Their willingness to provide honest feedback contributes mightily to this series.

Jerry L. Johnson: I want to thank my wife, Cheryl, for her support and willingness to give me the time and encouragement to write and edit. I also thank my equine herd, Joey, Hope, Zelda, Ruby, Pip, Rome, Bray, Tommy, Mister Mule, Hershey, Maddy, and Oprah for helping provide peace in my life.

George Grant, Jr.: I dedicate this book and all my work to my wife Beverly F. Grant. Thank you for your love, support, and encouragement.

REFERENCE

Johnson, J. L., & Grant G., Jr. (2005). *Casebook: Substance abuse.* Allyn & Bacon.

CHAPTER 1

A Multiple Systems Approach to Practice in Trauma-Informed Care

Jerry L. Johnson and George Grant, Jr.

IN HIS TEXT, we help readers build practice knowledge, values, and skills to work with clients presenting with trauma-based problems and diagnoses, in the context of a trauma-informed care approach to treatment. Clients may present with a single trauma-based diagnosis, multiple trauma-based diagnoses, trauma-based issues that are not diagnosable, or with co-occurring substance use and/or other disorders.

We define *trauma* as exposure to experiences that cause intense physical and psychological stress reactions. According to the Substance Abuse and Mental Health Services Administration (SAMHSA, 2012), trauma results from an event, series of events, or set of circumstances that is experienced by an individual as physically or emotionally harmful or threatening and that has lasting adverse effects on the individual's functioning and physical, social, emotional, or spiritual well-being. As stated above, people may present with a single specific traumatic event, whereas others, especially those seeking mental health or substance abuse services, have been exposed to multiple or chronic traumatic events.

According to the *Diagnostic and Statistical Manual of Mental Disorders*, 5th Edition (DSM-5), trauma occurs when a person experiences or is exposed "to actual or threatened death, serious injury, or sexual violence" (American Psychiatric Association [APA], 2013, p. 271). Yet, the definition of psychological trauma is not limited to diagnostic criteria; that is, many practitioners have ceased considering trauma-related symptoms as indicators of a mental disorder. Instead, these clinicians consider these symptoms as a normal part of human survival instincts or as "adaptive mental processes involved in the assimilation and integration of new information with intense survival emphasis which exposure to the trauma has provided" (Turnbull, 1998, p. 88). These normal adaptive processes only become pathological if they are inhibited in some way (Turnbull, 1998) or if they are left unacknowledged and therefore untreated (Scott, 1990).

Others define trauma more broadly. For example, Horowitz (1989) defined it as a sudden and forceful event that overwhelms a person's ability to respond, recognizing that a trauma need not involve actual physical harm to oneself; an event can be traumatic if it contradicts one's worldview and overpowers one's ability to cope.

The art and science of accurately assessing, diagnosing, treatment planning, and intervening successfully with clients presenting with trauma-based issues is difficult. This effort is made more difficult when trauma-based problems interact and exacerbate with co-occurring substance use disorders. Not only are treatments complex, but the complexity and difficulty is exacerbated by the short turnaround time many organizations and funding sources (i.e., private health insurance, etc.) require for reimbursement. Because accurate assessment and diagnosis is crucial if treatment is to be successfully matched to client need (Johnson, 2004), these skills are important to know, understand, and master.

In this text, we provide a rare opportunity to study the processes and strategies involved in meeting, engaging, assessing, and treating unique clients, all with at least one trauma-based problem, taken from the caseloads of experienced practitioners. We include five cases, each written with deep and rich case detail designed to plunge readers into the thinking, planning, and approaches of the practitioners/authors. We challenge you to study their thinking and methods, to understand their clinical decision-making, and then to think critically using your own background and experience to discover and propose alternative ways of working with the same clients. In other words, what would you do if you were the primary practitioner responsible for these cases? Would you approach these cases in a similar or different manner? What are your reasons for any differences?

Before diving into the cases, this chapter introduces the Advanced Multiple Systems (AMS) practice perspective, along with the Guiding Practice Principles underlying the AMS. We include the AMS and its principles for three reasons. First, AMS can be a guide to help assess and analyze the cases in this text. Each case chapter will ask you to complete a multiple systems assessment, diagnosis, treatment, and intervention plan. The AMS provides a theoretical and practical approach for these exercises. Second, we hope you find that the AMS makes conceptualizing cases clearer in your practice environment. Third, the AMS and the Guiding Practice Principles offer an experience-based way of thinking and acting about and with clients across the practice spectrum. The AMS and the Guiding Practice Principles offer young and experienced practitioners alike a time-tested way to think about and approach clients in clinical and other practice settings, and they provide the foundation on which successful practice rests.

We do not believe the AMS is the only way, or necessarily even the best way for all practitioners to think about clients. We simply know, through experience, that the AMS and the Guiding Practice Principles are an effective way to think about practice with clients from diverse backgrounds and with different needs. Although there are many approaches to practice, the AMS offers an effective way to place clinical decisions in the context of client lives and experiences, giving engagement and treatment a chance to be productive.

ADVANCED MULTIPLE SYSTEMS (AMS) PRACTICE

Sociological Roots

Whether the point of interest is a great power state or a minor literary mood, a family, a prison, and a creed—these are the kinds of questions the best social analysts have asked. They are the intellectual pivots of classic studies of (person) in society—and they are the questions inevitably raised by any mind possessing the sociological imagination. For that imagination is the capacity to shift from one perspective to another—from the political to the psychological; from examination of a single family to comparative assessment of the national budgets of the world; from the theological school to the military establishment; from considerations of an oil industry to studies of contemporary poetry. It is the capacity to range from the most impersonal and remote transformations to the most intimate features of the human self—and see the relations between the two. Back of its use is always the urge to know the social and historical meaning of the individual in the society and in the period in which he (or she) has his quality and his (or her) being (Mills, 1959, p. 7; parentheses added).

Sociologist C. Wright Mills provided an important description of the sociological imagination. As it turns out, Mills's sociological imagination is also an apt description of the AMS. Mills believed that linking people's "private troubles" to "public issues" (p. 2) was the most effective way to understand people and their problems, by placing them in social and historical context. It forces investigators to contextualize individuals and families in the framework of the larger social, political, economic, and historical environments in which they live. Ironically, this is also the goal of clinical practice (Germain & Gitterman, 1996; Longres, 2000). Going further, Mills (1959) stated:

> We have come to know that every individual lives, from one generation to the next, in some society; that he (or she) lives out a biography, and that he (or she) lives it out within some historical sequence. By the fact of his (or her) living he (or she) contributes, however minutely, to the shaping of this society and to the course of its history, even as he (or she) is made by society and by its historical push and shove (p. 6; parentheses added).

Mills (1959) proposed this approach to help understand links between people, their lives, and the larger environment. Yet, while laying the theoretical groundwork for social research, Mills also provided the theoretical foundation for an effective approach to clinical practice. This suggests three relevant points directly related to clinical practice.

1. It is crucial to recognize the relationships between people's personal issues and strengths (private troubles) and the issues (political, economic, social, historical, and legal) and strengths of the multiple systems environment (public issues) in which people live. This includes recognizing and integrating issues and strengths at the micro (individual, family, extended kin, etc.), mezzo (local community), and macro (state, region, national, and international policy, laws, political, economic, and social) levels during client engagement, assessment, treatment, and aftercare.

2. Understanding these relationships can lead people toward change. We speak here about second-order change, or, significant change that makes a long-term difference in people's lives; the kind of change that alters the fundamental rules of an existing system, helping people see themselves differently in relationship to their world. Second-order change is often forced from the outside of the system (or person). This level of change becomes possible when people make links across their world in a way that makes sense to them (Freire, 1993). In other words, clients become "empowered" to change when they understand their life in the context of their world, how often their lives have been limited or defined by that world, and realizing they have previously unknown or unimagined choices in how they live, think, feel, believe, and act.

3. Any assessment, clinical diagnosis, or treatment plan excluding multiple systems links does not provide a holistic picture of people's lives, their troubles, and/or their strengths. The opportunity for change lessens when client history is overlooked. A practitioner cannot learn too much about their clients—their lives; their attitudes, beliefs, and values stemming

from their local environment; the influence of important relationships; and their sense of hope for a better future.

AMS OVERVIEW

First, we define the foundational concept, the multiple systems perspective. Understanding these ideas provides the foundation for a common language and idea of the concepts used throughout the remainder of this chapter.

Multiple Systems Perspective

Generally, a systems approach emphasizes the connectedness between people and their problems to the complex interrelationships existing in their world (Timberlake et al., 2002). To explain these connections, systems theory emphasizes three important concepts: wholeness, relationships, and homeostasis.

Wholeness refers to the way various parts or subsystems interact to form a whole. This idea asserts that systems cannot be understood or explained unless the connectedness of the subsystems to the whole is understood; that is, the nature of the relationships within the system and the roles people play within that system. In other words, the whole is greater than the sum of its parts. Moreover, systems theory also posits that change in one subsystem will affect change in the whole system.

Relationship refers to the patterns of interaction and overall structures existing within and between subsystems. The nature of these relationships is more important than the system itself. That is, when trying to understand or explain a system (individual, family, or organization, etc.), how subsystems connect through relationships, the characteristics of the relationships between subsystems, and how the subsystems interact provide clues to understanding the whole, and the problems needing treatment.

Hence, the application of systems theory is primarily based on understanding relationships. In systems (families, individuals, etc.), problems occur *between* people (relationships), not *in* them. Even individual diagnoses are looked at by how they affect self and others, along with how the symptoms and/or behavior is encouraged or maintained by relationships within the system. Hence, from this perspective people's internal problems relate to the nature of the relationships in the systems where they live and interact.

Homeostasis refers to the idea that systems strive to maintain and preserve the existing system, its rules and relationships, the status quo. For example, family members assume roles that serve to protect and maintain family stability, often at the expense of "needed" change, or their own individual health and well-being.

The natural tendency toward homeostasis in systems represents what we call the "dilemma of change," where a dilemma is a series of choices, none of which are obviously good (Johnson, 2004). This is best described as the apparent conflict occurring when clients approach moments of significant change. People struggle with the dilemma of change: Should they change, risking the unknown, or try remaining the same, even if the status quo is unhealthy or unproductive?

When individuals within systems change, this forces others within the system to change as well, even if only in relation to the individual trying to change. So, if a mother with a long-term substance use disorder suddenly finds sobriety, her newly found life will require everyone else in the family to change in relation to her, even if they do not want to change. This often starts a series of relationship reactions, sometimes leading to the reinstatement of homeostasis that could come in the form of mother relapsing to ensure the family status quo.

What do we mean then, by the term *multiple systems*? People (clients) are part of and interact with multiple systems simultaneously. These systems interact on many levels, ranging from the micro level (individual and families), the mezzo level (local community, institutions, organizations, the practitioner and their agency, etc.), to the macro level (culture, laws and policy, politics, oppression and discrimination, international events, etc.). How these various systems come together and interact comprise the "whole" that is the client. The nature of these interactions and relationships often helps explain the nature of a client's problems.

In practice, the client (individual, couple, family, etc.) is not the "system," but one of many interacting subsystems in a maze of other subsystems constantly interacting to create the system—the client plus elements from multiple subsystems at each level. It would be a mistake to view the client as the whole system, or that individual problems are not affected by other aspects of the system (family and beyond).

This level of understanding—the system as the whole produced through multiple system interactions—is the main unit of investigation for practice. It is too narrow to consider the client as a functioning independent system with peripheral involvement with others existing outside of their intimate world. These issues and relationships work together to help shape and mold the client who, in turn, shapes and molds their relationship to the other subsystems. Yet, the person-of-the-client is but one part of the system in question.

For example, an African American student may have every intention of being a top academic performer in his mostly White high school. During class one day, the teacher asks something of the student, leading him to question the teacher on her reasons for asking. In this young man's family and culture, it is not unusual to talk loudly, more loudly than what is often considered "normal" in a White environment.

The student's tone and volume encourage his White teacher to believe the student is being challenging or even threatening, depending on her subjective experience with students of color. The student is immediately sent to the principal's office for "acting out" and being "threatening," although he simply asked for clarification in the ways of his family and culture, but not his teacher's. This student then risks becoming labeled as "oppositional" among the other teachers, who his teacher talks to every day. He also risks being referred for therapy or counseling to treat his "oppositional defiant disorder." In this case, multiple systems interacted against what our fictional student believed and was taught about his right to question and seek clarification about teacher requests. Interacting systems collided to create a problem where none existed.

The AMS provides an organized framework for gathering, conceptualizing, and analyzing multiple system client data to help practitioners proceed with the helping process. Beginning with culturally responsive client engagement, a comprehensive multisystem assessment points toward a holistically based treatment plan that requires practitioners to select and utilize appropriate practice theories, models, and methods—or combinations thereof—that best fit the client's unique circumstances and needs.

The AMS is a perspective or framework for understanding clients. It relies on the practitioner's ability to use a variety of theories, models, and methods in their routine approach with clients. For example, an AMS practitioner will have the skills to apply different approaches to individual treatment (client centered, cognitive behavioral, etc.), family treatment (structural, narrative, Bowenian, etc.), couples therapy, group therapy, and to make arrangements for specialized care, if needed. They will also act as an advocate on behalf of their client.

Practitioners must also know how to determine, primarily through the early engagement and assessment process, which theory, model, or approach (e.g., direct or indirect) would work best for each client. Hence, successful practice using AMS relies heavily on the practitioner's ability to competently engage and assess client problems and strengths. Practitioners develop a sense of their client's personal interaction and relationship style—especially related to how they relate to authority figures—when determining which approach would best suit their circumstance. For example, a reserved, quiet, or thoughtful client or someone who lacks assertiveness may not be well-served by a directive, confrontational approach, regardless of the practitioner's preference. Elsewhere we provide a more detailed exploration of the AMS perspective (Johnson & Grant, 2006, 2007).

DIMENSIONS OF THE AMS ASSESSMENT

This section lists and provides brief explanations of the dimensions of information needed to operationalize the AMS from a client data collection and assessment perspective. Collecting client information according to the following dimensions will provide the multiple systems data needed to develop a systemic understand of each client.

Dimension 1: Client Description, Presenting Problem, and Referral

Beyond a physical and demographic description of clients, it is important to understand, from the client's perspective, the problems that have led to the first session. The practitioner shouldn't focus only on the problems that referral sources claim, but should also learn the client's idea of the presenting problem. Whatever the client says is the problem, is the problem that must be addressed first.

A good practitioner also should understand how a referral was made, when, and for what reason. If it is a mandated referral (i.e., court, probation or parole officer, etc.), it is helpful to discover the client's reaction to the referral. It is also important to explore the events or circumstances that led to the referral at that particular moment in time.

Dimension 2: Treatment/Therapy History

This dimension includes discussion of any type of therapy, counseling, education, or more intensive treatments, inclusive of any problem. That is, the practitioner explores past treatments for substance use, mental health, and other issues for the client and family members.

More than a place to record dates, places, and lengths of stay, this conversation should be targeted at what clients "thought" about their experiences. What did they like and dislike about the treatment, therapists, counselors, and/or programs, and what is the reasoning behind their beliefs? New clients should also be asked about their expectations of therapy and therapists. An experienced clinician can use this conversation to learn a lot about how best to engage new clients, based entirely on their report of past treatment experiences.

Dimension 3: Substance Use History

Given the prevalence of co-occurring disorders across the practice spectrum, especially in trauma-related cases, it is important for practitioners to gather substance use information about their client and their family, regardless of the client's presenting problem and/or the specialty of the organization. In this discussion, practitioners focus on age of first use of alcohol and other drugs for "recreation," substances used in the previous 30 days (including prescribed drugs), and their favorite substances used in what combinations. Careful attention should be paid to the substances that clients mix together, hoping to understand if the combination of substances can lead to an accidental overdose.

If there is evidence of regular and patterned substance use, it is also important to discover if clients (or their family members) have ever been diagnosed with a substance use disorder. Based on their understanding of the role substance use, as a co-occurring disorder, can have on other problems, experienced practitioners do not perform any assessment without first exploring the possibility of substance use issues.

Dimension 4: Mental Health History

Data collected in this dimension focuses on symptoms, behaviors, thoughts, and feelings regarding both mental health functioning, potential mental health disorders, and personal histories of trauma. Practitioners can use one of the many mental health screening instruments available, including instruments designed to understand exposure to traumatic events and experiences. If there is evidence of trauma exposure, here is where practitioners explore the occurrence of events or activities leading to trauma reactions in clients. As part of this dimension, practitioners explore past or present evidence of abuse and neglect (sexual, physical, emotional, domestic), exposure to violence, or being the victim of violence.

Practitioners should also seek to learn about suicidal thoughts and gestures in the past or present; tendencies toward violence against family, strangers, etc.; and other kinds of physicality that can stem from issues of mental health. It is also important to help understand the connections, if any, to the reports of mental problems and their substance use history.

Dimension 5: Family History

Taking a family history helps place the client and their problems in the context of their family, defined as anybody the client considers "family." The most effective family history is one that provides a look at three generations from the client presenting for therapy. Beyond the details of who is living or deceased, married or divorced, the practitioner explores the quality of relationships, problems across members and generations, and the level of support clients believe they receive from their families.

Experience teaches that problems, especially trauma-related and substance abuse problems, tend to "run" in families, across subsystems and generations. A three-generation genogram with problems noted on the genogram provides clinicians with a quick and comprehensive look across the family that often helps explain the client in different ways. Practitioners cannot collect "too much" family history and background.

Dimension 6: Social Support and Engagement

In this dimension, practitioners explore with clients their social connections and the value clients place on those connections. The overarching question to answer here is: "When your life hits the skids, who do you call for support?" Clinicians look to assess the degree to which people are connected to their community in productive ways, or whether they are disconnected, isolated, and/or alone.

The practitioner will explore the client's support group attendance, social clubs, friends, family, and other groups they may be involved in, now and in the past. Clients should also be asked about their membership at places of worship, their military history, coworkers, and/or any other group or people who they have found to be supportive. If they have quit these connections, it is important to discover their reasons for quitting. In addition, clients should be asked about their hobbies and what they like to do for fun. Have their interests narrowed over the years? Often, as problems become serious, people abandon activities, groups, and people, making their life narrow, losing the opportunity for positive social support (Johnson, 2004).

The supportive nature of engagements often deemed negative and counterproductive, like street gangs, should not be ignored. These groups exist because they provide disaffected people with a sense of purpose, connection, structure, rules, and meaning. That is, street gangs and these groups exist largely because their members cannot or do not find these important and meaningful connections in their families and communities. Involvement in these groups demonstrates how important meaningful social connections are to people.

Dimension 7: Culture

Although we provide a more extensive discussion of culture in practice later as a Guiding Practice Principle, it is important to inquire about the client's cultural values, beyond race, gender, ethnicity, sexual preferences, and faith traditions. Culture represents more than demographics. That is, how do the client's cultural values shape choices, behaviors, values, and meaning (Johnson, 2000)? Practitioners must be aware that one's culture presents a fertile area for relying on stereotype and personal bias. Understanding a client's culture has more to do with the ability to gather personal information from diverse clients than on a basic understanding of larger cultural groups and their tendencies. Practitioners are not concerned about how "Mexican families" operate, but rather about how the Mexican family in their office, who is right in front of them, operates and believes (Johnson, 2004).

Dimension 8: Biopsychosocial Connection

Developing an understanding of the impact of the biopsychosocial connection in clinical practice can be difficult. Certainly, in addition to the external effects of multiple systems on people, there is also the person as system to consider. After many years of trying different ways of explaining the biopsychosocial connection unsuccessfully, I heard the following explanation that makes the relationship clear. For those readers sensitive to the use of the following analogy, I apologize. However, students have suggested that this analogy makes the biopsychosocial interaction clear.

1. A person's biological dimension (including genetics), *loads the weapon*;
2. A person's psychology (personality, coping mechanisms, attitude, etc.), *aims the weapon*; and,
3. A person's social environment (friends, family, support, etc.), *pulls the trigger*.

Again, I apologize for the use of weapons as analogy in a text like this, but if you think about it, it provides an apt description of how these three dimensions work together. Ironically, treatment, especially with clients experiencing co-occurring disorders, often works in the opposite order. That is:

1. Help clients create a supportive and helpful social environment to stop problem behaviors, or to stop pulling the trigger (i.e., substance use, mental health symptoms, ignoring medications, fighting, etc.).
2. Once the behavior has changed or ceased (periods of sobriety, calm, fewer symptoms, etc.), we can begin working on the persons aim towards problems, or psychology involved by teaching new coping skills, relapse prevention, anger management, etc., through therapy.
3. Our profession does not have the technology, other than perhaps through medication, to change people's biological or genetic makeup.

Staying with the above analogy, although it is not possible to "unload the weapon," it is possible to help clients stop "pulling the trigger" on problematic behaviors through social support to work on the underlying issues in therapy to change how people "aim the weapon."

The biopsychosocial perspective is composed of several elements. Longres (2000) identifies two dimensions of individual functioning, the biophysical and the psychological, subdividing the psychological into three subdimensions: the cognitive, affective, and behavioral. Elsewhere, we added the spiritual/existential dimension to this conception (Johnson & Grant, 2006). Understanding how the biological, psychological, spiritual and existential, and social environment interact is instrumental in developing an appreciation of how individuals influence and are influenced by their environment.

GUIDING PRACTICE PRINCIPLES

The AMS is based on several Guiding Practice Principles derived from the current professional practice literature and the editors' more than 80 years of combined practice experience. The Guiding Practice Principles are the core—the guts, as it were—of the AMS practice perspective.

Over the years, we have searched for the core of excellent practice. Hence, we developed the Guiding Practice Principles as the foundation of AMS as our way to approach this core. Here, Guiding Practice Principles (GPPs) are defined as those precepts, ideas, attitudes, and practices used to guide an ethical, receptive, respectful, welcoming, and competent approach to clients and client problems regardless of the specific issues, culture, worldview, professional theories, models, or methods, professional disciplines, or practice settings. The GPPs are fundamental ways of thinking and acting by human service professionals that, if consistent, transcend theory, model, or method. The GPPs are not tied to a particular practice theory, model, or method, and they are not bound by practitioner and client culture, practices, and beliefs. Practitioners may use any intervention or treatment choice to specifically match their client's culture or background, if that choice is deemed ethical and not in violation one or more of the GPPs.

Like a professional code of ethics, the GPPs are guidelines for thinking and decision-making. GPPs rarely describe specific rules or actions, but rather the larger goals of professional human interaction and relationship. Accordingly, practitioners can utilize whatever best practice or evidence-based theory and/or method is deemed appropriate to help clients. The GPPs provide a helpful filter for practice decision-making.

GUIDING PRACTICE PRINCIPLES EXPLAINED

First Practice Principle (Umbrella Principle): Healthy outcomes (and lives) are directly related to people's connections to helpful, supportive systems, across a lifetime.

The First Practice Principle is universal—it applies to everyone. That is, everyone who is either seeking a better life through therapy, counseling, and/or recovery or who lives a well-adjusted, healthy and happy life abides at some level to the First Practice Principle. Healthy people maintain lifelong, positive, and variably intimate connections with helpful, healthy, and supportive systems throughout life.

We define helpful and supportive systems as any person, people, group, organization, program, etc., a person finds helpful and supportive, has the person's best interests at heart, and is one in which the person feels positively engaged. Although the specifics and the nature of helpful and supportive systems change across a lifetime, the value of these connections is difficult to question (Johnson, 2004). They are the foundation of personal resilience. These relationships are the "difference that makes a difference" in treatment, recovery, life, and happiness.

Helpful and supportive systems also include counselors, therapists, and human service programs. But it is so much more in real life. Most people's "helpful and supportive systems" include everything from close friends and relatives to social clubs and groups, leagues, places of worship, coffee friends, support groups, etc. More important, a system is only helpful and supportive to the extent clients believe it is and *is willing to use it.*

It is not enough to say clients have "access" to helpful and supportive systems. We all have access to helpful and supportive systems. It does not matter that helpful and supportive systems are available—they are everywhere, both personal and professional. It only matters if a person is willing to seek and accept help and support from said system. Without personal investment and belief in its value as support, it is not helpful and supportive.

For example, it is only a partial step to give a client a list of support groups in the local area. Working to satisfy the tenets of the First Practice Principle also includes discussing with clients what support groups are about, the reasons why it may be important to attend, and the reasons why making friends and/or finding a sponsor in those groups is important. Based on their knowledge of the client, the practitioner should discuss with the client before they attend what parts of the meetings the client may find difficult or objectionable as a way of removing excuses for not attending.

Why all this effort? Because we know attendance alone, without steps toward engagement in the process, will not provide long-term help and support. If you've heard the saying that people can "be lonely in a crowded stadium," then the importance of this discussion should be clear. One cannot be lonely in a crowded stadium, or at a support group, if they are engaged with others and talking to people. To repeat, engagement, not access, is the key to successful social support in the First Practice Principle.

Hence, the First Practice Principle is the umbrella under which all else in professional practice falls. It is so important to understand and fundamental to long-term life success that the Final Practice Principle states: **When all else fails, never do anything with and/or to a client that violates the First Principle**. Successful practitioners approach every client situation with the First Practice Principle in mind, whether they know the specific definition or not.

What does this mean in practice? Those abiding by the First Practice Principle believe that no matter how much or how little progress clients make, how resistant or unmotivated they may appear, or whether they do anything at all toward changing while in the practitioner's care, they ensure that clients do not leave their professional relationship angry, insulted, disillusioned, negatively labeled; or hostile toward help, helpers, and/or helping systems. At the very least, abiding by the First Practice Principle means helping set clients up for future success by not driving them away from care and/or helpers out of personal or professional frustration at the client's lack of engagement, motivation, or change.

The First Practice Principle requires both short- and long-term thinking. Is anything happening in therapy, or am I, as the practitioner, acting in such a way with my client today that may damage or make less likely that they will be open to engaging with helpers and/or helping systems later in life when they might be more ready to change? In other words, how one is treated today will impact them in many important ways later. The First Practice Principle simply requires helpers do everything within their power to ensure that the said impact is positive.

Although we discuss client motivation later, it is important to understand the developmental nature of change, and people's willingness to change. That is, people progress through different developmental stages related to depth and severity of their problems, acceptance of their problems, the need for change, the motivation to change, and the courage and willingness to embark on a difficult and sometimes painful process called change (Johnson, 2004). Some make it; some do well and disappear, finding success through other services or support; some do well in the short term only to fade away; and, unfortunately, some never make progress and/or regress.

Often, when client progress lags, stalls, or never begins, often out of frustration, therapists often directly and personally confront clients about their lack of progress, engagement, or motivation with rude, accusatory, or even personally hostile remarks (Johnson & Grant, 2005).

The epitome of frustration occurs when therapists or counselors talk to clients, beginning with the phrase, "What you need to do is ..." When I hear students or practitioners talking to clients in this way, I simply ask them, "Who in your life has the right to talk to you in that way?" Rarely do they have an answer. This approach is usually borne out of the practitioner's need to control, or be paternalistic, thinking of troubled clients more as children than struggling people.

The net result of these frustration-borne tactics is to drive clients away from therapists, treatment programs, and perhaps the helping profession in the future. Why would someone ever want to seek therapy again after being treated in these ways? They probably would not.

In service of the First Practice Principle, the practitioner's job is to ensure, as much as possible, that when clients fade away from treatment or never get started at all, they do so based on personal choice and not because they have been driven away through unreasonable behavioral expectations, bad attitudes, inappropriate professional labels, misguided confrontation, attempts at control, and/or the practitioner's professional or personal frustrations at their lack of progress.

Given the First Practice Principle's requirement of lifelong connections, it is good for practitioners to realize they are only a small part of the larger network of possible helpful systems a person needs during their lifetime. Unfortunately, we in the helping professions often see ourselves as far more, sometimes to the detriment of clients needing to establish their own personal networks.

Although the professional's role is often short on the timeline of lifelong connections, it can be the most important step in the process if they see to it that their clients make, foster, and utilize these connections during and after their time in therapy. That is, professional helpers play a seminal role in the work of the First Practice Principle, largely because they become the client's initial "helpful" system. They are often the gatekeeper for help and lifelong change. How they interact with and treat people at perhaps the most vulnerable moment in their lives often determines the extent to which they will want to pursue other helpful systems in their lives in the future.

Hence, if practitioners learn to treat even the most reluctant, angry, or resistant client with dignity, respect, and compassion, it is possible that they may more readily engage with their next therapist or program and/or find helpful and supportive systems in their communities. Not because the next therapist or program is necessarily "better" or "more skilled," but because the previous relationship formed the groundwork for clients to move developmentally closer to being ready for the excruciating work of changing their lives. Working to abide by the First Practice Principle may be more important in the long run than it is in terms of positive short-term, therapeutic outcomes. The First Practice Principle is for life, not short-term gain.

The First Practice Principle consists of two important elements, each speaking to different aspects of the principle. Indeed, it speaks to the importance of client engagement and the value of hope in people's lives.

CLIENT ENGAGEMENT

Fundamental to the First Practice Principle is the ability to rapidly develop rapport leading to client engagement. In this text, client engagement

> occurs when you develop a trusting and open professional relationship that promotes hope and presents viable prospects for change. Successful engagement occurs when you create a social context in which vulnerable people (who often hold jaded attitudes toward helping professionals) can share their innermost feelings, as well as their most embarrassing and shameful behavior with you, a total stranger, over a relative short period (Johnson, 2004, p. 93).

Successful practice, regardless of setting or problems, is built on the foundation of trusting, respectful, and emotionally intimate relationships with clients (Johnson, 2004). Clinical models and/or interventions are not effective without successful client engagement. Clients have no reason to accept help at a personal level from a therapist if they do not first like them, and then come to trust and respect them.

For example, I ask students to ponder how vulnerable, truthful, and motivated they would be with a therapist they did not like, or come to trust and respect; would they accept help from anyone they did not trust or who did not treat them with dignity and respect? This is fundamental human relationship dynamics. To a new client, the therapist is a total stranger. They have no reason to trust or respect the therapist upon first meeting. Simply having a college degree or an office with a "shingle," or because someone was ordered to treatment by a judge, does not change basic, fundamental human relationship dynamics.

Becoming skilled in the nuances of successful client engagement is based on the fundamentals of being genuine, available, and focused on clients. Most important, it is based on being friendly, open, welcoming, and polite. Practitioners must exhibit these behaviors even when clients are hostile, angry, and resistant. When practitioners are nice and friendly, clients are not angry with them personally, but rather with their own personal circumstances that led them to therapy.

Successful client engagement comes through understanding and accepting people's perceptions of their reality, and not the "objective" reality of the practitioner. Seeking to understand how people perceive their world, problems, and the people around them increases the likelihood that they will feel understood. This culturally appropriate approach contributes to a professional relationship based in the client's life and belief systems.

In short, understanding people's perceptions leads practitioners to understand each individual client's definition of "common sense." It is important to remember that "common sense" is only common and sensible to one person. There is no general definition of common sense. Common sense does not exist outside of people's social, environmental, family, and cultural context. It is unique to every person, depending on where they live and come from.

Being mindful of the definitions people learn from their culture underlies not only what they do but also what they perceive, feel, and think. This knowledge places practitioners on the correct path to "start where the client is." It emphasizes the cultural uniqueness of each client and the need to understand each client in their own context and belief system, not the practitioner's context or belief system.

Different people attribute different meaning to the same events, even within the same family or community. One cannot assume people raised in the same family will define their social world similarly. For example, the sound of gunfire in the middle of the night may be frightening or normal, depending upon where a person resides and what is routine and accepted in their specific environment. Moreover, simply because some members of a family are unfazed by nightly gunfire does not mean others in the same family will not be traumatized by it.

Additionally, people use language differently based on established or evolving cultural beliefs. For example, alcohol consumption is defined as problematic depending upon how the concept of an "alcohol problem" is socially constructed in specific environments. Clients from so-called drinking cultures may define drinking six alcoholic drinks daily as normal, whereas someone from a different cultural background may see this level of consumption as problematic. Similarly, people will define trauma and traumatic events differently based on their personal culture, family environment, experiences, and upbringing. For example, children who grew up in war-torn countries will define and experience witnessing death differently than most children growing up in the United States.

It is worth repeating that upholding the First Practice Principle requires the ability to engage clients in open and trusting professional relationships. The skills needed to engage clients from different backgrounds and with different personal and cultural histories are what drives practice; that is, it is what determines the difference between successful and unsuccessful practice. Advanced client engagement skills allow the practitioner to elicit in-depth, personal information in a dialogue between client and practitioner (Johnson, 2004), providing the foundation for strengths-based client empowerment leading to change.

FOSTERING, BUILDING, OR REDISCOVERING HOPES AND DREAMS

Early in my career, I learned a lesson so important that it became a hallmark of my practice approach. It helps me effectively engage clients from all walks and ages, races, ethnicities, genders, with multiple problems; the motivated, unmotivated, mandated and hostile alike. It centered my approach on client motivation, long before models and methods came along to help with this (which we will discuss later). What I learned is:

Clients do not seek help because of their problems. They seek help because they lost hope of being able to solve their problems on their own (or in their own social networks).

Accordingly, helping professionals are not only in the problem-solving business, but also in the "hope" business. What, not in the problem-solving business? When someone comes to us because they drink too much, isn't it our job to get them to drink less or quit drinking? That's problem solving, right?

Well, yes and no. Of course, as practitioners we want to help people change by solving their problems. There is no doubt about this. This might be the reason most of us endeavor to join this profession in the first place, to help people with their problems. Yet, most clients, even those with significant levels of personal denial, already know they need to change something, even if they will not admit it. Often, they already know what must change; they simply are not ready to admit it to us, mainly because they are not ready to assume responsibility to change. If all we needed to do is encourage people to change, and have them do it, this would be easy work. Unfortunately, that is not how it works.

Our success, or skill, is not telling someone who drinks too much they need to quit drinking. Almost anybody can figure that out. The real skill—or art—of practice is getting clients to act even when they initially do not want to change.

That is, before solving problems, the main task of practitioners is helping convince people, at the deepest level possible, that change is not only positive and desirable, but more important—possible.

First, an experienced practitioner helps clients discover, perhaps for the first time, that change is possible. When clients learn that they, too, can change, that a better life is not just for "other people," they can become motivated to solve problems in the short term and maintain short-term changes over the course of their lifetime.

Let's be clear; problems get solved by models, methods, and interventions. However, here we speak of the groundwork needed *before* models, methods, and interventions can work. To accomplish this, we first discover people's sense of hope; hope for a better future, hope for change, and hope they can be effective change agents in their own lives. Here, *hope* is defined as a person's expectation for the possibility of a better tomorrow; a sense of the future that develops over time and is a function of interactions between people and their environments.

While there is little consensus in the professional literature about what hope is, whether it is innate to the human condition and/or how it is experienced (Polgar, 2017; Snyder, 2002), all agree that having hope provides a sense of optimism for the future. An optimism that leads people to believe the difficult and painful journey toward a better life might be worth it. That is, hope for better, hope for different, and/or hope that change is even possible, and good. A sense of hope, as defined here, is the foundation of motivation to change. With it, change is worth a try. Without it, why bother?

Of course, for many people the prospect of hope for a better tomorrow is difficult, if not impossible, to imagine. Their lives and existence preclude them from having hope for anything except, perhaps, survival. Whether it be from poverty, pain, violence, trauma, discrimination/racism, war, or their overall social environment, we cannot assume our clients know what it means to have a sense of optimism for the future; they are often devoid of the ability to dream.

According to Polgar (2017), "Most, if not all, who avail themselves of social work services live under siege conditions" (p. 271). That is, most clients find themselves under such significant personal and environmental stress, perhaps feeling under attack by their world, that they end up focusing only on existing. People living under siege seek survival. They are often unable to visualize or imagine a positive future or engage in the kind of reflection required to realize, develop, or enhance hope for their future. Hence, people living under environmental siege can, at best, experience hope as an expectation there may be a tomorrow, but certainly not a better one (Polgar, 2017).

There are many people who do not understand, or worse yet, cannot allow themselves to believe in the idea a better life is possible and attainable. Perhaps their circumstances disrupted the ability to hope and dream from the beginning, or it was stolen or extinguished at an early age and never restored. Without a sense of hope and the ability to dream, people will not undertake the effort to change their lives with the sense of determination and motivation often required.

Yet the loss of hope is usually larger than an individual problem. It also suggests a loss of hope in the ability of their friends, family, and other support networks to help as well. As I say to my students and workshop audiences, a lack of problems is not what separates us from our clients. Usually, what separates us is the ability to call on people we trust and love when life gets difficult; people who will support, challenge, and comfort us. These support people will have our best interests at heart and help lead us away from difficulty toward something more positive. Many people coming for professional help do not have this buffer; what we believe constitutes resilience. In our practice, we define resilience as the quality of one's social support network and one's willingness to use it. The better the support network, the more resilient people become.

Moreover, it helps to understand that the process of asking for or accepting professional help defines in many ways people's lack of, or loss of, hope. For some, needing outside help in their lives is to admit that they do not "have what it takes" to solve their own problems. Asking outsiders to help can be an outright violation of their personal, family, or community cultural norms. That is, asking for help is akin to admitting failure or weakness and can lead to a sense of shame and humiliation. Without taking these issues—hope, humiliation, and cultural norms—as a starting point for practice, change will most likely not occur.

People come for services discouraged, sometimes lost, having either abandoned their hopes and dreams or never knowing that hopes and dreams were possible. Understanding this is, in our view, the core of practice wisdom. That is, without hope, either rekindled or newly discovered, long-term change is out of reach. Without hope, the kind of positive, healing, and powerful therapeutic relationship that leads to change becomes difficult. Hence, a respectful and trusting therapeutic relationship is more important in promoting positive clinical outcomes than specific therapeutic models or interventions (Johnson, 2004; Johnson & Grant, 2005).

Principle A: Clients Are People, Too

The main point of this principle is simple, yet often not practiced. "Clients are people, too" is not intended as funny or cute, but serious. Practitioners who embody Principle A in their worldview and practice approach will find success with client engagement and relationship building. This principle is important, respectful, and offers clients a sense of dignity at what could be their most vulnerable moment. Principle A is an integral part of Principle B (Practice Privilege) discussed below, but it also makes sense on its own. The best way to earn a client's trust and respect is for practitioners to act in trustworthy and respectful ways. There really is no other way to accomplish this feat. Therefore, Principle A, "Clients are people, too," is defined as:

> *Simply, practitioners should never expect their clients to act in ways the practitioner would not act in similar circumstances and under similar pressures. In fact, practitioners should never expect clients to act in ways practitioners do not act presently, in their private lives.*

I must ask, have you ever been late for an appointment or a class when your lateness meant nothing more than you were just late? You were not late because you were "resistant" to your instructor or acting out in some meaningful, subconscious way. You were late ... period. If so, then why in the helping profession do we put so much time and effort into defining why our clients are sometimes late for their appointments? Even if they are late to every session, perhaps given their life circumstances it's a major accomplishment to get themselves to your office. Perhaps they do not have reliable transportation. I've had a client tell me that their "ride" wanted sexual favors in exchange for the ride, and they refused, causing them to miss the session completely.

Are there times when lateness or absence is a sign of avoidance ... sure. But without an open discussion with your clients about it and simply jumping to the conclusion that they are late just to make you mad means that you do not think your "clients are people, too." Sometimes, people have good reasons to be late or miss a session that have nothing to do with the therapist or the session. It just did not work that day.

Although the lateness example is oversimplified, it makes the point of this principle. People coming for therapy, by definition, have problems they cannot solve on their own (see the First Practice Principle). Depending on their problems and circumstances, they may be under heavy pressure and stress from substance use, mental health challenges, children, divorce, poverty, lack of transportation, violence, abuse, neglect, etc. These are all serious issue that compromise people's ability to respond, process, follow through, and live up to a behavior contract or therapy plan as we think they should as motivated clients. Moreover, our client's lives can be toppled by what may seem to us middle-class therapists to be the "smallest" things. We can claim "poor coping skills," but the fact remains our clients are often dealing with more than we will ever know or understand. Given the severity and difficulty of some client's lives, it is a miracle of coping that they can even get up in the morning, let alone make every session on time and fulfill a therapy contract from day to day.

When a client struggles to live up to our standards, first ask yourself the question: How would I respond under the same circumstances? This is called developing empathy. Have I ever not followed through on a work task? Have I ever been unfocused because of troubles in my personal life? Have I ever left my home "a mess" because I was too tired to clean it up? Have I ever been short-tempered with my partner, spouse, or kids because of my stress and not because of them? Have I ever slept late, been late, skipped or taken a day off just because I felt like it instead of "being a responsible adult"?

If the answer is "yes" to any of these questions, then why is it "something deeper" when our clients do the same things? Give your clients the same benefit of the doubt we expect from others and ourselves: Have empathy for people trying to navigate life. Discuss it with them, find out what happens to cause them to not follow through, and most of all, be open to cutting them some slack. After all, clients are people, too!

Principle B: Check Your Practice/Professional Privilege at the Door

Social privilege is a special, unearned advantage or entitlement that is used to one's own benefit or to the detriment of others. It provides unearned access to resources that are only available to some people because of their social group membership, with immunity granted to or enjoyed by one group above and beyond the common advantage of others (https://www.nccj.org/resources/social-justice-definitions2020). The idea of identifying the social privileges of certain groups (i.e., rich White males) is an important conversation related to inequities and social justice. Social privilege is bestowed upon certain groups in certain situations by the larger system of forces and history, over many years, often to the detriment of everyone not in in the privileged groups. Let us take a moment and explore how this occurs.

STRUCTURAL AND HISTORICAL SYSTEMS OF PRIVILEGE AND OPPRESSION: WHO HOLDS THE POWER?

Often embedded in laws, policies, and social institutions are oppressive influences such as racism, sexism, homophobia, and classism, to name a few. These structural issues play a significant role in the lives of clients (through maltreatment, racism, and discrimination) and in clinical practice. How people are treated (or how they internalize historical treatment of self, family, friends, and/or ancestors) shapes how they believe, think, and act in the present. Oppression, operationalized through privilege, affects how people perceive that others feel about them, how they view the world and their place in it, and how receptive they are to professional service providers. Therefore, culturally respectful and responsive practice must consider the impact of structural systems of oppression, social privilege, our practice privilege, and injustice on clients, their problems, strengths, and potential for change.

Oppression and privilege are a by-product of socially constructed notions of power, privilege, control, and hierarchies of difference. It is created and maintained by differences in power. Those who have power can force people to abide by the rules, standards, and actions the powerful deem worthwhile, mandatory, or acceptable. Those who hold power can enforce particular worldviews; deny equal access and opportunity to housing, employment, or health care; define right and wrong, normal and abnormal; and imprison, confine, and/or commit physical, emotional, or mental violence against the powerless (Freire, 1993; McLaren, 1995). Most important, power permits the holder to "set the very terms of power" (Appleby, 2001, p. 37). It defines the interaction between the oppressed and the oppressor, and between the practitioner and client. In the practice world, we as professional practitioners hold the power—we have the privilege to enforce in our world in the same ways as dominant groups in the larger world.

Social institutions and practices are developed and maintained by the dominant culture to meet its needs and maintain its power. Everything and everybody are judged and classified accordingly. Even when the majority culture develops programs or engages in helping activities, these efforts will not include measures that threaten the dominant group's position at the top of the social hierarchy (Freire, 1993). For example, Kozol (1991) wrote eloquently about how public schools fail by design, and Freire (1993) wrote about how state welfare and private charity provide short-term assistance while ensuring that there are not enough resources to lift people permanently out of poverty.

Oppression and/or privilege is neither an academic nor a theoretical consideration; it is not a faded relic of a bygone era. Racism did not end with the civil rights movement, and sexism was not eradicated by the feminist movement. Understanding how systems of oppression work in people's lives is of paramount importance for every individual and family seeking professional help, including those who belong to the same race, gender, and class as the practitioner.

Systems of oppression ensure unequal access to resources for certain individuals, families, and communities. However, although all oppressed people are similar in that they lack the power to define their place in the social hierarchy, oppression based on race, gender, sexual orientation, class, and other social factors is expressed in a variety of ways. Learning about cultural nuances is important in client assessment, treatment planning, and treatment (Lum, 1999). According to Pinderhughes (1989), there is no such thing as culture-free service delivery. Cultural differences between clients and practitioners in terms of values, norms, beliefs, attitudes, lifestyles, and life opportunities affect every aspect of practice.

Although larger social inequities are often discussed in terms of privilege, rarely have the helping professions examined and interrogated how professional, or "practice," privilege operates in the relationships between practitioners and clients, clients and helping organizations, and how practitioners mediate the existing systems of oppression between clients and the larger social control systems (courts, CPS, mental health, etc.).

In the wrong hands, clinical training and practice brings the potential to exercise practice privilege to the detriment of our clients. Our professional degrees, licenses, certifications, and roles brings the power to define, label, and diagnose. We have the power to influence court decisions, parental custody decisions, existing relationships, and people's well-being. We make recommendations, give advice, judge, and decide our client's futures and possibilities for change. In the wrong hands, we can dominate and define people's lives and the lives of their children well into the future, if not forever. This is the power of practice privilege.

This power is bestowed by the state and society as ours because we are members of this profession. We earn the right to be in our professional roles through education and training, but we do not earn the right to use it to shape and dominate other people's lives or to determine normal from abnormal, right from wrong, or healthy from unhealthy.

This notion of practice privilege must be considered, processed, and discussed in professional circles, much like larger issues of social privilege. One of the insidious and consistent hallmarks of privilege is that the people who have it do not know it exists, or when they exert it on others. This is difficult enough in daily life, but potentially harmful among professional practitioners.

Oblivious practitioners can wield practice privilege to the detriment of clients in professional practice, without knowing it. Fighting one's privilege takes bringing the unknown to the fore, examining one's ideas and practices in a way that interrogates the extent to which our profession and our professionals wielding practice privilege that reinforce our client's place down the social hierarchy. Without a close, serious, and vulnerable exploration of our practices, much like we ask clients to do every day, we seriously cannot examine practice privilege, leaving us to blindly treat our clients in ways that reinforce their place as having opinions and beliefs that do not matter as much as those of the privileged few.

Principle C: Culturally Respectful and Responsive Client Engagement

Earlier we defined client engagement as a mutual process occurring between clients and practitioners in a professional context, created by practitioners. In other words, creating the professional space and open atmosphere that allows engagement to flourish is the primary responsibility of the practitioner, not the client. Practitioners must have the skills and knowledge to adjust their approach toward specific clients and the client's cultural context, not vice versa. Clients do not adjust to us and our beliefs, values, and practices—we adjust to them. When that occurs, the foundation exists for client engagement. Relationships of this nature must be performed in a culturally welcoming and responsive manner. Yet, what does this mean?

Over the last two decades, social work and other helping professions have been concerned with cultural competence in practice (Fong, 2001). Beginning in the late 1970s the professional literature has been replete with ideas, definitions, and practice models designed to increase cultural awareness and promote culturally appropriate practice methods. Yet, despite the attention given to the issue, there remains confusion about how to define and teach culturally competent practice.

As stated earlier, over the years many different ideas and definitions of what constitutes culturally competent practice have developed, as indicated by the growth of the professional literature since the late 1970s. To date, focus has primarily been placed in two areas: (1) the need for practitioners to be aware or their own cultural beliefs, ideas, and identities, leading to cultural sensitivity, and (2) learning factual and descriptive information about various ethnic and racial groups based mostly on group-level survey data and analyses. Fong (2001) suggests that culture is often considered "tangential" to individual functioning and not central to the client's functioning.

To address this issue, Fong (2001) builds on Lum's (1999) culturally competent practice model that focuses on four areas: (1) cultural awareness, (2) knowledge acquisition, (3) skill development, and (4) inductive learning. Besides inductive learning, Lum's model places focus mainly on practitioners in perpetual self-awareness, gaining knowledge about cultures, and skill building. Although these are important ideas for cultural competence, Fong (2001) calls for a shift in thinking and practice "to provide a culturally competent service focused solely on the client rather than the social worker and what he or she brings to the awareness of ethnicity" (p. 5). Fong (2001) suggests an "extension" of Lum's model by turning the focus of each of the four elements away from the practitioner toward the client. For example, cultural awareness changes from a practitioner focus to "the social worker's understanding and the identification of the critical cultural values important to the client system and to themselves" (p. 6). This change allows Fong (2001) to remain consistent with the stated definition of culturally competent practice, insisting that practitioners

> operating from an empowerment, strengths, and ecological framework, provide services, conduct assessments, and implement interventions that are reflective of the clients' cultural values and norms, congruent with their natural help-seeking behaviors, and inclusive of existing indigenous solutions (p. 1).

Although we agree with the idea that "to be culturally competent is to know the cultural values of the client system and to use them in planning and implementing services" (Fong, 2001, p. 6), we want to make this shift the main point of a culturally competent model of client engagement. That is, beyond what should or must occur, we believe that professional education and training must focus on the skills of culturally competent client engagement that are necessary to make this happen;

a model that places the ability to gather individual client cultural information at the center of practice. We agree with Fong (2001) that having culturally sensitive or culturally aware practitioners is not nearly enough. Practitioner self-awareness and knowledge of different cultures does not constitute cultural competence. We strive to find a method for reaching this worthy goal.

Here, cultural competence does not mean practitioners will become competent in other people's cultures. This is not only impossible with limited exposure, but to assume it is possible is evidence of out-of-control practice privilege, discussed earlier. We do not learn a "special" set of skills allowing us to transcend history, time, and our own culture to rapidly become competent in some else's culture.

Here, the central issue revolves around practitioners participating in inductive learning and the skills of grounded theory. In other words, regardless of practitioner beliefs, awareness, or sensitivities, cultural competence comes with the ability to gather the information necessary to understand their client's cultural values and meanings, and "ground" their theory of practice in the cultural context of their client. They develop a unique theory of human behavior based on the cultural beliefs and practices of each client. Culturally competent client engagement does not happen by assessing the extent to which client lives "fit" within existing theory and knowledge about reality, most of which is middle class and Eurocentric at its core (Johnson, 2004). Cultural competence:

> *begins* with learning about different cultures, races, personal circumstances, and structural mechanisms of oppression. It *occurs* when practitioners master the interpersonal skills needed to move beyond general descriptions of a specific culture or race to learn specific individual, family, group, or community interpretations of culture, ethnicity, and race. The culturally competent practitioner knows that within each culture are individually interpreted and practiced thoughts, beliefs, and behaviors that may or may not be consistent with group-level information. That is, there is tremendous diversity within groups, as well as between them. Individuals are unique unto themselves, not simply interchangeable members of a specific culture, ethnicity, or race who naturally abide by the group-level norms often taught on graduate and undergraduate courses on human diversity (Johnson, 2004, p. 105).

Culturally competent client engagement revolves around the practitioner's ability to create a relationship, through the professional use of self, based in true dialogue (Freire, 1993; Johnson, 2004). We define *dialogue* as, "a joint endeavor, developed between people (in this case, practitioner and client) that move clients from their current state of hopelessness to a more hopeful, motivated position in their world" (Johnson, 2004, p. 97). Elsewhere (Johnson, 2004) we detailed a model of culturally competent engagement based on Freire's (1993) definitions of oppression, communication, dialogue, practitioner self-work, and the ability to exhibit worldview respect, hope, humility, trust, and empathy.

To investigate culture in a competent manner is to take a comprehensive look into people's worldview—to discover what they believe about the world and their place in it. It goes beyond race and ethnicity (although these are important issues) into how culture determines thoughts, feelings, and behaviors in daily life. This includes what culture says about people's problems; culturally appropriate strengths and resources; the impact of gender on these issues; and what it means to seek professional help (Leigh, 1998).

The larger questions to be answered are how clients uniquely and individually interpret their culture; how their beliefs, attitudes, and behaviors are shaped by that interpretation, and, how these cultural beliefs and practices affect daily life and determine lifestyle in the context of the larger community. Additionally, based on their cultural membership, beliefs, and practices, practitioners need to discover the potential and real barriers faced by clients in the world. For many clients of color and other minority groups, their worlds are defined by racism, sexism, homophobia, and ethnocentrism that enforce limitations and barriers that others do not face.

What is the value of culturally competent client engagement? Helping clients discuss their attitudes, beliefs, and behaviors in the context of their culture—including their religious or spiritual belief systems—offers valuable information about their worldview, sense of social and spiritual connection, and/or practical involvement in their social world. Moreover, establishing connections between their unique interpretation of their culture and their daily life provides vital clues about people's belief systems, attitudes, expectations (social construction of reality), and explanation of behaviors that cannot be understood outside the context of their socially constructed interpretation of culture.

Principle D: Motivation Matters

Earlier we discussed the importance of assessing client's hopes and dreams for a better future as setting the stage for change. This, along with building a trusting, respectful, and culturally appropriate therapeutic relationship, all serve to enhance and bolster client's motivation to change. Without the proper motivation, comprising all we have discussed to this point, clients will continue to lack progress and/or success in therapy.

> *Remember our core belief: Clients do not change because of models, methods, or interventions alone. They change because they are helped into a trusting and respectful therapeutic relationship based on enhancing their dignity as human beings, have hope they can*

change for the better, and the motivation to endure the process of change. All of this is accomplished in the context of helpful and supportive systems of support to build personal resilience.

Here we look at ways to accurately assess a client's motivation for change. Miller and Rollnick (2002) suggest that clients with different stages of motivation, or change, require helpers to approach them differently, depending on the needs of their current stage of change and the needs to progress from earlier to later stages along the motivation continuum. The authors further state that "problems of clients being unmotivated or resistant occur when a counselor is using strategies inappropriate for a client's current stage of change" (p. 16).

In the 1980s, Prochaska and DiClemente (1982, 1984, 1986; DiClemente & Prochaska, 1985) developed the transtheoretical model, commonly known as the stages of change model, based on their work with people trying to quit smoking. This model is based on how and why clients, either alone or with help, succeed at changing their addictive behavior. Subsequently, the stages of change model has been adapted for other addictive behaviors such as food and alcohol and other drugs (Connors et al., 2001; DiClemente & Hughes, 1990; DiClemente, 1991). Previously, we expanded the stages of change to include mental health disorders, trauma disorders, and other disorders (Johnson, 2004).

There are six stages of change to be assessed during an assessment and treatment process. It is important to note, however, that the stages are fluid, meaning clients move from one to another, often needing between four and six "trips" through the stages before discovering long-term change (Miller & Rollnick, 1991). The stages of change are (1) precontemplation, (2) contemplation, (3) preparation, (4) action, (5) maintenance, and (6) relapse. The client's stage of change is assessed and determined for each diagnosable and treatable problem, during each session. That is, if the client has two diagnosed co-occurring disorders (e.g., substance use and mental health), they are assessed along the stage of change continuum for each problem, during each session. These are described, along with assessment indicators, below.

Stage 1: Precontemplation
In the precontemplation stage, people have not yet considered the possibility they have a problem(s) or refuse to consider the possibility they may have a problem(s). Most often, clients in the precontemplation stage present with what appears as classic denial. These clients are often labeled resistant, recalcitrant, unmotivated, or not ready for treatment. They often refuse or make it difficult to perform an assessment because they either have not considered their behavior as problematic or refuse to entertain a discussion about it. These clients often are mandated by outside systems, including the legal system, employers, or their families, but

not always. Rarely will people in the precontemplation stage voluntarily submit themselves for treatment of any kind.

DiClemente (1991) has suggested four subtypes of clients in the precontemplation stage. Called the "four Rs" (DiClemente, 1991, p. 192), they include reluctance, rebellion, resignation, and rationalizing precontemplating clients.

Certain clients will fit the category of *reluctant precontemplators*. People in this category genuinely do not know or understand they have a problem(s) or even need to consider changing. These individuals are not as resistant as they are reluctant. Clients in this category will appear genuinely surprised, baffled, or taken aback by the suggestion they may have issues of any kind. They will appear as if they have never considered the possibility despite problematic behavior and significant negative life consequences.

The *rebellious precontemplator* is resistant—resistant to being told what to do, to having their problems pointed out to them, and to most anything the practitioner does, except agree with them. If clients argue with nearly every question, refuse to respond or respond only in a hostile manner, and/or exhibit other oppositional behavior, it is quite possible that they are a rebellious precontemplator. The best way for the practitioner to approach these individuals is to offer choices and/ or give the appearance that they are not really trying to change them or "telling them what to do."

Resigned precontemplators have usually given up on the prospect for change and appear overwhelmed by their problems. Often, these individuals will want to tell the practitioner how many times they have tried and failed to quit, how nothing seems to work, and/or how they may be "destined" to be a drug addict. These clients lack hope. Throughout the conversation, the practitioner should make it known that it is not too late for them to make a positive change.

Finally, *rationalizing precontemplators* have "all the answers" (p. 193). These individuals do not consider the possibility of change because they "have it all figured out." They know someone who has bigger problems, have plenty of reasons why their problem is not a problem, or believe they would be fine if people would simply leave them alone. Rationalizing precontemplators can sound a lot like rebellious precontemplators, with one exception, the rationalizing precontemplators will be intellectual, whereas rebellious precontemplators will be angry and emotional. If the practitioner begins to feel like they are in an intellectual debate with the client about the extent of their problems, then the client is probably a rationalizing precontemplator. These clients need to be approached as such, asking them to explain how they came to their conclusions. Contradictions between what is said and what is happening in their lives must be pointed out and clarified.

Stage 2: Contemplation
The contemplation stage is characterized by ambivalence (Miller & Rollnick, 2002). Clients in this stage are open to the possibility that they have problems

to work on and change may be needed. However, they have not yet decided to change and appear hesitant to make a commitment. This is a critical stage to recognize and one that can be quite frustrating, especially when the practitioner misreads the client and thinks that they are ready to change immediately. Miscalculations of this type often drive clients away or back into the precontemplation stage.

Clients in this stage will often state they know they should change and understand they have problems. They will give several reasons why they "should" change, but do not. The major difference is people in the contemplation stage acknowledge that a vague problem exists and something "should" be done about it. To facilitate this ambivalence into a productive relationship, the practitioner will help the client explore past treatment failures, their fears about changing and staying the same, and offer hope that they can succeed. Clients in this stage, according to DiClemente (1991), lack a sense of self-efficacy needed to commit to a life-changing process. In this case, not only is it our job to assess this stage, but to enhance it by employing approaches to help clients believe they have "what it takes" to succeed.

Stage 3: Preparation

Clients in the preparation stage are already in the process of deciding to "stop a problem behavior or to initiate a positive behavior" (DiClemente, 1991, p. 197). These individuals have made a concrete decision to change. These are highly motivated individuals, ready to make a serious effort toward change. Clients in the preparation stage normally have already begun making changes or recently tried to change. They bring a serious commitment to their situation that was not seen in earlier stages. The practitioner's challenge is to enhance their motivation, offer support and linkages to resources needed to further their chances of success, and to discuss with them the potential barriers to change that may have to be confronted along the way. Helping clients through this anxiety and normal hesitation is critically important during this stage.

People in the preparation stage worry less about jargon, and more about what to do. How can you tell the difference between clients in the preparation stage and those who are not? Listen for reports about previous action, concrete plan development, and whether they have reasons for why they cannot begin the process immediately. In the context of the dilemma of change, people in the preparation stage will have misgivings, hesitancies, and fears about what they are trying to accomplish. They will not usually be adamant about the need to change, nor will they dismiss the notion that change is difficult and frightening. Therefore, if clients are adamant about the need to change and unwilling to address the dilemma of change, it is likely that they have not reached this stage.

Stage 4: Action

People assessed to be in the action stage are committed to a course of action toward change (good or not). They have passed the point of decision-making and are taking steps to change their life. If clients in the determination stage commit to and begin a plan of action (DiClemente, 1991; Prochaska and DiClemente, 1982, 1984, 1986), they move from that stage to the action stage. Hence, the action stage is characterized by the client implementing their plan.

Stage 5: Maintenance

Occasionally clients will present in the maintenance stage, primarily for support. However, many of these clients find the support they need in community support groups, in their churches, synagogues, or mosques, or among family and friends in the community. The maintenance phase is the last stage of successful change. Over time, clients slowly replace old ineffective behaviors with new patterns. As the new behavior patterns, attitudes, and beliefs become firmly entrenched, old patterns dissipate. However, it is important to note that this takes time, perhaps years to accomplish. Clients who submit themselves for assessment at this point are usually trying to avoid and prevent a relapse.

Stage 6: Relapse

Clients will often present for assistance when they relapse. These clients have cycled through the stages, often more than once, and achieved a period of maintenance through action. However, in any kind of treatment, relapse is a common and normal occurrence (Denning, 2000). People, for one reason or another, often slip back into behaviors as they try to solidify their hold on their new lifestyle. These clients often come for assistance just after relapsing, with a weakened self-efficacy, guilt feelings, and a sense of resignation. The indicators of someone in the relapse stage are obvious. These are people who have been changing for any period who want to prevent a full-fledged relapse, while continuing to make progress.

However, assessing the client's stage of change does not stop with the assessment. It is an ongoing part of the treatment process. Again, clients do not cycle smoothly through the stages, and relapse is a regular and expected occurrence in therapy, whether substance use or mental health. Also, remember that clients should be approached differently based on their motivation stage. For example, a client in the rebellious precontemplation stage cannot be approached harshly and directly. A more indirect approach that relies on slowly and gently pointing out discrepancies in their story is a better approach.

Last Principle: When All Else Fails, Never Do Anything That Violates the First Principle!

This principle speaks for itself. If it will make your relationship oppositional, or if you are frustrated with your client's lack of progress, remember … Just. Don't.

Do. It. In the end, if all else fails, practitioners can simply, be nice, friendly, welcoming, and respectful. This attitude may just help save a life someday because they remember how nice you were when it comes time to seriously seek help.

SUMMARY

In this chapter you were introduced to the Advance Multiple Systems (AMS) practice perspective. This approach, although not a specific practice method, provides a foundation for conceptualizing and thinking about clients from a multiple systems perspective, particularly as it related to understanding, engaging, assessing, and treatment planning for the cases included in this text.

The chapter also presented the Guiding Practice Principles of the AMS. These principles, like a professional code of ethics, offers a process for clinical decision-making throughout the treatment process. We place high value on the quality of relationships and solid personal choices always made in the client's best interest. We discussed the positive value of practitioners working to become the kind of professional who promotes trusting and respectful therapeutic relationships as the foundation for successful practice. We believe the best practitioners are personally insightful, attending to their personal biases, practice privilege, and relationships in a way that enhances their client's chance to succeed.

In the end, the following paragraph provides an excellent summary of the values and practices discussed in this chapter.

Core Beliefs

Clients do not change because of models, methods, or interventions alone. They change because they are helped into a trusting and respectful therapeutic relationship based on enhancing their dignity as human beings, have hope they can change for the better, and the motivation to endure the process of change. All of this is accomplished in the context of helpful and supportive systems of support to build personal resilience.

REFERENCES

American Psychiatric Association. (2013). *Diagnostic and statistical manual of mental disorders* (5th ed.). Author.

Appleby, G. A. (2001). Dynamics of oppression and discrimination. In G. A. Appleby, E. Colon, & J. Hamilton (Eds.), *Diversity, oppression, and social functioning: Person-in-environment assessment and intervention.* (pp. 36–52). Allyn & Bacon.

Connors, G. J., Donovan, D. M., & DiClemente, C. C. (2001). *Selecting and planning interventions: Substance abuse treatment and the stages of change.* Guilford Press.

Denning, P. (2000). *Practicing harm reduction psychotherapy: An alternative approach to addictions.* Guilford Press.

DiClemente, C. C. (1991). Motivational interviewing and the stages of change. In W. R. Miller & S. Rollnick (Eds.), *Motivational interviewing: Preparing people to change addictive behavior* (pp. 191–202). Guilford Press.

DiClemente, C. C., & Hughes, S. O. (1990). Stages of change profiles in outpatient alcoholism treatment. *Journal of Substance Abuse, 2,* 217–235.

DiClemente, C. C., & Prochaska, J. O. (1985). Processes and stages of change: Coping and competence in smoking behavior change. In S. Shiffman & T. A. Wills (Eds.), *Coping and substance abuse. (p. 176–194)* Academic Press.

Fong, R. (2001). Culturally competent social work practice: Past and present. In R. Fong & S. Furuto (Eds.), *Culturally competent practice: Skills, interventions, and evaluations. (p. 1–10)* Allyn and Bacon.

Freire, P. (1993). *Pedagogy of the oppressed.* Continuum.

Germain, C. B., & Gitterman, A. (1996). *The life model of social work practice* (2nd ed.). Columbia University Press.

Horowitz, M. J. (1989). Posttraumatic stress disorder. In American Psychiatric Association Task Force on Treatments of Psychiatric Disorders (Ed.), *Treatments of psychiatric disorders: A task force report of the American Psychiatric Association* (pp. 2065–2082). American Psychiatric Association

Johnson, J. L. (2000). *Crossing borders—confronting history: Intercultural adjustment in a post–Cold War world.* University Press of America.

Johnson, J. L. (2004). *Fundamentals of substance abuse practice.* Brooks/Cole.

Johnson, J. L., & Grant, G. (2005). *Casebook: Substance abuse.* Allyn & Bacon.

Johnson, J. L., & Grant, G. (2006). *Casebook: Mental health.* Allyn & Bacon.

Johnson, J. L., & Grant, G. (2007). *Casebook: Sexual abuse.* Allyn & Bacon.

Kozol, J. (1991). *Savage inequalities: Children in America's schools.* Crown Publishers.

Leigh, J. W. (1998). *Communicating for cultural competence.* Allyn & Bacon.

Longres, J. F. (2000). *Human behavior in the social environment* (3rd ed.). F. E. Peacock.

Lum, D. (1999). *Culturally competent practice.* Brooks/Cole.

McLaren, P. (1995). *Critical pedagogy and predatory culture: Oppositional politics in a postmodern era.* Routledge.

Miller, W. R., & Rollnick, S. (1991). *Motivational interviewing: Preparing people to change addictive behavior.* Guilford Press.

Miller, W. R., & Rollnick, S. (2002). *Motivational interviewing: Preparing people to change addictive behavior* (2nd ed.). Guilford Press.

Mills, C. W. (1959). *The sociological imagination.* Oxford University Press.

National Conference of Community and Justice. (2020). Social justice definitions. https://www.nccj.org/resources/social-justice-definitions

Pinderhughes, E. (1989). *Understanding race, ethnicity, and power*. Free Press.

Polgar, A. T. (2017). Hope theory as social work treatment. In F. J. Turner (ed.), *Social work treatment: Interlocking theoretical approaches* (6th ed., pp. 222–275). Oxford University Press.

Prochaska, J. O., & DiClemente, C. C. (1982). Transtheoretical therapy: Toward a more integrative model of change. *Psychotherapy: Theory, Research, and Practice, 19*, 276–288.

Prochaska, J. O., & DiClemente, C. C. (1984). *The transtheoretical approach: Crossing traditional boundaries of therapy*. Dow Jones/Irwin.

Prochaska, J. O., & DiClemente, C. C. (1986). Toward a comprehensive model of change. In W. R. Miller & N. Heather (Eds.), *Treating addictive behaviors: Processes of change* (pp. 3–27). Plenum Press.

Scott, J. C. (1990). *Domination and the arts of resistance: Hidden transcripts*. Yale University Press.

Snyder, C. R. (2002). Hope theory: Rainbows in the mind. *Psychological Inquiry, 13*(4), 249–275.

Substance Abuse and Mental Health Services Administration (SAMHSA). (2012). SAMHSA's concept of trauma and guidance for a trauma-informed approach. HHS Publication No. (SMA) 14-4884. Substance Abuse and Mental Health Services Administration.

Timberlake, E. M., Farber, M. Z., & Sabatino, C. A. (2002). *The general method of social work practice: McMahon's generalist perspective* (4th ed.). Allyn and Bacon.

Turnbull, G. J. (1998). A review of post-traumatic stress disorder; Part I: Historical development and classification. *Injury, 29*, 87–91.

CHAPTER 2

Charles Bayou and Hurricane Katrina

Dianne Green-Smith

CHARLES "CHUCKIE" BAYOU is a 77-year-old African American male who came to see me for therapy because he was having nightmares and exhibiting what he called "extreme sadness." When I met Charles, he was living with his daughter in the Midwest after being forced from his home and community in the Lower Ninth Ward of New Orleans by Hurricane Katrina and its aftermath a few months earlier.

Charles had been "missing," out of touch with his family for 7 days in the immediate aftermath of Katrina. He spent those days housed in the Louisiana Superdome, without access to a cell phone or other means of communication. Charles was a proud African American and had retired after being a laborer in the New Orleans area for most of his life. He had successfully raised his children and was an excellent grandfather to his many grandchildren. Charles's wife of many years was suffering from dementia and was living in the Midwest where her daughter could see that she received the services she needed.

His daughter, Gilda, accompanied him to my office for the initial visit. According to Gilda, her dad was reluctant to come to therapy because of "old teachings" such as "what happens in the home stays in the home" and "we should keep our dirty laundry to ourselves." Gilda interpreted this to mean that "our family business is our business and should not be blasted to the world." This made it difficult to convince Charles that attending therapy would be helpful, or appropriate.

Gilda also said her dad is a God-fearing man who "believes he should talk to his pastor at his home church instead of talking to some young person up North who does not know anything about old Black people from the South." In the wake of these teachings and beliefs, Gilda was worried about her father enough to still encourage him to seek help from outsiders.

When they arrived for the first session, Charles stayed behind and did not look up for introductions. At his daughter's insistence, Mr. Bayou introduced himself, "Most people call me Mr. Chuckie … you can call me that if you like."

I extended my hand to Mr. Chuckie, thanking him for coming.

"My name is Dianne Green-Smith. I'm one of the therapists here. Please call me Dianne. You folks can take a seat where you think you will be comfortable. Based on the initial information I received from your daughter, I understand you are from New Orleans. You know, I have relatives living near New Orleans and I go there often. Spent lots of time there when I was young. New Orleans is a culture of its own … a place full of life!" I said with a smile.

With my smile, I noticed the stress lines on his forehead ease, and his shoulders seemed to relax. His body seemed to relax, perhaps an indication he might be talking to somebody who would understand him.

"What brings you here Mr. Chuckie?"

Working from an empowering and strength-based perspective, I respected Mr. Chuckie as the head of his family by asking him first, why he was meeting with me. I understood that some of his story [narrative] would be told by his daughter, Gilda. However, I needed to honor Mr. Chuckie's role as patriarch if I were to have a chance to engage him in treatment. The construction of his narrative had begun when he began to realize he had entered a safe environment and had nonjudgmental family support and love.

This was Mr. Chuckie's first time coming to therapy. It was an uncommon phenomenon to him. Gilda indicated that she attended therapy in the past and that she was familiar with how it worked. She said it was helpful for her, but that it took a long time for her to connect with someone who did not understand her culture. She said she found herself educating her therapist on simple nuances of Black people and she did not want her dad to experience anything connected to racism or cultural imperialism.

I acknowledged her concerns and shared that both myself and the agency worked from a strengths-based perspective, practiced from a culturally aware stance, and understood the impact of discriminatory practices on people considered minorities in the larger culture. I also acknowledged that therapy was foreign to Mr. Chuckie, and that coming for help did not mean he was weak or less of a man. As I was about to learn, his life history was a testament to this being untrue about him.

Besides, I said, "I'm Black … I'm from the South … and I understand!"

As in all first sessions, I discussed the therapeutic process from an agency perspective and of my clinical paradigms. An administrative person already did the initial intake paperwork; therefore, there was no need to discuss payment, insurance, and missed appointments.

To ease some of Mr. Chuckie's concerns about sharing personal information with a stranger and going to someone outside of the church, I shared some of my background and experiences as a Black person from the South. We talked about the issues of "airing our dirty laundry" and how damaging our "dirty laundry," or keeping secrets, might be on individuals and family members when it's not shared.

We acknowledged the short- and long-term harmful effects on one's mental health and relationships of keeping secrets.

We also discussed the role of the church and the many historical and traditional roles and skills of Black pastors. In Mr. Chuckie's world, and most Black communities, the Black pastor is an acknowledged leader in the community. We talked about specific scripture that claims everyone has a gift; some are evangelists, teachers, counselors, doctors, lawyers, etc., and how people should utilize people in their giftedness. That included counselors and therapists.

As I spoke with Mr. Chuckie, I sensed a further loosening of his traditional paradigms. I was becoming, albeit quite early, a person who could be trusted; an ally who can hear his truth without judgment. We talked about issues of confidentiality, particularly related to doing harm to oneself, since it appeared Mr. Chuckie could be depressed and potentially suicidal.

As I talked with both Mr. Chuckie and Gilda about approaches to therapy, I refrained from using jargon, and spoke in terms that were meaningful to them. From the intake form, I knew Mr. Chuckie was rescued from the Superdome after Katrina. This could have been particularly traumatic, so I needed to be the kind of person who he might become comfortable telling his story to. I practice from the "use of self" perspective. That is, I listen attentively to individual narratives to gain knowledge about attachment issues and object relatedness in terms of early or recent trauma, I also listen to client's verbal and nonverbal languages to understand what gives meaning and purpose to their lives, for aspects of their unique cultural background.

I am also intently listening to people's stories of systemic and environmental oppressions, their individual and collective resilience, and their psychological and spiritual strength. I want to understand, from their narratives, how they survived yesterday and what gives them hope for today and tomorrow. After sharing how the therapeutic process works, I turned my attention to Mr. Chuckie and Gilda and, their stories.

QUESTIONS

1. Given what you know about Mr. Chuckie, Gilda, and their current situation, what issues would you consider as you prepared to meet them for the first time?

2. Before progressing, please study Hurricane Katrina, reviewing what happened during and after the storm. Look deeply into the conditions and treatment residents, especially African American residents, received before, during, and after the storm and resulting floods.

3. Review media coverage, looking for how the media, both local and national, portrayed the storm and its residents, especially those residents

caught in the aftermath at the Superdome and the New Orleans Convention Center.

4. Critically review literature discussing and analyzing the government response (local, state, and national) to the storm, during the run-up, during, and immediately after the resulting floods.

5. Mr. Chuckie presents several unique challenges pertaining to client engagement. How would you prepare to build rapport and engage him in therapy, especially if you are not African American or have no personal connections to New Orleans or the South?

6. What percentage of your time do you spend working on and/or practicing your engagement skills? List several ways you can improve your practice engagement skills.

HURRICANE KATRINA: UP CLOSE AND PERSONAL

As Mr. Chuckie and Gilda began telling their story about the impact of Hurricane Katrina on their family, I became aware of muscle tension in my shoulders and of my drifting thoughts. You see, several of my extended family were also greatly affected by Hurricane Katrina. My family happen to live on higher ground in a small town on the West Bank of the Mississippi River. Yet, they had to evacuate to a local school for shelter. Fortunately, my relatives only spent 2 days at the shelter, able to return to their unaffected homes, unlike Mr. Chuckie and thousands of others.

I was surprised at my almost immediate physical reaction to their stories. I knew right then, that if I chose to work with Mr. Chuckie, and I knew I would, it would be imperative for me to utilize supervision and case consultation to deal with and manage any issues I may have pertaining to countertransference and/or vicarious trauma.

I believe in the value of body work and how mental health issues are experienced physically by clients and clinicians. Van Der Kolk (2015) talked about the importance of monitoring muscle tension by being attuned to a client's (and clinician's) visceral experiences in therapy. That is, being aware of body sensations and facial expressions are helpful gauges to be used during a therapeutic process.

In my case, I had a personal, physical reaction to their stories about Katrina. Although we might not have had the same experience, each of us in that therapy office had experienced pain, fear, and loss from Hurricane Katrina. Therefore, it was my responsibility as an experienced and competent practitioner to ensure that my personal feelings and experiences did not diminish my ability to help Mr. Chuckie and Gilda with their issues. They were, after all, paying for professional services, and it was my job to give them the best services possible. That is what good supervision and case consultation is for in our business. I intended to use it with case.

I was glad that Gilda decided to stay in the session and participate with her dad. I thought it might make it easier to get Mr. Chuckie to participate if he could see his daughter doing so. Plus, after learning I had personal connections to New Orleans and some of the surrounding cities, I believe both Gilda and her dad felt safer talking to me. As I had hoped, Gilda talked first. She was immediately upset.

"You know about our people [African American] and the people back home. … You know our people had no option but to stay put [during Katrina], regardless of what was said and ordered. Where were people supposed to go? Where do you go when you are poor, used to the storms happening, and stuff like that … had survived many bad storms in the past, and besides … you think it [the storm] is only going to be for a day or so! She paused, appearing contemplative. What did the government expect?"

I looked at both Mr. Chuckie and Gilda and said, "Because there have been several storms and hurricanes in New Orleans, I imagine things become routine. I imagine people might take a few basic items with the thought they would return home in a day or two."

Both Gilda and Mr. Chuckie nodded. Mr. Chuckie grunted, "Yep, that's about the size of it."

Gilda continued her story, providing details about the structure of her family and how her dad came to live with her in recent months. As an attuned clinician, I instinctively leaned forward as I listened attentively. I nodded appropriately, demonstrated empathy in my nonverbal personal body language and vocal expression. I was attuned to their body language, facial expressions, and guttural sounds. Additionally, I remained aware of the tightness in the back of my neck and my shoulders, places where I hold my anxiety. I shifted my position, wanting to rub my neck, but didn't.

I relaxed my shoulders and made genuine and authentic statements to Gilda: "Gilda … I understand the stress you experienced while you watched Katrina play out on television. I sense the tension you experienced in your body might have been insurmountable at times. As you said … and from my own knowledge of living Black with minimal income … it's true. There is no place to go when you don't have money, when you don't have adequate transportation, and when you think nothing is really going to happen."

We paused. It appears my statement reflected their truth. I allowed the silence to settle us, our bodies and minds. Perhaps we wondered why everyone didn't understand the realities of our world.

My intent was to be person centered according to Carl Rogers (1995): to be nonjudgmental, congruent, empathic, and fully engaged. This session allowed time for some of Mr. Chuckie's anxiety to not only ebb and flow, but to dissipate as Gilda talked about her experiences with Katrina. Because Gilda had time to process some of her thoughts with her family prior to the session, the sting of her pain was not as pronounced as it would have been had she come as soon as her dad came to live with her.

LANDING AT THE SUPERDOME

According to Gilda, her father was "caught-up" in the hurricane because he grew frustrated with the evacuation process. After heeding the order to evacuate, he hitched a ride with his granddaughter and her children on their way out of the Lower Ninth. According to Gilda, the traffic was dense, and cars were creeping along Veterans Highway.

Mr. Chuckie chimed in, adding that this "slow creep" seemed to last "forever." Not only did cars creep, but traffic often came to a standstill, and stalled, and stalled. These standstills lasted so long people would get out of their cars and talk. During one of many standstills on the highway, Mr. Chuckie happened to see one of his buddies, who worked for the fire department, on the other side of the highway headed back into the city. He asked his friend for a ride back to town. Over Gilda's objections, Mr. Chuckie jumped into his friend's car and headed back to his house. He said he was relieved to be out of the "traffic mess" and on his way to his own home, back in the Lower Ninth Ward in New Orleans.

Gilda confirmed his story. "The other driver was a fire person who had to report to work. He dropped my dad close enough to his house, and since my dad walked about 5 miles a day, he had no problems walking the seven or eight blocks home. Once home, he ate the food that he cooked that day, sat on the front porch, watched cars go by, and waved at his neighbors as they left the neighborhood ... Didn't you daddy?"

She looked at her dad and narrated their story with tears in her eyes. Mr. Chuckie pulled out his handkerchief, wiped his daughter's tears, and held his head down. Sitting side by side on the sofa, they held hands as though to take in the enormity of the situation. Gilda continued, "After the storm ... my daddy was missing for an entire week. ... No one knew where he was. He didn't have any cell phone minutes and couldn't call out."

She said that week he was missing was a very difficult and painful one for her. She sighed and heaved a little, and the grip between their hands tighten. "I didn't know if he was alive or dead in his house. Nobody could get to the house without a boat in those days."

I reached across and touched both of their hands to show support. "This was a sad and painful time for you and your entire family. Sounds like no one knew where anyone was ... or were even alive. I know it is difficult to talk about. Do you want to say more?"

Gilda agreed. She said she went to work each day as usual, but every night she watched the news on television, hoping to get a clue about what happened to her father. Every station showed something about the hurricane and its aftermath. She continued, "I saw Black men walking in waist-deep water. I saw people in watercrafts … anything they could get their hands on. I saw women with their children in buckets, anything floatable. I saw people standing on their roofs waving sheets asking for help. My heart went out to those people. They were helpless and seemed hopeless, desperate even. … I knew how they felt because I was also feeling hopeless and helpless. All I could do was watch and pray and walk around like a zombie. … I watched hard, looking for my father, but I didn't see him. Several times I thought I saw him, but it wasn't him."

Gilda was worried about him; she didn't know if he had made it out safely, or if he had died in the house. Her voice was low, as if reliving the trauma from this horrific experience. She teared.

Gilda said she heard from her nieces and her brother, who had also been displaced by Katrina. Since they had cell phones, she was able to speak to them from time to time. While she knew one sister was safe and with her children, for several days she did not know the whereabouts of her other sister. She was perplexed, because even after the hurricane, she had not received information from anyone about the whereabouts of her sister, Skinny. Not expecting an answer, but hoping for some explanation from her dad, Gilda mumbled aloud, "I do not know why my sister was not traveling with her children and grandchildren." If Mr. Chuckie knew the answer to this question, he did not provide one. He was silent.

I did not want to get sidetracked in this session. Hence, I said, "There appears to be some unknown factors associated with the hurricane; not knowing where your father was and not knowing why your sister was not with her children. What we know right now is that your sister is safe. I'm wondering if we could stay with your father's story and deal with Skinny's story later. Perhaps she could address your concerns over her whereabouts in a private conversation."

I continued, "Right now, Mr. Chuckie seems to be carrying some heavy thoughts and feelings just hearing your story and your pain associated with the hurricane as it relates to him. It might be too much of a burden for Mr. Chuckie to talk about an additional concern right now."

Sensing Mr. Chuckie was hearing firsthand about Gilda's experience of searching for him during the 7 days he was housed in the Superdome for the first time, I decided it might be too painful for Mr. Chuckie to talk about what he knew or did not know about Skinny. As with any trauma, it was necessary in this case for Mr. Chuckie to feel emotionally secure in the therapeutic environment and in the therapeutic process. According to Berzoff and colleagues (2011), the therapeutic process can be conceptualized as a holding environment, a container that provides safety.

I acknowledged the difficulty that comes with the not knowing. I acknowledged Gilda's pain, her grief, and the traumatic experiences of those who were "caught" in Hurricane Katrina. Not wanting to add to her pain of not knowing, I wanted to return to Mr. Chuckie's story, since we were in therapy to help him.

After some thought, Gilda agreed it made sense to talk with her sister about her concerns privately. "Sometimes it's better to leave well enough along, but leaving things alone means having no answers ... I guess I will have to be content with the unknown right how. Even though I didn't know where she was at first, I eventually knew she was safe in her apartment."

I agreed. "Skinny was safe in her apartment. She did not have the same experience as your dad. She was not held captive in the Superdome. But, I empathize with your sister's situation and your pain of not knowing where she was for a significant time. The whole situation was sad and mishandled by our government. Social injustice and rampant inequality in our country was witnessed by the world. We can only hope things have changed for the better. We can hope to stop victimizing the victim."

This statement was helpful. It allowed both Gilda and Mr. Chuckie relief from some of their hurt and pain; that which each had experienced and internalized. This process allowed both to cast off some of the critical judgment of the situation they heard from others and outsiders. This session rendered an opportunity for each to release some of the pain and disappointment they might have harbored within, and against others or themselves.

We were all silent. I believe silence is critical in the therapeutic process. It allows clients time to think and reflect during which the therapist can demonstrate empathy and a supportive environment.

With that, Gilda shifted back to the main purpose of the session. She said her dad was missing for a week. No one knew where he was. The last anybody knew he got tired of sitting in the car and left to return to his home to eat. Gilda stopped talking and looked at her dad.

Trying to provide an explanation, Mr. Chuckie said he did go home, but left for the Superdome after he realized the neighborhood was virtually empty. No one was walking the street and there were no cars moving. Everyone was gone but him. The last neighbors he encountered asked him if he was going to leave. They said, "You know the hurricane is coming, and it might flood down here."

"It was like a ghost town ... like something I saw on television," he said.

I validated his thoughts. "That must have been scary seeing everyone leave and feeling alone."

With his face cast down, he cleared his throat as though to confirm what he heard. After a few seconds, Mr. Chuckie said that although the neighbors encouraged him to leave, he still believed the storm was probably not going to be "that bad." Besides, his house had already weathered Hurricane Betsey several years earlier (1965). He did remember his neighborhood being flooded back then after the levy at the foot of the canal broke. His daughter looked at him. She remembered that time. She muttered softly, reflecting.

I asked her to think about whether the memory she shared was fresh and if it connected emotionally with the experience that brought them to the office today. My intent was to keep her connected to her emotions and to recall how she worked through the emotional impact at that time.

Gilda nodded in agreement.

We returned to Mr. Chuckie's narrative. I asked how he made the decision to leave his home.

"It was quiet and getting dark … everyone was gone … the neighborhood was a ghost town, so I decided to drive to the Superdome for the night. I took a small bag of things with me—a jacket, a little change, and my medicine, the eye drops for my eye pressure, stuff like that. I thought I would be home the next day."

As Mr. Chuckie talked, his body became tense. Gilda became his comforter. I leaned in closely and touched both of their hands as they held each other's hand. I looked in both of their eyes to demonstrate empathy and attunement. In a voice reflective of the atmosphere in the room, I asked Mr. Chuckie if he wanted to share more of this experience.

He proceeded. "I tried to drive to the Superdome, but I could only go so far. There were cars all over the place … empty cars … so, I parked my car on the levy, and I walked the rest of the way to the Dome. I stayed there, in that awful place … it was nuts."

Mr. Chuckie, a proud man, fought not to cry. It got the best of him. He heaved and cried. His daughter touched his hand.

"It sounds like you endured a great deal of loneliness and pain, struggling with the decision to leave home to drive to the Superdome. You had no idea what to expect, and right now you don't have the words to fully express what those moments were for you."

Gilda added, "He always stops the story right here … at this spot! I do not know what happened in that Dome or what he saw in that place … but I know it's painful. The first night he was at my house, he screamed and became agitated. We calmed him down and reassured him everything was ok; that he was safe here. That was the only time he expressed pain. Since than he has locked down his emotions. I want to help my dad. But I am also struggling because I thought my dad was dead. I did not know where he was for a solid week."

I sat back, shifted my position, and leaned forward. I felt my body tense, especially in my shoulders. I was reminded of my need to process this session with my supervisor and peers. As the session was nearing an end, I asked the family if we could practice some calming strategies, but before doing these, I asked them, "What is the most important thing you want to work until our next session?"

Gilda said she wanted her dad to discuss his experiences in the Superdome. She wanted him to become less anxious and calm enough to sleep at night, and to feel comfortable talking with her and the rest of the family. Gilda also said she hoped her father could feel comfortable talking with me, the therapist.

I looked at Mr. Chuckie and asked him if he found it helpful to talk about how he experienced the hurricane, if he was comfortable talking with me, and if he wanted to come back for another session.

He said it wasn't "too bad" to talk, but still didn't know if anything would change by talking about it. I said that sometimes people find it easier to talk with a stranger than with a family member, and sometimes a therapist can help a person find a way to talk with their family.

Mr. Chuckie thought about this for a minute, and said he'd give coming back "a shot." I asked him what he wanted to work on, and he said he wanted to work on what his daughter thought he should work on. He said he needed to rest at night and needed to "get things off my mind."

We scheduled an appointment for the following week. Before ending, I introduced them to breathing and meditation exercises to aid in the calming of thoughts and to help release the tension each carried in various parts of their body. I also showed them a few calming and meditation apps for their cell phones. I suggested they could do the exercises together or separately.

Mr. Chuckie gave me a strange look, so I asked him if everything was alright or if I needed to explain what I said differently. Mr. Chuckie playfully said, "I don't know anything about an app. I don't have that stuff on my phone and I'm not about to learn it. I only use the phone to talk. I don't know where y'all people come up with that stuff."

I laughed, looked at Gilda, and said; "You're right ... please forgive me for thinking you used your phone for more than to talk with your friends and family members. Sometimes, I overlook differences in how each age group uses technology. Besides, Mr. Chuckie, you have such a young face. I forget you are 77, so close to 80." We all had a good laugh at my comment.

Instead of apps, Mr. Chuckie and I discussed ways he might practice mindfulness with his walking since this was an established activity he enjoyed. We discussed where he could walk in the neighborhood and established a schedule where he and his daughter might occasionally walk together.

Last, we practiced a communication strategy where each could express how experiences from Katrina affected them. Knowing Mr. Chuckie would most likely not write about his experiences during the week, I asked them if there was a way the conversations could be captured for future sessions. We brainstormed and decided Gilda would capture the conversations on her phone and would keep a journal. I believe parts of these conversations could be useful in future meetings.

Now that the first session with Mr. Chuckie is complete, please respond to the following questions before moving on with the case.

1. Make a list, with supporting evidence, of the main issues in Mr. Chuckie's life at the time of the interview. Include a list of his personal and social strengths that may be used as resources in the future pertaining to each of the issues listed.

2. Based on the case information so far, begin drawing a three-generation genogram (including important nonfamily members, if needed) to represent Mr. Chuckie's presented life and circumstances. Make any notes and figures on this genogram to aid in developing a wholistic view of this case.

3. What information was not discovered during this session? What would you have done differently throughout the assessment? Are there questions you would not have asked or pushed for more information on?

4. The author noticed her personal reaction to the session through body tension, realizing she was having her own reaction to the discussion, based on her personal and family experience with Hurricane Katrina. How do you determine if you are experiencing the beginnings of countertransference or are having a vicarious trauma response during your work with clients?

5. When you do have a personal reaction to a session, what course of action can you take to ensure excellent practice, and to practice self-care prior to the next session with your triggering client?

EXPERIENCING VICARIOUS TRAUMA IN THERAPY

I work at an agency where my clinical supervisor has an open-door policy. Fortunately for me, no one was in her office when I popped in, minutes after Mr. Chuckie and Gilda left. I asked if she had a moment to spare, as I needed to process the session I had just completed. As usual, she welcomed me into her office.

I talked with her about my family and friend connections to Hurricane Katrina, the family I just met, and my anger and frustration about how I believe discrimination and racism played a huge role in the way people in New Orleans were treated during—and after—the crisis.

My supervisor understands the notion of parallel process during supervision sessions. That is, she knows to create an environment where she works with me in the same ways she wants me to work with my clients. Hence, my supervisor listened empathetically and validated my perspectives. I told her how I found myself glued to the television during the days people were held hostage in an unthinkable inhumane environment (the Superdome) where they witnessed—or suffered—physical and sexual assault, medical crises, poor hygiene, and death. I talked about the humiliation these individuals must have experienced as they lacked adequate resources to address basic needs while living in a sports arena. According to reports, these were 7 days in hell. The New Orleans Convention Center may have even been worse, if that was possible.

I needed to talk about how the media and government officials labeled Black people as "looters," while describing White people involved in the same activities as people trying to obtain what they needed to meet their basic needs. While I had harbored anger about all of this for several months, meeting Mr. Chuckie on this day, knowing he lived that nightmare as an elderly Black man who had provided for his family for years, made my anger and pain surface.

The session with my supervisor gave me the opportunity to voice the pain and anger I had internalized the past couple of months. Watching live television coverage of the devastated areas of New Orleans from the hurricane and floods, I recalled crying tears of helplessness as people searched for separated and missing loved ones. I recalled crying while people waved banners (HELP ME) made of bedsheets, standing on rooftops begging for help. I cried as I saw Black faces walking knee deep in filthy water trying to get to a place of safety. I cried, too, as I saw covered dead bodies lying on the streets and propped up in wheelchairs in and around the Superdome and convention center. Lastly, I cried when I saw newscasters and camera persons show pictures of vulnerable women begging to be treated with humanity and compassion, by simply asking to have their children's basic needs met.

I also talked to my supervisor about the needs of women in those facilities, how they most likely had no hygiene items to address their menstrual flow, how they were targeted for sexual assault in those unsafe spaces ... how little babies and toddlers had to wear dirty diapers because the parents ran out of these things. The citizens of New Orleans, like the rest of society, had not envisioned the stay in the Superdome or convention center would last so long. Everyone was unprepared—especially government at all levels.

In exasperation I said, "Supplies, even the basics, were limited. No one was prepared for this level of devastation. The government ... our government ... failed to respond appropriately to this disaster in a timely manner, and from my perspective, the police overreacted. They responded out of fear and their own vulnerability and not out of concern for struggling people. These people, these first responders, were also adversely affected by the hurricane ... I get it ... they lost things, too. Their family members were also scattered about, but I am sure they were not caught in these inhuman public shelters."

My supervisor gave me the space and permission to cry. I was able to voice the pain I had internalized and not felt comfortable enough to discuss before. I cried, too, because I was ashamed by the negative thoughts I might have harbored along with the rest of society, thinking, "these people should have left the city when the mayor said to leave."

How could I be so cruel, so insensitive, and so elitist? I knew better! I had to admit my shame and come to grips with the notion that in some ways I was no different from the rest of the U.S. population. I was one of the "us" in the United States. I knew the people caught in this disaster did nothing to deserve the treatment they unfortunately experienced. Many people live from paycheck to paycheck or are unemployed. Many people rely on public transportation. Many people simply had no place to go! These unfortunates, these vulnerable people, most of whom were Black, ended up in that hell that was the Superdome, the convention center, or sleeping on highway overpasses, waiting for the authorities to come to their rescue.

My supervisor was keenly aware of how distraught I was at this moment. She asked a colleague to cover my next appointment. Then, she helped me utilize the same mindfulness and meditation skills I introduced to Mr. Chuckie and Gilda earlier. We practiced grounding techniques and calming strategies. We did not dwell on systemic societal practices that created the chaos resulting from Katrina, instead we talked about ways of changing supervision to focus on broader societal issues that influence treatment.

She helped me in many ways and made me more aware of the power of supervision to help clinicians work through issues they may share with clients. In this case, my experience with Katrina through my family, friends, and my identity as a Black woman from that region made me vulnerable to the effects of vicarious trauma the moment I met Mr. Chuckie and began hearing his story.

At our next group clinical supervision session, she allowed me to present my client and talk about issues of countertransference and vicarious trauma I had experienced. My colleagues were empathetic, expressed genuine regard, and validated my pain. They felt free to talk about similar experiences they had with vicarious trauma. It became evident that several colleagues had personal struggles they believed interfered with clinical treatment. We agreed to trust and support one another when we struggled with personal issues that could negatively affect the therapeutic process. We decided to incorporate time to discuss vulnerable topics in individual supervisory sessions and in clinical group sessions when warranted. In the meantime, we talked about strategies and advocacy projects we could implement to unpack the pain myself and others were experiencing.

Clinical supervision allows practitioners the opportunity to address concerns, feelings, behaviors, thoughts, and unaddressed trauma that can be triggered when working with clients who have similar issues. Supervisors and other staff can become more sensitive and feel supported when they, too, are dealing with unaddressed traumas, fears, and other societal issues. Good supervision based in parallel process assists professional practitioners in their professional development thereby increasing their professional growth (Shulman, 2010). I learned in this case just how important supervision that is built on trust and empathy can be, not only for my clients, but for myself as a human being. Mr. Chuckie's case, at least so far, had taught me that I needed to care for myself if I hoped to be helpful to him.

QUESTIONS

1. Search the professional literature about vicarious trauma and counter-transference and its effects on clinical practice and clinicians' mental health. What does the literature say about this subject that pertains to this case and your personal professional practice?
2. Find a group of trusted peers. Participate in a serious discussion about a time when you have experienced many of the same issues the author has described. Because this happens to all practitioners involved with clients, do not be ashamed to admit your experiences and talk them through. Take this opportunity to learn from other's experiences.
3. What strategies and supports have you, or will you, put into place to help navigate the personal aspects of clinical practice? Discuss your plans and ideas with peers and mentors in your professional life.

SECOND SESSION

Mr. Chuckie's second session occurred 2 weeks later. Gilda was unable to participate at the start of the session but told her dad she would make every effort to join before it ended. Knowing Gilda might arrive later, I informed the office person to let me know when Mr. Bayou's daughter arrived. It was an opportunity for me to get to know Mr. Chuckie better without Gilda present. I thought Mr. Chuckie might share more of his story, and I was interested to learn if his story differed from what Gilda had said in the previous meeting.

Mr. Chuckie was sitting in an end chair in the waiting room with his hat in his hand. He looked a little anxious and unsure of his surroundings. Another person was in the waiting room. Occasionally, clients seem reluctant to make eye contact with others perhaps due to the strangeness of the environment or wanting to respect each other's reason for being there. Or, perhaps people are uncomfortable being in a counseling center waiting room.

At any rate, Mr. Chuckie smiled and stood as I entered the room. He appeared to relax after seeing a familiar face. Due to my southern culture and having a desire to give my client a comforting hug, I quickly regrouped, smiled to self, and extended my hand to Mr. Chuckie. I decided the hug could wait.

I led him to my office and offered him a seat. There was a sofa and a chair in the office. He chose the chair perhaps because it provided a secured self-contained space, and at his age perhaps it was easier to get in and out of. I asked if he wanted a bottle of water or a cup of coffee. He accepted the water and said he stopped drinking coffee a while ago because of his overactive bladder. I laughed and told him to let me know if he needed to use the bathroom.

It was important to ensure Mr. Chuckie was comfortable, so I engaged in small talk before moving into the issues for counseling. Because it had snowed a little that week, I asked Mr. Chuckie how he handled the snow.

He laughed, "I don't know why people live up here. I could not walk outside the day it snowed. I did not have boots, just tennis shoes. A couple of days after it snowed, Gilda took me shopping for a heavy jacket and a pair of boots. She said the weather here is unpredictable and she wanted me to be prepared for the next snowstorm. I told her I did not want to spend a lot of money on those things because I'm not planning on being up here too long … in fact, I've already been here too long. I'm ready to go home to warm weather. I don't want to be in the snow!"

Mr. Chuckie said this statement again with emphasis, "I don't want to be here in the snow!"

"I understand how you feel about the snow," I said. I proceeded to tell him about my first snow experience and how I also did not have the right shoes, the right type of coat, and my children did not have snowsuits. I shared that I didn't even know how to walk in the snow … that I was slipping and sliding … looking like a nut!

Both of us laughed at how unprepared southern newcomers are in cold snowy weather the first time around. After I reflected on my statement about newcomers, I was aware there was more to Mr. Chuckie's statement about not wanting to spend a lot of money on boots and coats. Mr. Chuckie was ready to return home. He wanted the comfort of his familiar community.

I asked him if there was anything pressing on his mind we should talk about first before we talked about the reason he came to see me 2 weeks ago. He said he received some papers from FEMA about his house in New Orleans, and his daughter was helping him complete the forms. He said he didn't understand the forms and didn't understand "Road Home."

It turns out, Road Home is a program funded by the federal government that provides federal grant money to help Louisiana rebuild, through grants, or sell houses severely damaged by Hurricane Katrina, and now Hurricane Rita. He said he was grateful his daughter was helping him because the whole thing was confusing and complicated.

I told him that I had heard about the Road Home project, and it sounded complicated to me, too. "I'll bet having Gilda to help complete the forms is a great asset and you might want to keep her involved during the entire process," I said.

"You're right about that. I won't sign my name to anything without talking to my daughter and my son. They understand that stuff more than I do. Hell, I don't want to sign away my house or my property."

I agreed. "Everyone needs to be careful about any papers they receive. You are being wise to seek the assistance of your son and daughter. I'm sure they respect you for this and I'm sure it's not a problem for them."

For the first time, Mr. Chuckie spoke of his wife, claiming she did not understand about the flooding that took place. He claimed she has dementia and needs constant assistance. He said he is glad she lives in Michigan with family, because it would have been hard to take care of her in New Orleans, especially after all the damage.

"Besides ... I'm up here now because the people in New Orleans have not allowed the people from the Lower Ninth Ward to go back to their homes yet."

I asked him to tell me whom he meant when he said, "the people." That is, I asked Mr. Chuckie, "Who are the people you believe are not allowing the residents from the Lower Ninth Ward to return home?"

"I think the mayor doesn't want people to go to their homes ... I heard the police were stopping people from going to their homes. I guess they closed the bridges so people could not cross the canal."

I knew some areas of the Lower Ninth Ward, but I wanted Mr. Chuckie to be specific. I asked which bridges.

"They closed the St. Claude and Claiborne Bridges, so some people tried to cross that other bridge, the um, the um, hell, what's that bridge ... oh yeah, the Florida Walk Bridge. They stopped people from crossing that bridge, too. I heard only the police could get across the bridge because they thought the entire area was dangerous."

He also said it was "dark" in the Lower Ninth because there was no electricity. He also believed some of the streets might be cracked and caved in from the water. He heard from friends that they [the police] were still looking for dead bodies in some homes. They wanted to finish searching all the homes and businesses before people could go back and look at their property.

"I know people want to go home ... but it makes sense to keep residents safe," I said.

"I don't know what I will find when I go back. My other daughter was able to go back because she lived uptown. Maybe I can stay with her until I find a place to live," said Mr. Chuckie.

"Your other daughter?" I asked.

"Yea, Skinny is back home and she lets me know what she knows and hears from time to time."

Getting reliable information is helpful, I said. It can help you make decisions, especially when you know the information is coming from credible sources.

Mr. Chuckie nodded but appeared contemplative, not animated as he talked about going home. I allowed his mood to encapsulate the space. His breathing ebbed and flowed at different rhythms. His eyes were downcast. I could tell he was sad and expressed to him my observations of his apparent sadness.

"Can you tell me where in your body you feel tension?" I asked.

"Yeah ... I have a headache and my chest hurts a little ... don't worry, my heart's good ... I just had a physical when I got here from New Orleans." He said the Red Cross made sure he had good health care.

"It's good to know that your heart is ok. ... Are you comfortable doing some tension-reduction exercises with me right now?"

After agreeing, we did tension-reduction and calming exercises, breathing and body scanning until he relaxed. This process helps the client to stay present and not become overwhelmed by the memory of past experiences (Van Der Kolk, 2015).

I asked Mr. Chuckie more about the FEMA Road Home papers. I wondered if the presence of these papers influenced his thoughts today.

He claimed the papers were confusing, and he did not know what to do about his house. According to Mr. Chuckie, he has the choice of selling his property or rebuilding on it.

"I don't' know what to do ... I don't want to make the wrong decision." He took a deep breath and said, "I'll just have to wait and see ... I won't know anything until I get there." "I just have to wait and see," he said again.

I did not rush him during this session. I offered time for him to reflect on what he knew and to openly express what he was uncertain about. He had freedom to express his thoughts without judgment.

Using a constructivist framework (Carpenter & Brownlee, 2017), Mr. Chuckie was able to narrate his story from his lens.

I said to him, "It must be difficult to be in limbo; to not be allowed to go home ... and to worry about what might or might not be there. It's also got to be scary to worry about dead bodies still being in homes and not knowing if some of these bodies are people you know."

I gently touched Mr. Chuckie's hand to ease the trembling and tension I observed. In the first session with Mr. Chuckie and his daughter, I observed the calming effect of touch. Therefore, I utilized this technique with Mr. Chuckie. Not only did I want him to become physically calm, but I wanted the therapeutic space to be a secure holding environment that felt safe.

Without prompting, Mr. Chuckie said he heard most of the information about the Lower Ninth Ward's situation from the television news and Skinny. He repeated that he will not really know how things are there until he returns home.

"I'm worried because I don't know what the house might look like. I had to leave everything behind when I left for the Superdome. All my papers are there ... everything ... pictures, memories ... you know. I hope my stuff is still in the house ... I hope nobody stole my stuff," he said.

He thought for a moment. I could see stress lines burrowed across his forehead. "I guess everything is messed up since the waters were in the house for a long time. You know the house is made of wood and siding with sheetrock inside ... In fact, the house was in another flood ... yeah, that was Hurricane Betsy around 1965 or so, something like that. We didn't live there, but my wife's aunt lived there. In fact, we got that house after the aunt's son died. We paid the back taxes. That's how we got that house ... It's been in the family for a long time. It was a double, but we fixed it up and made it a one family home. It didn't cost much then. Now I have to get money to fix the house or something ... Maybe that's what this Road Home thing is about."

Mr. Chuckie fell into silence. I thought it important to allow it to linger. He needed space to process all he had just said. I didn't want to rush things. I thought it was important for Mr. Chuckie to give voice to his concerns, to externalize his thoughts, and to have the time to reflect on his statements. After a few silent seconds that seemed more like minutes, I reflected what he said: "Sounds like there is a lot of uncertainty about the status of the house ... in fact your whole life. It sounds like you aren't quite sure about the condition the house is in or about what it might cost to repair or rebuild it ... heck, whether you can even live in it the way you have always lived. I also hear the house has been in your wife's family for a while, and that's important to you."

I looked directly at Mr. Chuckie and said, "I understand your concern about the unknown, about being so far away from home and not be able to see how New Orleans looks with your own eyes. That must be difficult and scary and hard to make any decisions ... It sounds like there are many factors to consider here. Based on what I've observed and heard about the process with Road Home, I believe you will have time to make decisions that will ultimately work well for you and your family. You have your son and daughters helping you with decisions regarding the home and property. Would you consider sharing more of these thoughts with them? I believe they are committed to helping you. From where I stand, they appear to be supportive ... I'm wondering, how you see their involvement"?

Mr. Chuckie acknowledged that his children have been helpful, and that he would not be here if it had not been for them. "I know I can depend on them."

"I'm sure if you speak with your friends they will most likely agree with the statement you just made, that your children are dependable," I said.

I looked at the clock. We had but a few more minutes left in the session. I asked if there was something else he might have on his mind. "Are you resting better at night?"

Mr. Chuckie said he was sleeping a little better, mainly because he had begun talking more with his daughter about his experiences at the Superdome. He claimed he was mad at himself because he got out of the car and left his daughter's car during the evacuation. "I hated that it was taking so long … we were in the car over 4 hours … a ride that is normally 20 to 25 minutes … It made no sense to me at the time," he said.

I nodded at him as a way of reassuring him, and to hopefully encourage him to continue talking.

"Now you know the food at home was not that important … I guess I didn't think … I didn't think it would get that bad. I'm sorry my daughter and everybody had to worry about me like that. I should have stayed in the car … but it's done now, nothing I can do about it now. I didn't have any minutes on my phone, and I couldn't call anybody … I was stuck."

He paused, appearing to be in deep thought. I allowed him space for his thoughts to take shape, and said, "Seems like something is on your mind. Do you want to talk about it?"

"When I was at the Dome, I ran into my neighbor, Al. He lived around the corner. He had that 'sugar,' you know … and he didn't have his medicine. He only had one shoe and he didn't have his teeth with him. I didn't see him the first day I was there, but when I saw him I didn't feel alone. We kept one another company. I took care of him … made sure he was safe. When food was brought in, I made sure he ate. When doctors came, I saw to it that they gave him treatment … You know, it wasn't safe in the Dome. I slept on the floor on cardboard. Other times, I slept in the stadium chairs next to my buddie. We were always together. There was a lot of screaming in that place … there was no peace."

He paused. "Did you know that somebody actually jumped from high up in the stadium and killed himself … just jumped to their death, for all of us to see! It really was like being in hell on earth."

"Oh Mr. Chuckie, I am so sorry you had to experience all that you saw and heard at the Dome. No wonder you are having difficulty sleeping. There is so much pain and real fear bottled up inside of you. I am so glad you are here talking with me. I know you are not really enjoying Michigan, but I believe you are safe here for now. In time, I believe you will return to your New Orleans, and I hope the city will have the resources needed for everyone to thrive. Thank you for sharing this story."

I continued, "You said you've had the opportunity to talk with Gilda about some of these things. I'm glad you can talk about these things together. The sharing of these horrific events is the beginning of healing, not just for you but for her as well."

I wanted to assist Mr. Chuckie in changing his narrative and suggested he close his eyes if he was comfortable, and to try saying to himself: "I am in a safe place now. I don't have to worry about the things I worried about in the Dome." Before we started this self-talk, I suggested we do some mindfulness exercises to become grounded and to release felt tension. Mr. Chuckie participated in the process.

Our session was about to end. It appears that Gilda was unable to make it. I asked Mr. Chuckie if he felt ok waiting for his daughter in the waiting room.

"I'm fine ... thanks ... I'll give her a call to see how long I'll have to wait. By the way ... that breathing stuff has been working ... It's not hocus pocus ... Gilda and I have been doing it whenever we get a chance, and she got that thing on her phone like you asked," he said.

With that, our session ended. I really hoped I would see him again in a couple of weeks.

THIRD SESSION

In 2 weeks, both Mr. Chuckie and Gilda attended the session. Mr. Chuckie seemed in excellent spirits on this day.

"This is my last time coming to see you ... they are finally opening up the Ninth Ward ... I'm leaving in a couple of days. I'm gonna stay with my other daughter ... she has a small place, only one bedroom, but I'll get an air mattress or something and sleep on that. It a' do for a while ... Yea, I think everything a' be alright," he said.

I asked if he was anxious or worried about how he might find things in New Orleans, particularly in the Lower Ninth Ward.

"I'm a little worried, yeah, but I'm ready to go back home. I know my house is destroyed, and I'll have to look for another place to stay at some point ... I can't stay with my daughter forever," he said.

I looked at Gilda to see how she felt about her dad's move.

"I'm ok with dad going back home," she said. "He needs to see for himself how the living situation is there. We've talked with people who have gone back already, and with people who have visited the Lower Ninth Ward. We know it's bad there. We've seen stuff on the news, too, but that's not the same as seeing things with your own eyes. We know the Lower Ninth is like a ghost town ... It's a mostly Black community, and like many things that's mostly Black, that area is not a priority for the city."

I nodded and she continued, "There is no power there ... no electricity, no lights ... nothing. It's just empty homes, tall grass, junk that floated out of homes ... houses setting on top of houses ... cars setting on top of cars ... trees uprooted. It's like living in another country, but this is the United States".

"You seem sad," I noted.

"I am not just sad" she said. "I'm angry and hurt, and at the same time, I'm also hopeful. My dad is lonely here. When he walks in the neighborhood, he walks alone. He doesn't have 'hanging out' buddies here. No one honks their horn in recognition of him here. It's like he doesn't exist … he has no one to talk trash with … you know, whatever his generation talks about … who knows!"

She continued, "I've taken him to a men's Bible study group here, but he finds the men stuffy and 'righteous.' There is no connection for him here … I really am OK with him going back home. It's just that I'm sad about the house … and that his expectations won't be met."

"Can you say more about this?" I asked.

"Well, just like he had to evacuate his home, and just as he found himself in a different environment, so did his buddies and his church members. Only a few people have a place to return to in New Orleans. It's not like his friends lived on the West Bank or in part of New Orleans that did not flood. I'm afraid he will be lonely and depressed. I'm afraid he won't know what to do … and even if he knew what to do, I'm afraid there would be no resources there for him. You know, he's from that generation of Black men who learned to survive on their own … even if it was dysfunctional, they survived!"

I turned to Mr. Chuckie who was quietly listening to the conversation. "It seems both of you have some degree of anxiety about you returning home to New Orleans. While it appears both of you see returning home as the right thing to do, at the same time both of you are a little concerned about what you might or might not find there."

"I know it's going to be hard … but I have to go back. This is not home … New Orleans is home," he said.

"I understand," I said. "I appreciate both of your concerns. Both are valid reasons to return or not to return. I've watched the news regarding updates on reviving the city, and Gilda is right. There are not too many places to live. The Lower Ninth is not habitable. At least, you, Mr. Chuckie, can stay with your other daughter for a while."

I continued, "What would you do if you found retuning home was not what you expected? What would you do if your buddies were not there or the house and those items you were concerned about were missing?" I wanted Mr. Chuckie to begin thinking of other options … something that would be palatable for himself and his family.

Mr. Chuckie said, "Well," and cleared his throat. "I know everyone won't be back, but some will. It'll be good to see my friends and people from church. I know other people, too, people who live uptown and back of town. It's already spring in New Orleans. I can't take this cold weather anymore … I just need to go home. I didn't think I would be here this long. Besides, my daughter said things are getting better every day. I don't need much," he said.

Gilda looked at her dad and said, "It's OK, Daddy, I know you're not happy here. I know you are lonely here. I just want you to know how I feel. I know you grew up with little, and I know you know how to survive and make do. You didn't grow up on a 'bed of ease.' I know you will make it … so, don't worry about leaving momma because she's OK. Besides, there is no reason for her to return. She has dementia anyway and there are no resources for her there. I just want you to come back and visit her. As for the house, we'll help you with this. You don't need to make any decisions about the house or the property right way … Let's take one step at a time."

As the session was coming to an end, I said to Mr. Chuckie, "Are you ok with Gilda's concerns and with her belief in what you can do?"

Again, Mr. Chuckie said he was ready. "I already packed my clothes and have my train ticket. My granddaughter, Skinny's daughter, is picking me up from the train station. I'm ready."

From a constructivist perspective, Mr. Chuckie has a narrative of strength and resilience. Even when he experienced traumatic situations in the past, he was able to work through those experiences in ways that enhanced his ability to move forward. Giving voice to his traumatic experience with his daughter, and within this therapeutic holding environment, Mr. Chuckie was able to safely integrate his current experience into his dominant narrative (Jirek, 2016).

Returning home will allow him to strengthen his narrative. He anticipates receiving support from established relationships in his church and with his life-long buddies; men he worked with as laborers on the river front, who learned to "take the bitter with the sweet," and with men who learned to provide for their families with the resources that were available to them in ways that maintained their positions as head of home.

I thanked Mr. Chuckie for sharing his experiences of survival with me, particularly his experiences related to Hurricane Katrina. I validated his right to self-determination by telling him he demonstrated fortitude and remarkable strength to turn a poorly thought out decision to return to New Orleans when people who were evacuating into a decision to go to the Dome that led to life instead of death. Despite how bad it was in the Superdome, he survived, when so many did not.

Leaving his home and a community that experienced environmental devastation, and going to a place where rescue was possible, was an act of bravery in the midst of chaos, I said. I encouraged Mr. Chuckie to practice any calming strategies that suited his level of comfort. I also encouraged Mr. Chuckie to keep his phone charged, to call Gilda and to share with her the good and the bad things he found about returning home.

I looked at Gilda who nodded and confirmed my summary. Gilda said, "When we get home, let's set up days and times when we will touch base. As a matter of fact, let's talk each day at least for a few minutes. Are you ok with this Daddy?"

I told Mr. Chuckie I would be happy to research the availability of therapy for him if he was open to talking with someone back home, just in case things got a little tough and overwhelming. Knowing how Mr. Chuckie saw the role of his pastor, I encouraged him to reach out to his pastor for support. Notwithstanding the importance of his friends, I encouraged Mr. Chuckie to touch base with his friends on a regular basis, and to feel comfortable asking hard questions, having frank and real discussions.

I wanted to provide Mr. Chuckie with a way to normalize his thoughts and feelings. I wanted him to know he was not alone. Mr. Chuckie said yes to these suggestions. He said he would talk with Gilda several times a week about everything New Orleans, even about his feelings that might be negative or positive.

I thanked Gilda for coming with her dad, and I encouraged her to come for herself, that she, too, was psychologically and socioculturally affected by Hurricane Katrina. Even prior to her leaving, I asked her if she wanted to make an appointment. She said not at that point, but that she had the agency's number and that she would utilize therapy if she continued to feel overwhelmed with her father's experiences, but said she would consider coming for therapy as she experiences the caustic narratives of other family members.

QUESTIONS

1. Based on the information in this case, what is your opinion about Mr. Chuckie's decision to return to New Orleans? Provide specific reasons why you agree or disagree with his decision.
2. Based on the information in the case, how do you think the author handled the situation and Mr. Chuckie's decision? Again, be specific.
3. Based on what you know about Mr. Chuckie and the conditions in New Orleans in the immediate months post-Katrina, what concerns, issues, or worries do you have about how Mr. Chuckie will handle his return? Make a list of his possible issues and strengths that may either hinder or help his adjustment to returning home.

TWO WEEKS LATER

Gilda called and left a message prior to my arrival at the office. She seemed in a panic. "My dad called me from New Orleans very early this morning, about 6:00 AM. He was crying incoherently and mumbling. He said he wanted to die. I know it's early, and you're probably not at work, but please call me as soon as you get this message."

I called Gilda back as soon as I received the message. I began by acknowledging the painful conversation she had with her dad that morning and validated her concerns and fears. Since my schedule that day made it impossible to see her in person, I offered some time on the telephone immediately and an in-person appointment the following day. She accepted.

As she recounted the disturbing call from her father. I helped her develop strategies to help ensure his immediate safety, including getting her sister in New Orleans involved. She said she would call her sister, discuss it with her, and check to see how both her father and sister were holding up.

The next day, Gilda came for her appointment appearing emotionally and physically drained. I asked her if it was ok to give her a hug as both of us culturally understood the importance and healing power human touch. She agreed. I embraced her softly, allowing her to feel comforted.

In a gentle but validating voice, I said, "You look exhausted. I'm sure yesterday was hard for you. How are things going with Dad?"

From Gilda, there was rested quietness. Again, the therapeutic environment provided safety. It held, comforted her, and allowed healing to begin. "I hope things have calmed down for your father today. Your presence here indicates he survived yesterday. Where do you want to begin? You are free to talk about your dad, yourself, and anything else that's important to you right now. You can also just sit and relax; breathe and reflect. This is your time to use as you wish and as you need."

It was important for me to let the Gilda know she was important, and although her dad was the initial client, she, too, suffered through the trauma and lingering effects of Hurricane Katrina.

Gilda proceeded to talk about the previous day being "horrible." "I shouldn't have gone to work … I couldn't concentrate at all. It was my job's yearly retreat and the agenda was full. I got really irritated because my colleagues focused on trivial stuff … I found myself becoming really sad and angry."

"How did you handle this?"

"I could not contain myself … I was feeling restless and vulnerable all at the same time."

At some point, while her colleagues were talking "about nothing, but making it seem so important," Gilda had "finally had enough." Before she could stop herself, she burst open, saying, "You know … there are important things going on in the world and here we are talking about much of nothing." Gilda claims the room went silent.

Gilda shared bits of the conversation she had with her dad earlier that morning. While some of her colleagues listened with hearts of compassion, others were patronizing, lacking true empathy. "I felt exposed, misunderstood. People who were not personally affected by Katrina don't really understand how it impacts loved ones watching from a distance … what it's like to hear of the suffering of those inside and outside the Superdome who suffered through the chaos of that week … and are still suffering. These families had enormous loss … they were stigmatized and blamed for being ill-prepared or not following instructions to evacuate. They were victimized and humiliated. They were stuck in the Superdome, in the convention center, in their homes, and God knows where else!"

I nodded, shifted my position, and made sure my facial expressions demonstrated empathy and concern. I listened, affirmed, and allowed her to talk about what was important. She needed to share her story in a place where she felt supported and understood.

"About Dad … I barely understood what he was saying. He scared me. I didn't know what was going on. I was sleeping and he caught me off guard. I asked him to calm down and to speak slowly. I said, 'Breathe, Daddy, just breathe.' I stopped talking and waited for his crying and heaving to stop and said, 'What's the matter, Daddy?' He said he just couldn't take it anymore. He kept repeating this over and over, 'I can't take it anymore!'"

Gilda wanted to know what he couldn't take but said her father could not stop crying and she knew she couldn't comfort him on the phone, so she asked him to put Skinny on the phone. Gilda asked her sister, "Why is Daddy crying?"

Skinny said, "He wants to kill himself."

Gilda appeared deeply saddened and scared as she told her story. She cried and felt overwhelmed. I validated her sense of helplessness, "I know this is difficult for you, knowing your father is in a great deal of emotional pain as he struggles with being back in New Orleans, and seeing devastation from the hurricane. It's most likely hard for your sister to live with and see your father struggle with the devastation that occurred in his beloved city, the loss of his home, not knowing where his friends and other family members are … yes, it is hard for everyone. But, he called … he reached out to you just as he said he would … and, no, you don't have answers, but you were there. And Skinny was there. Your father is alive right now. Can you share what you did next?"

Gilda looked at me and said, "I called his pastor, and the pastor said, 'Bro Bayou looked fine to me the last time I saw him. He'll be fine! It's hard, but he'll be fine!'" Gilda did not seem to find solace in those remarks.

Mr. Chuckie was active in his church and believed in spiritual healing. She said the pastor would probably not mention the phone call to him, and she would not mention her conversation with the pastor to her dad. She said she would rather not upset him or embarrass him if he was simply having a moment. "I sure hope the pastor follows up after my dad," she said.

"We can explore resources for mental health," I said. "We can check to determine the role of the Red Cross, and we can check to see if there are other emergency services there or nearby. It's been 5 months since the hurricane, so most definitely something is available."

As we explored mental health resources. We understood these resources might be limited. Because her dad was staying with her sister, and since the sister's daughter was also in New Orleans, we knew both individuals would be resourceful in keeping their dad safe. We said we would talk with the sister about symptoms to look for with her dad and provide her with the location of emergency services. We would also encourage her sister about when it would be appropriate to call the police.

Gilda was satisfied with the strategies we outlined. We considered future appointments to help her work through the impact of this trauma on her life. In the meantime, I called Gilda the day after this session and provided her with information on the Red Cross and the role they would play in an emergency. I also provided her with information on other emergency places close to where her dad was living. She said her dada seemed better, but that she was still concerned.

"Imagine how devastating it must be for a man of his age, to really understand that the life he had built for so many years was gone," she said.

I couldn't agree more.

QUESTIONS

1. React and respond to Mr. Chuckie's crisis described in the last section of the case. Based on your list of issues and strengths prior to him returning to New Orleans, how predictable were the circumstances described in the case?

2. Let's assume for a minute that you were the therapist who Mr. Chuckie was referred to in New Orleans. Based on the information from the entire case, what strategies would you employ to be helpful?

3. What further information would you need to determine the best course of action, that is, to formulate diagnoses, a treatment plan, an intervention plan, and a safety plan?

4. Based on your list of issues and strengths, write a one-page narrative assessment that could guide your initial meetings with Mr. Chuckie.

REFERENCES

Berzoff, J., Flanagan, L.M., & Hertz, P. (2011). Why psychodynamic theories? Why biopsychosocial context? In, (J.Berzoff, LM Flanagan, & P. Hertz (eds), *Inside out and outside in: Psychodynamic clinical theory and psychopathology in contemporary multicultural contexts* (3rd ed). pp. 1–18. Rowman & Littlefield.

Carpenter, D. E., & Brownlee, K. (2017). Constructivism: A conceptual framework for social work treatment. In F. J. Turner (Ed.), *Social work treatment: Interlocking theoretical approaches* (6th ed., pp. 96–116). Oxford University Press.

Jirek, S. L. (2016). Narrative reconstruction and post-traumatic growth among trauma survivors: The importance of narrative in social work research and practice. *Qualitative Social Work*, *16*(2), 166–188.

Rogers, C. (1995). *On becoming a person: A therapist's view of psychotherapy*. Houghton Mifflin.

Shulman, L. (1998). *Interactional supervision*. NASW Press.

Van Der Kolk, B. (2014). *The body keeps the score: Brain, mind and body in the healing of trauma*. Penguin Books.

CHAPTER 3

Trauma-Informed Care with a Transgender Adolescent

Ash Herald

INTRODUCTION

IN THIS CHAPTER, Ash Herald describes three clinical sessions with an adolescent client named Jordan. Embedded in the case description is client information at multiple levels needed to complete the items listed and described below. Herald also provides important current best-practice literature review, where appropriate. However, they mostly omitted "clinical assessment thinking"; that is, they report mostly on the client's comments and circumstances, leaving most clinical thinking, conclusions, diagnostics, final assessment report, and treatment plan for readers to determine.

It is for the readers to read and study the case description, perhaps discuss the case with peers and colleagues, and, when finished, complete the following sections as part of the overall clinical assessment:

1. **Narrative assessment:** Readers will write a complete narrative assessment, encompassing all client data, including clinical hypotheses and conclusions. This narrative must be wholistic and consistent with the clinical diagnoses made earlier (Johnson, 2004).
2. **Clinical diagnoses:** Readers will use the client information to make clinical diagnoses. There will be at least one substance use disorder and at least one mental health disorder. There may in fact, be more.
3. **Stages of change:** Readers will determine the relevant stage of change for each clinical diagnosis, along with the justification for said change (see Chapter 1 for more on the stages of change).
4. **Treatment plan:** Using the information from above, in combination with knowledge of treatment modalities, intensities, and methods, readers will develop a treatment plan for Jordan moving forward. The treatment plan will include treatment goals, measurable objectives, and a rationale for each section.

5. **High-risk aftercare and intervention plan:** Based on Jordan's presentation and life circumstances, readers will decide how his case will be handled in the event of any high-risk activities and behaviors, and how these will be handled by the professionals and through recommendations or referrals for the client.

Remember that all assessment and clinical conclusions, diagnoses, and decision-making must be based on data contained in the case. That is, although it may be appropriate to speculate about issues based on new information learned later in therapy, any documented conclusions must have data as its foundation. Conclusions without data represents the practitioner's implicit or explicit bias, out-of-control subjectivity, too much reliance on personal life experience, or simply overconfidence. Please take steps to help avoid making clinical decisions based on practitioner life experience, beliefs, attitudes, and thoughts. This exercise is good practice about an issue that professionals must be aware of throughout their clinical careers.

Jordan's case is an interesting, challenging, and timely case to consider. Good luck!

MEETING JORDAN

Jordan was first referred to me by his parents, who were seeking private therapy for what they described as "sexual confusion" and problems at school, where he had been cutting class. I was working with a program that frequently saw LGBTQA+ (Lesbian, Gay, Bisexual, Transgender, Queer, Questioning, Asexual, and other sexual minority) adolescents, and, believing we would "fix" their "daughter," the parents ensured that we took their insurance, and then asked to have Jordan admitted to our therapeutic program.

I informed his parents I would be happy to talk to Jordan about the problems he was having at school, but we did not practice conversion therapy (a practice aimed at attempting to force LGBTQA+ people into living as cisgender, heterosexual people), as it is not ethical (World Professional Association for Transgender Health [WPATH], 2012). Jordan's father replied on the phone, "Whatever … please just get my daughter to talk about what's wrong. She needs to go to school." Apparently, Jordan was going to fail the semester if his attendance didn't improve in the next couple of months. I agreed to meet with Jordan and looked forward to hearing his story.

Jordan's parents both spoke with me on the phone prior to his visit referring to him by his given name, Catherine. He was a 15-year-old whose gender was assigned female at birth. Jordan was the only child of his white, cisgender, heterosexual, and middle-class parents. Jordan attended a private Christian school where his parents paid tuition. They spoke of his "sexual confusion" with agitation and what I gathered were feelings of embarrassment.

"She keeps stating she's a boy *at public events*. The other parents think we're not raising her right," his mother said to me, sounding frustrated. "But it's not our fault! She's so defiant."

They mentioned that Jordan had become a "disciplinary problem," starting with a suspension over an incident in the school cafeteria some months ago. Neither parent would say what Jordan had been suspended for, though both expressed they wished Jordan would "behave appropriately."

WORKING WITH LGBTQA+ ADOLESCENTS

LGBTQA+ people experience trauma at a much higher rate than their heterosexual, cisgender, and gender-conforming counterparts (Graziano & Wagner 2011; McCormick et al. 2018), including bullying (Beckerman & Auerbach, 2014; McCormick et al., 2018) and sexual assault (Cramer et al., 2012; McCormick et al., 2018). This victimization places LGBTQA+ youth at a greater risk for depression and posttraumatic stress disorder (PTSD) (Mustanski et al., 2016).

Gender-nonconforming youth (youth whose gender expression does not conform to the gender they were assigned at birth) specifically have a greater lifetime risk of PTSD (Roberts et al., 2012). Thus, while it is appropriate to incorporate trauma-informed care approaches to avoid retraumatization (i.e., a re-experiencing of the trauma) for any set of clients, this is especially relevant for LGBTQA+ clients.

Additionally, LGBTQA+ clients are at increased risk of experiencing minority stress. Minority stress is the enduring, chronic stress experienced by social minorities in stigmatizing environments due to social attitudes, including experiences of violence and discrimination (Balsam et al., 2013; Eckstrand & Potter, 2017). Research has indicated that the daily, repeated experiences of minority stress result in a higher likelihood of mental illness (Balsam et al., 2013). This being the case, minority stress can also exacerbate or compound any other trauma an LGBTQA+ person faces.

The majority of LGBTQA+ clients I have worked with have experienced several discriminatory and/or traumatic events. This means these clients often seek to ascertain during therapy whether a clinician holds any implicit or explicit bias before divulging personal information. Research indicates that this is common (McCormick et al., 2018). For LGBTQA+ people, this is a sensible precaution; historically, mental health professionals have stigmatized and pathologized LGBTQA+ people and their experiences (McCormick et al., 2018).

Trauma-informed care is an ideal choice for working with this population, then, as it is contextualizing rather than pathologizing, viewing symptoms as responses to a broader context and environment, and not a result of the person (Hales et al., 2018).

Nevertheless, a trauma-informed care approach alone may be inadequate to the task of engaging LGBTQA+ clients. McCormick et al. (2018) state that it is not enough to be nondiscriminatory; for the best outcomes, clinicians must be actively LGBTQA+ positive and supportive, and ask questions in ways that are affirming. Second-guessing a youth's self-identification may be viewed as rejection and can cause undue harm. It should further be noted that "LGBTQ identities are not symptoms of trauma or problems to be solved. It is an LGBTQ youth's experiences with discrimination and oppression that are the problems," and therefore interventions should focus on addressing that oppression and providing LGBTQA+ youth space to heal (McCormick et al., 2018, p. 162.). To avoid adding to the traumatization and minority stress experienced by LGBTQA+ clients, it is important for practitioners to interrogate their own feelings regarding sex, gender, and sexuality before working with these clients.

Transgender Adolescents

Before we go any further, we should cover some terminology relating to the transgender population in general. (Please note that these definitions are currently in use by the WPATH in the most recent [2012] edition of the *Standards of Care for the Health of Transsexual, Transgender, and Gender Nonconforming People*, and may be updated in the future.)

> **Gender dysphoria:** Distress that is caused by a discrepancy between a person's gender identity and that person's sex assigned at birth (and the associated gender role and/or primary and secondary sex characteristics).

> **Gender identity:** A person's intrinsic sense of being male (a boy or a man), female (a girl or woman), or an alternative gender (e.g., genderqueer).

> **Gender role or expression:** Characteristics in personality, appearance, and behavior in each culture and historical period that are designated as masculine or feminine (i.e., more typical of the male or female social role). While most individuals present socially in clearly male or female gender roles, some people present in an alternative gender role such as genderqueer or specifically transgender. All people tend to incorporate both masculine and feminine characteristics in their gender expression in varying ways and to varying degrees.

Sex: Sex is assigned at birth as male or female, usually based on the appearance of the external genitalia. When the external genitalia are ambiguous, other components of sex (internal genitalia, chromosomal and hormonal sex) are considered in order to assign sex. For most people, gender identity and expression are consistent with their sex assigned at birth; for transsexual, transgender, and gender nonconforming individuals, gender identity or expression differ from their sex assigned at birth.

Transgender: Adjective to describe a diverse group of individuals who cross or transcend culturally defined categories of gender. The gender identity of transgender people differs to varying degrees from the sex they were assigned at birth.

Transition: Period when individuals change from the gender role associated with their sex assigned at birth to a different gender role. For many people, this involves learning how to live socially in "the other" gender role; for others this means finding a gender role and expression that is most comfortable for them. Transition may or may not include feminization or masculinization of the body through hormones or other medical procedures. The nature and duration of transition is variable and individualized.

Not included in the WPATH Standards of Care (2012), but nevertheless important, is this term:

Cisgender: People whose gender identities match the ones they were assigned at birth (i.e., people who are not transgender).

An important note about the above terms is that sex and gender are different. Although colloquially they are sometimes treated as synonymous, sex refers purely to biological aspects of a person related to the development of reproductive organs, and gender refers to social roles, expression, and identities that may be associated with a specific sex. It should be noted that such roles and expression can vary widely between cultures, so how a person identifies and experiences their gender can vary as well.

Thus, as mentioned above, transition is a very individualized process. Not all trans people experience gender dysphoria, and gender dysphoria is not a prerequisite to seeking to transition. Some trans people may wish to transition socially (i.e., to present as their gender to others, but not medically), or to pursue some aspects of medical transition but not others (WPATH, 2012). If your client is seeking to transition, your role as a clinician is to support their decisions about their transition, to act as an advocate and resource, to be a safe person with whom they can examine all possible outcomes, and empower them to decide which is best for themselves; this is informed consent in action.

Hence, the lives and experiences of trans people are very diverse, and continued scholarship is needed to improve evidence-based practice. Existing research often focuses on trans people from North America and Western Europe, which means trans people of other cultural backgrounds may need support and resources not currently discussed in literature (WPATH, 2012). The healthcare system in the United States often requires clinicians to act as gatekeepers and may require clinicians to supply letters of recommendation for insurance companies to approve coverage for medical transition. Some advocates are rightly concerned this system places the decision of how to transition in the hands of clinicians rather than the trans person themselves (Urquhart, 2016). Working with trans clients will mean listening to them first and foremost and being prepared to act as staunch advocates for their rights and self-determination.

TRAUMA-INFORMED CARE WITH LGBTQA+ ADOLESCENTS

Trauma, as it is understood currently in clinical settings, is much more severe than typical stress; it refers to events or experiences that involve exposure to actual or threatened death, serious injury, or sexual violation (Basham, 2016).

Fallot and Harris (2009) discuss the far-reaching impacts of trauma, noting that trauma is pervasive, broad, and touches many different areas of life, from mental health, to physical health, to a person's relationships and more. Trauma can have deep and reverberating impacts on a person, and trauma can and does occur in service contexts; care providers must be careful not to *retraumatize* their clients. Moreover, trauma can affect service providers; it is intense emotional labor to work with someone who has been through a traumatic experience, and providers are often pressed to "do more with less," which may overwhelm their coping abilities (Fallot & Harris, 2009).

To address these concerns, Fallot and Harris outline five core values essential to any trauma-informed care framework: safety, trustworthiness, choice, collaboration, and empowerment.

Safety refers directly to physical and emotional safety. The accessibility and safety of the areas where service delivery takes place, how navigable a given building is, how welcoming a building's appearance and staff is, whether exits are visible and easily accessible, and who is present during service delivery are examples of considerations that establish both physical safety and a feeling of safety. Establishing a safe environment where one may become comfortable sharing sensitive, personal, and often painful information about themselves and their lives is key to effective trauma-informed care. Given that transgender youth are particularly vulnerable, establishing a safe clinical environment is important for enhancing their resilience (Torres et al., 2015). Safety is considered before and throughout the therapeutic process.

Trustworthiness refers to things like task clarity, consistency, and interpersonal boundaries. Trustworthiness is something a service provider must clearly demonstrate to their client, by communicating clearly and following through. Clearly explaining what a client can expect, the practitioner's reasoning for their suggestions, respecting informed consent, explaining and respecting boundaries, and acting in ways consistent with their words are examples of demonstrating trustworthiness, which helps engage clients. Trustworthiness must be demonstrated throughout the therapeutic process.

Choice is the effort to maximize the client's choices and control. Considerations to maximize choice include making provisions for the client to be contacted in a manner of their choosing, giving clients the opportunity to select the type and frequency of services they would like to have, and making client priorities central in treatment planning. Trauma can overwhelm the system of care that often gives people a sense of control in the world (Basham, 2016), so arranging services in a way that allows them to maximize their choices engages them in services, while emphasizing respect of their personal agency. Choice is considered throughout the therapeutic process.

Collaboration focuses on working as a team and sharing power. Examples of collaboration include ensuring that clients have a significant role in planning and evaluating the agency's services, including giving client concerns substantial weight, having client concerns validated, and cultivating a culture of doing things "with" rather than "to" or "for" a client. This includes expressing a conviction that the client is the ultimate expert on their life own experience and encourages clients to take an active role in their treatment. Collaboration happens throughout the therapeutic process and is especially relevant during treatment planning.

Empowerment means that services prioritize empowering the client and a focus on skill-building. This means that a client's strengths and skills are emphasized, that the client is validated and affirmed at each meeting, and that the client's growth is prioritized over maintenance or stability. Service providers should express a realistic optimism that clients can reach their goals and succeed.

To successfully address the trauma-informed care pillars (Fallot & Harris, 2009), I combine a trauma-informed care approach with a feminist approach to therapy when working with LGBTQA+ clients. A feminist approach focuses on therapy that is collaborative in nature as well as emphasizing client agency and self-determination (Sommers-Flanagan & Sommers-Flanagan, 2015), all priorities shared with the trauma-informed care approach. Familiarizing oneself with feminist and queer theory, as well as how LGBTQA+ experience differs for people of different races, ethnicities, classes, and levels of ability can help understand the depth of client experiences.

These approaches invite LGBTQA+ clients to be a part of the decision-making process, and to have more input and control over the pace and scope of the therapeutic practice. This helps build rapport and facilitate engagement. By empowering the client in this way, a clinician can demonstrate respect for a client's self-determination, and belief in their ability to face adversity as well as possible, a component in strengths-based approaches which can be the key factor in a person's recovery (Turner, 2011).

QUESTIONS

1. Given what you know about Jordan and his presenting problems, what issues would you consider as you prepare to meet him for the first time?
2. Because client engagement is critical in clinical situations, and especially in a case dealing with issues of gender and sexuality, how would you prepare yourself to engage Jordan in therapy?
3. What are the most important factors in client engagement with LGBTQA+ adolescents?
4. What percentage of your time do you spend working on and/or practicing your engagement skills? List several ways you can improve your practice engagement skills.
5. Before reading the next section, how do you prepare to work with clients whose issues, problems, and/or circumstances may challenge your personal, professional, or political values and/or worldview?

FIRST MEETING

Jordan came in on time, having been dropped off by his parents, and was quiet as we walked to my office. He was wearing rumpled cargo pants and a loose T-shirt, with his brown hair pulled back in a tight ponytail. I offered my name and added my pronouns. "I go by they and them. What do you go by?"

Jordan's eyebrows rose, and he smiled slightly. "I'm Jordan, he/him." He watched me closely. "I identify as a boy. That cool with you?"

"Sure is. It's nice to meet you, Jordan."

The practice of stating one's pronouns is becoming common in communities seeking to be welcoming to trans people. To quote McCormick et al. (2018), "efforts to use inclusive language and … the names and pronouns [he, she, they, etc.] with which a young person identifies can be critical in fostering a sense of safety and security for LGBTQ youth (P. 161)." This is particularly important when you consider that a client's name and pronouns may not be respected by other people in their life. From my own experience, it always helps me feel more comfortable when another person initiates this exchange. It proves they intend to treat me with respect. My initiation seemed to have a similar effect on Jordan, whose shoulders visibly relaxed.

As we continued down the hall, I pointed out the locations of the all-gender restrooms and emergency exits, "in case you need them."

Jordan nodded. As we entered my office, Jordan's eyebrows rose again. "Wow," he commented.

On the walls of my office are a rainbow Pride flag, and the blue, white, and pink Transgender Pride flag. If you provide services in an office, you have the advantage of preparing your space to be welcoming and safe to your clients; working with LGBTQA+ clients frequently, it made sense to have the Pride flags present and visible and communicated that it was an LGBTQA+ positive setting.

I waited until Jordan sat down, allowing him to choose which chair he wanted to sit in, and settled myself in the other. While he slumped in his chair, he did not cross his arms or otherwise close off his body language. I interpreted this as a lack of enthusiasm, but not a refusal to engage.

I started by explaining confidentiality. Jordan interrupted to ask, "So you can't even tell my parents? Unless somebody is going to get hurt?"

"That's correct," I confirmed.

"We'll see," Jordan said lightly, settling back in his seat.

Jordan was warning that he did not trust me to keep his secrets. Adolescents, being minors, often have very little control over the circumstances of their own life. Jordan was no exception. It also made me wonder if some other adult had betrayed Jordan's trust.

Part of how I cultivate a safe environment is by explaining that everything is voluntary. "These sessions are about you. If you don't want to talk, we can just sit here for an hour or read a magazine. If you decide you're okay with talking to me, we can stop at absolutely any time, just say the word. If there's a topic you don't want to discuss, just say so. And if there's a topic you don't want to discuss now, but might be willing to come back to later, just let me know."

"You're serious?" He asked.

"Yep."

"You're not going to make me do anything? We can just sit here and stare at the wall if I want?"

"Yep."

Jordan nodded a few times, still examining me. "Okay. And we can stop whenever I want?"

"That's correct."

"Okay, then ... I guess we can talk for a bit. But if it's not working for me then I'm going to stop."

"Good!" I agreed. Jordan's relaxed back in his chair, nodding slightly. As I had hoped, control over the session had put him at least a little more at ease. Hopefully, this would also reinforce for Jordan that participating in therapy was his choice, and not an obligation.

I went on to explain what I tend to call the "two-experts" approach to therapy, an approach informed by feminist theory (Sommers-Flanagan & Sommers-Flanagan, 2015).

"So ... I like to think we're two experts working together. I got a degree to show that I have expertise in empowering people to make change in their lives, and you're the expert on your own life. Nobody knows your life better than you, so we work together with what we know to find solutions for the stuff you're dealing with."

"Uh huh. Yeah." Jordan muttered, looking off at the wall. "Look, I know my parents told you what they think the problem is, let's just get this over with."

"Hey," I said gently. Jordan made eye contact with me, his face blank and tired.

"Yeah, your parents have told me what they think we should talk about. But it's *your* life, I'd rather know what *you* would like to change. I'm not living your life ... I don't know what you're facing ... and I'm open to hearing that maybe your parents don't know either."

Jordan's eyes seemed to tear up a little. "Yeah. They don't."

"I want them to hear you, and I want to hear you. I'm not here to lecture you. We're two experts working together. Can you lend me your expertise? Tell me what you've been dealing with?"

Jordan nodded and sat up a little. "At least you call me by my actual name." He took a deep breath. "Okay. Yeah."

Jordan talked a little about trouble sleeping, concentrating, and feeling jumpy all the time, summarizing his experience. "Like I'm freaking out, all the time, like any loud noise will just throw me. But I'm always tired because I sleep like shit—uh, like crap ..."

"You can swear," I said. Jordan smiled.

"You can, too!" He gave me permission. "But yeah, it's like I'm always wired and exhausted at the same time. I can't focus on anything. It sucks. Even just thinking about going to school makes me nauseous and nervous and I can't go in the cafeteria anymore."

"Do you eat lunch elsewhere?"

"Not really. I just skip lunch. And sometimes classes. I do all the homework, but what's the point of sitting in a chair if I'm just gonna vibrate out of my seat? Or listen to some asshole call me, uh, names for an hour? Half the time I feel like I need to run out of the room and puke."

"Have you always felt like this in school?" I asked.

Jordan shrugged. "No. I mean, sometimes nervous, but not like this."

"Can you think of when you started feeling like this?"

Jordan sighed. "Like, 6 months-ish? After I got suspended, I guess."

"What happened there?"

"According to the principal," Jordan rolled his eyes, "I 'started a fight' in the cafeteria." He made air quotes with his fingers.

"But you didn't start a fight," I prompted.

"No! But nobody wants to hear that. Nobody wants to hear that some assholes decided to …"

Jordan stopped short, squeezing the sides of his chair and glaring at the floor. Mention of the cafeteria incident caused Jordan to freeze in a way that looked to me a lot like an adrenaline response, what we call "fight, flight, or freeze."

Responses to conflict are culturally determined; we all have physiological stress responses, but the way we behave in response to physical stimuli varies based on our background and experiences (Basham, 2016). "Fight, flight, or freeze" is common among White Americans, and I wanted to avoid triggering that response with any further discussion of the incident. Discussing that incident had to be his choice, on his own terms, when he was ready. More than that, I did not want to retraumatize him by forcing him to talk about the incident if it had been traumatic, so I decided to try reorienting him to the present.

"It's okay. Just breathe … and feel your feet on the floor." I said. "Take your time."

Jordan took a minute; I audibly heard him count to five before he looked back up. "I don't wanna talk about this right now."

"That's totally okay, we can talk about other stuff."

"Look, I just don't wanna be at school, okay? It sucks. I hate it. I don't wanna deal with it."

SCHOOL CLIMATE FOR LGBTQA+ STUDENTS

The GLSEN, an organization that advocates for greater LGBTQA+ inclusivity in K-12 schools in the United States, conducts a school climate survey every 2 years. The results of these surveys consistently show K-12 schooling in the United States to be, in varying degrees, hostile to its LGBTQA+ students.

According to GLSEN's 2017 report (the most recent at the time of this writing), schools are often hostile environments for LGBTQA+ students. LGBTQA+ students surveyed often felt unsafe or uncomfortable at school because of their sexual orientation, gender expression, or gender. Responses to feeling unsafe at school included missing school (sometimes for several days), avoiding gender-segregated spaces (such as bathrooms or locker rooms), avoiding school functions and extracurriculars, and changing schools. Almost all LGBTQA+ students reported hearing homophobic remarks or negative remarks about gender expression at school, with 71% of students hearing negative remarks about gender expressions specifically from school staff.

Additionally, GLSEN found that LGBTQA+ students frequently encountered harassment or assault, ranging from the more common verbal assault (being called names or threatened) to the less common physical harassment and assault (pushed or shoved, punching, kicking, or injury with a weapon). Over half of LGBTQA+ students were sexually harassed at school, including unwanted touching. Most students who were harassed or assaulted did not report the incident to school staff, usually because they believed intervention would not be effective, or would make the situation worse. Most students who did report an incident stated that school staff did nothing in response or were told to ignore it. Some students were disciplined (detention or suspension) after reporting.

School environments are particularly hostile for transgender and gender-non-conforming (GNC) students; trans and GNC students are often prevented from using their name and pronouns and required to use bathrooms and locker rooms of their assigned-at-birth sex, rather than the ones that appropriately match their identified gender. Students who were victimized because of their gender expression were much more likely to have missed school, were more likely to have been disciplined at school, and typically had higher levels of depression (GLSEN, 2017).

In short, school is often a hostile place for LGBTQA+ adolescents in the United States. While some schools may be open to advocacy for GLSEN-recommended policies to make their environment more welcoming, it is important to support a transgender client regarding any struggles they are having at school. It is also critical to encourage and support students finding and using affirming support networks outside of the school environment.

COPING AND PREVIOUS TREATMENT HISTORY

I absolutely did not want to push Jordan in any way, especially since this was our first session and we'd barely begun building rapport. Also, I had stated earlier that Jordan could change the topic at any time, and I had to respect that. It would be up to Jordan to shift this boundary when he was ready, so I asked instead if he'd seen any clinicians before me.

"Uh, not really. I got sent to the school counselor a few times, but she was mainly interested in telling me to let bullies do whatever they wanted and then go to class like nothing happened ... super helpful." Jordan rolled his eyes.

"So, when you're dealing with stuff like this, or even when you're just feeling bad, what do you do to feel better?"

Jordan shrugged. "Exercise."

"Exercise?"

"Yeah, I'll just, like, run a lap or two around the track, do crunches in the parking lot, see how fast I can walk to the convenience store and back ... you know ... whatever."

"That's a lot of activity! You exercise every day?"

"Oh yeah, probably like five or so times a day. Like I do stuff in my room when I'm at home ... better than trying to talk to my parents. That shit goes nowhere."

"You're careful about injuries and things like that?"

"Oh yeah, I always do stretches and stuff. I get a lot of blisters on my feet, you know, because my school shoes aren't good for running and stuff, but I gotta keep exercising. Gotta do *something*, you know? I'm wired ... but I'm tired ... and I have to *do* something, or I get, like, fidgety ... then I feel like I'm gonna fall asleep wherever I am. Gotta keep moving."

"So, you exercise to keep the jitters at bay?"

"Oh my god, 'the jitters'? You must be like a million years old. But yeah, I do."

"Do you have people who support you, too, when you're feeling bad? Since your parents and the school aren't all that supportive?"

Jordan talked at some length about friends he met online in social media communities, "even my closest friends at school get weird about my name and pronouns, but online there's a lot of other people dealing with the same thing I am. We trade pics and talk about what clothes to wear."

"Other LGBTQ+ kids?"

"Yeah, other trans kids. Like my friend Cecilia is still learning dress styles, but I learned that growing up, so I tell her to look for A-line skirts to help her pass better. I don't have much chance to look at boy's clothes, so she explains the measurements and stuff to me, so maybe I can pass as a guy someday." Jordan looked at me curiously.

"You're not freaking out. Last time I said this to an adult they like, cringed."

I shrugged with my hands up. "I'm trans, too. Nonbinary. That's why I said my pronouns are they/them. What you're talking about sounds familiar to my own experiences."

"I wondered," Jordan grinned. "Just checking."

Jordan was testing me. He was comfortable with being trans. He also knew that I knew he was trans. Yet, based on my pronouns, he tested my comfort level to see if I was real.

I must have passed, because Jordan switched topics. He began talking in more detail about his sleeplessness, the thing he said he really wanted to deal with.

"The nightmares are the worst," Jordan mentioned. "I can't sleep ... and when I do sleep, my dreams are always nasty. Like I'm being chased, right? Like I hear dogs howling, like I'm being hunted ... it's always people from school chasing me. There's these four jerks who follow me around school all the time ... and now

I must deal with them stalking me in my sleep, like seriously? Can I get a break from this shit?"

Our session was ending, and I needed to address Jordan's stated priorities. I asked Jordan if he'd be willing to keep a notebook, and every day write down the date, how well he slept, and how jumpy he felt that day. I wanted him to look for patterns that might help us figure out together how he could sleep better.

He agreed, saying it sounded like a useful first step in addressing his jitters and insomnia. When I asked what he thought he'd like to talk about next week, he shrugged.

"I dunno … how to get through school and sleep at night without feeling like I'm going to explode, I guess? And … can you not talk to my parents about any of this yet, seriously? I want to be ready to handle, uh, however they react."

"Completely fair. Like I said, this is just between us unless I think you or somebody else is gonna get hurt. I can just tell them I think it's going well, if they ask, if that's okay with you?"

"Oh yeah. Thanks," Jordan said, looking relieved.

"Thanks for talking with me, Jordan. What questions do you have?"

"Nothing right now, I guess."

"Great. I'll see you next week!"

Jordan waved as he left the office, pulling out his phone. "Yeah, for sure! See ya."

Jordan verbally agreed to come back next week, which I took as positive progress. If Jordan kept coming to see me, we could work together to navigate his situation.

Family Rejection

We should note here a dilemma: Jordan's parents asked that he be called the name on his birth certificate. Between this and what Jordan will talk about in the second session, we can see that Jordan was experiencing family rejection. Family rejection occurs when families fail to provide support and acceptance to their LGBTQA+ members. Research indicates that family rejection increases the risk of suicidal ideation (serious thoughts about suicide), substance abuse, and/or denial of appropriate bathroom or housing access for the rejected family member (Klein & Golub, 2016; McCormick et al., 2018; Narang et al., 2018). Family rejection experiences are common across socioeconomic statuses, though the form family rejection takes, and how an LGBTQA+ client handles family rejection, can vary (Robinson, 2018; Schmitz & Tyler, 2018).

By contrast, when an LGBTQA+ person has family support, the likelihood of suicidal ideation decreases, and other mental health symptoms improve as well (Simons et al., 2013; Wilson et al., 2016). Also, they are less likely to engage in risky behaviors, such as substance abuse (McCormick et al., 2018), and they report higher levels of life satisfaction (Simons et al., 2013). For transgender people specifically, being called by their chosen name and correct pronouns can be a protective factor against the risks (Russel et al., 2018).

Research emphasizes what many already know: we all have a better shot at a happy life with a family who unconditionally loves and supports us, regardless of gender identity. It appeared that while Jordan's parents supported Jordan generally—they were worried about him and wanted him to do well in school—they were not providing him with the support he really needed. Despite his parents' wishes, Jordan's health and well-being were my priority. Research supports the notion that respecting his autonomy and calling him by his correct name are essential. And more than that, it was his right to decide who he was for himself, and to have me respect that.

QUESTIONS

1. What is your attitude about LGBTQA+ clients? What factors contribute to this attitude? That is, where did this information come from: practice experience, practice literature, personal experience of family bias, instructor bias, or some other place? Do adolescent LGBTQA+ clients like Jordan deserve the same right to self-determination as other clients, or does that right change because of their legal minor status? Search your attitudes and beliefs to uncover the possibility of negative implicit or explicit bias toward this population.

2. The author took a nonconfrontational approach, more concerned with engaging Jordan than getting his entire story. Yet, many practitioners would believe a more direct approach is what clients need. This is more than simply a theoretical or style difference. The professional literature is beginning to produce a body of research that specifically addresses this difference. Therefore, as you prepare for the second meeting:

   a. Explore the practice literature looking for evidence of the efficacy of both a nonconfrontational approach and a confrontational approach in trauma-informed care, especially with LGBTQA+ clients. Develop a position based on a balanced exploration of all sides of this argument.

   b. Based on the information given in the first session, generate a list of Jordan's problems and strengths.

   c. What is your initial assessment? Write a concise, one-paragraph narrative as if you are writing an article abstract of this session.

   d. What areas of Jordan's life need further exploration in the next session, and how do you plan to approach these issues when and if he returns?

SECOND SESSION

Once I believe rapport is established, I want to explore a client's support structure with few prompts. I let my clients decide how many details to offer, unprompted. In my experience, the volume of information a client offers voluntarily often reveals how much influence they have on their own life. This tells me which relationships in their life might need the most attention.

I greeted Jordan for our second session. He handed me his notebook, noting sleepless nights and high anxiety almost every day. When I asked how he was doing, Jordan made an exaggerated groaning noise, and said, drawing the word out, "baaaaaaaaaaaad." He smiled slightly. That he was telling me his honest feelings in a humorous way told me he was ready to engage, at least a little.

I asked what doing bad meant. He mentioned that his parents grounded him from Skype (a webcam software for talking online) and were generally "hassling" him about his online friends. His parents said they were "bad influences."

"They're mad I don't have close friends in real life ... like I'm friendly with some people at school but I don't hang out with them really. They think my Internet friends are making me trans, but that's not how it works! We found each other because we're dealing with the same thing, it's not like a virus I picked up. Being trans isn't the flu."

Jordan's Family and Trustworthy Adults

I took this opportunity to ask more about his relationship with his parents. Jordan's mother, Lisa, was 42, and his father, Charles, was 45.

"They were both raised to be really religious, and it shows," Jordan commented. "Dad's dad was a preacher, and Mom's parents were a doctor and a nurse, but like, only for rich people. Like they were contracted for specific people, I think that's how they met. I haven't asked my mom and dad much about family history. Hard to ask them about anything at this point."

I asked if it had ever been easy to ask them about anything. Jordan frowned and shook his head.

"Nah. I mean, it was better when I was pretending to be a girl. But trying to come out as trans, they've met me with like ... silence. Like I'll say something about it and they just won't respond."

"Won't respond how?"

"Like, won't respond ... no words or faces or anything ... they just go on with whatever they were doing like I didn't say anything at all. It's like they think if they ignore me being trans it'll just go away. They misgender me and call me by the wrong name constantly. Any time I try to get them to take me shopping for dude's clothes or anything they don't react. It's like talking to a wall, except that wall is supposed to be my mom."

"Well that sounds frustrating," I observed.

"You have NO idea. My parents care about me because I'm their kid, but not because I'm *me*. You could swap me out with literally any other kid and as long as mom gave birth to 'em it'd be the same, you know? I'm pretty sure they wish that was the case … that I was some other kid. But I'm not, like, I'm me and they will not listen to me at all."

"And both your parents feel this way?"

"I mean, I assume so. They both do the silent treatment thing," Jordan sighed. "I mean, I guess it could be worse. I know people that have been kicked out of their houses … having to stay with friends or in shelters or whatever. Maybe this is weird, but sometimes I wish my parents would just kick me out, though? Like it'd be better than living in this weird half-state where I could scream, and they'd act like I wasn't there. I feel like a ghost."

"It's hard to feel like you exist when people don't acknowledge your existence," I commented.

"Yeah, exactly. It's annoying. And weird!"

"Do your parents know that you have trouble sleeping, and high anxiety?"

"I told them … but I got the brick wall treatment. I mean, they didn't even bring me here until the school called about me cutting class. They know … but just because someone hears you doesn't mean they're listening; you know?"

Jordan seemed to answer my questions honestly, often accompanied by sarcastic humor. I made no effort to contradict or question his feelings here; Jordan's feelings were authentic, and it was important he knew he could express himself honestly.

When I asked about staff and teachers at school, he immediately said they were not to be trusted, offering no further detail. Jordan remained unwilling to discuss adults he knew at school. He clearly did not want to elaborate, instead reiterating that his parents had pulled him from all extracurriculars when he had tried to come out as trans, leaving him with no mentors, cut off from possible outside support. I didn't push him to elaborate when he declined, respecting that boundary.

Instead, I asked about what extracurriculars he was involved in previously. He said he participated in track and field, and an after-school literature club. When I asked if he thought his coach or literature club teacher would be amenable to supporting him, Jordan just laughed.

"I tried talking to the lit club teacher about anything important exactly once. She went to the principal. I got suspended." He stretched. "Can we not talk about this right now? Talking about school makes me feel antsy … ask me something else."

I asked about his extended family. Jordan explained who they were and offered his opinion on how supportive they would be. He had one still-living grandparent, a grandmother on his mother's side. She lived a couple states away, and Jordan stated he spoke to her only at family events, never one on one. "I think if I tried to tell her I was a dude now my parents would scream," Jordan said. "They regard my gender as this family shame. Grandma probably wouldn't get it anyway. She says weird homophobic stuff sometimes."

I asked if he had aunts and uncles, and he explained his mom was an only child, but his dad had a sister. His aunt, her husband, and their kids (ages 6 and 9) lived on the other side of the country, and he saw them only once every couple of years around the holidays.

"My cousins are little kids; I doubt they even know what being transgender is. My aunt and uncle would be disgusted with me, I'm sure … they are, like, super religious, more than my parents even."

When I asked if his parents took him to church, Jordan shook his head.

"They used to, but not since I told them I was a boy and insisted on wearing T-shirts instead of blouses and stuff. Which is cool with me, church wasn't really for me, and it gives me some time Sunday morning to not feel like my parents think I'm the lady in the attic in Jane Eyre."

"You really liked literature club, huh?" I asked.

"Yeah, when I could go. I read books at home a lot now. Nice little escape from feeling trapped."

His tone was a little sardonic. Jordan clearly resented being pulled from all his clubs, and understandably felt trapped and isolated at home.

"Man, you really don't have a lot of helpful adults around." I stated, affirming what he'd said earlier.

"Nope! You're basically the only adult who hasn't told me I'm a freak, so thanks," he summarized.

Jordan's Biggest Support: His Online Friends

I went to ask Jordan more about sources of support in his life, since family and other adults in his life didn't seem like much.

"Yeah, I think I mentioned my friends last week? The ones I know from online?"

Jordan explained that he was part of a ring of blogs on Tumblr, a microblogging website, and a couple of groups on Facebook, where trans adolescents and young adults shared resources and information.

"Cecilia is probably the friend I'm closest to, we share a lot because our families are so similar and she's about my age. She's stuck in a Catholic school right now and it's like gender dysphoria hell for her. She must sneak out of her house to visit friends where she can dress up and stuff. But there's Connor, they're on puberty blockers and they're a couple states away, they're a senior in high school, and they're nice, funny. Jennifer is graduating high school and really wants to stay in the girl's dorm at her school next Fall but she's running into rude people, I'm trying to message her every day to encourage her. And Kevin, who's like 21, I think? He's on T [referring to testosterone, hormone replacement therapy for someone seeking masculinizing therapy] and he talks about the body changes and stuff and what I can expect when I get there."

I pointed out that, at 21, Kevin was an adult, and Jordan rolled his eyes.

"I mean yeah, but he's hardly someone with authority over me, is he? He's more like a big brother. The Facebook group is trans people who are in high school and college, and he's still in college. I really don't see Kevin as someone who's like, an adult I look to for guidance, really, just more like someone who can answer the questions I have about being a trans dude."

Jordan chatted about his friends, who he held in genuine high esteem for a while longer, even showing me some jokes about trans life his friends had sent him on his phone. It seemed clear to me that if school was hostile, and home wasn't supportive, then Jordan was drawing most of his strength from his friends online.

"Keep in touch with your friends, they sound like good support," I advised.

"No joke," Jordan said. "They're about the only ones."

INFORMATION COMMUNICATION TECHNOLOGY AND RESILIENCE FOR TRANS AND GNC YOUTH

Clinically speaking, resilience is "successful adaption [sic] to adverse circumstances, including recovery from adversity and the ability to sustain well-being while facing adversity" (Eckstrand & Potter, 2017, p. 75). In other words, the ability to overcome the tough stuff in life. Resilience factors are things that enhance that ability.

Eckstrand and Potter (2017) state that information communication technology (e.g., smartphones, social media, and the Internet) appears to be tremendously important as a resiliency factor for trans and GNC youth in the face of minority stress. This is particularly true when they encounter barriers to information and support about their identity. The Internet can provide opportunities for these youth "to form community, build individualized support networks, develop coping skills, engage in identity development activities, increase perceived support, and seek information in an environment that is notably safer and more accessible than their daily lives (p. 63)" Particularly in the face of research that indicates contact with other trans and GNC people is important for positive gender identity development (Richmond et al., 2012), this technology can be a crucial factor in a youth's support system, as it is with Jordan (Eckstrand & Potter, 2017).

Adkins et al. (2018) note that online communities are particularly helpful in establishing hope for the future. Trans and GNC youth can meet other people who have been through similar circumstances, from coming out to transitioning to bullying to victimization, and see that they, too, can make it through these experiences and live a happy, productive life. The value of this kind of hope cannot be underestimated for a client's resiliency.

BODILY AUTONOMY

"So, to summarize, you've got some great friends looking out for you, but not a lot of adults willing to listen," I said. "Do you feel like the adults in your life were the primary obstacle to his success?"

Jordan nodded. "I mean, basically? I feel like I don't have control over my own, like, self."

"Like personal autonomy?"

"Yeah, exactly. Every decision I make has to be triple-checked by some adult who has no concept of what being a trans kid in a private Christian school is like ... half of them think I'm going to hell or something ... and they think that I should just tolerate other people telling me what to do with my body, it's stupid."

"What do you think having control over your body would look like, as opposed to how things are now?"

"Puberty blockers, for one." Jordan rubbed his forehead. "I get that my parents don't want to put me on HRT [Hormone Replacement Therapy, a common part of medical transitioning] right now, because they think it's a phase, but puberty blockers are safe and reversible. I just wouldn't finish estrogen puberty, and then later if I want to, I just go off the blockers and then can do whichever puberty I want ... why shouldn't that be my choice? If they make me finish girl puberty, then my transition is going to be that much harder."

Jordan had clearly investigated this topic, as his information on puberty blockers was accurate. He also was willing to accept limits on what he could do at his age to please his parents. That they were not willing to listen was understandably frustrating, and I told him so.

"Yeah, it sure is. And like, I'm trying to feel in control of my body all the time, because no one even respects, like, my personal space, much less the reality of my gender, and I can't even wear the clothes that are right for me, they won't let me get a haircut. The only thing I can control is like, how much I eat and push-ups in my bedroom."

We explored this line of reasoning for a bit, examining what Jordan felt was in his control, and a pattern emerged. Jordan mentioned, several times, that he was restricting how much he ate, as a way of exercising control over his body.

"So, when you skip meals, or only eat part of your dinner, does that make you feel like you have more autonomy?" I clarified.

"Yeah. It's my body, I should get to decide something, right? And it's healthy. I'm losing weight, my boobs aren't as obvious so I can maybe pass as a dude sometimes, maybe if I lose enough my period will go away, too. That's just a bonus, mainly it feels like self-discipline, you know. I can make my body do whatever I want it to. Other people can't."

"Have other people tried?" I asked gently.

"Uh yeah, only constantly, like every day. My anxiety doesn't come from nowhere." Jordan hunched forward and glared. He was reacting defensively, so I sat back and relaxed my posture to show I wasn't trying to attack him.

"I believe that, and I'm sorry you feel that every day."

"Maybe you are, but I know what you're gonna say, the school counselor tried to say the same thing when I was sent there for skipping lunch. Sometimes I skip meals, or I throw up after. Who cares? Lots of kids do that … and you can't complain about the exercising in my room. My parents pulled me from sports and everything, I must work out somewhere, right? And if I wanna not eat, then that's my business." Jordan folded his arms and narrowed his eyes at me.

With this, I noticed that Jordan appeared to be exhibiting a pattern. With some topics, Jordan often framed what he said as a response to what other people had already said to him. I guessed he probably would not have mentioned anything about his eating and exercise habits to his parents. He had mentioned this to the school counselor, but I wondered if he had mentioned it to his friends.

"What do your online friends think about you skipping lunch? Does Cecilia have an opinion?"

Jordan slumped a bit. "She doesn't like it. She seems worried, I keep telling her it's fine. Look, it's my body, okay? I can do whatever I want with it. Everyone keeps trying to take that away from me, and they *can't*." Jordan said it with a lot of finality.

"When you say people are trying to take that away from you, what do you mean?" I asked.

Jordan shrugged and rolled his eyes. "Well the last time I tried to talk about it I got suspended, so."

I asked Jordan if he would be willing to add days he skipped meals to his notebook, and he asked why. I said that I wanted to see if his skipping meals lined up with his anxiety or sleeplessness. "I'm just trying to find a pattern, to see if we can address how you feel. Eating affects your other body functions," I explained.

After asking me if his parents would see this notebook (not without his permission, I said), he agreed to take note of it.

"I really would like to be able to sleep," he said. "If tracking my meals can help, then I'll give it a shot.

DISORDERED EATING, TRAUMA, AND TRANSGENDER YOUTH

Although Jordan had not provided adequate detail to diagnose him with an eating disorder per se, it sounded to me like he did have some disordered eating habits developing as maladaptive coping mechanisms (i.e., things he did to cope that were not entirely healthy). This combined with the nightmares, sleeplessness, and hypervigilance (e.g., him being easily startled) convinced me that he was responding to trauma, though whether it was from minority stress or a specific incident, or a combination thereof, I was not yet sure.

Existing literature shows a relationship between trauma and eating disorders in adolescents (Hicks et al., 2018; Tagay et al., 2014). A study from Watson et al. (2017) seems to indicate that a large proportion of trans youth engage in disordered eating behaviors, including (but not limited to) fasting or vomiting to lose weight, such as Jordan expressed. Experiencing stigma in the form of discrimination or harassment or exposure to violence increased the likelihood of disordered eating behaviors in this study, mitigated only by positive social supports, such as a supportive school and family environment.

Given that Jordan had so little support at school and at home, it is unfortunately not surprising that he might have turned to disordered eating to regain some sense of control over his own situation. This combined with the fact that transgender survivors of trauma often feel stripped of the right to control their bodies (Richmond et al., 2012), and Jordan's insistence that his eating habits were an expression of autonomy, made me wonder if that cafeteria incident had been traumatic. My curiosity on this point was compounded because his insomnia started after the incident, he avoided discussing it in any detail, and his apparent fight, flight, or freeze response the first time I mentioned the incident.

Furthermore, Testa et al. (2017) found that gender-confirming medical interventions can, by way of reducing nonaffirming experiences, lead to increased body satisfaction, and thus decreased eating disorder symptoms. Jordan mentioned a desire to be perceived as masculine as a "bonus" for his current eating habits, suggesting that support transitioning might enable a change in his eating habits as well.

THIRD SESSION: DISCLOSURE OF TRAUMA

For our third session, I had expected to go over the contents of his notebook, and see if we could, together, pick out patterns to help reduce Jordan's day-to-day sleeplessness and anxiety. However, Jordan came in and, with barely a greeting, he began by saying that none of the adults in his life cared about him, because if they did, they would listen to him.

I considered this good for our rapport; he clearly felt comfortable telling me about what was troubling him, and given that he was grinding his teeth and appeared to be shivering he was feeling angry and wanted to talk about it. I wanted to follow his lead. I asked Jordan to tell me more about what prompted his feelings today.

"My parents made me go to the school building today ... like they took me to the front office and made me check in and told me I had to check in there in between every single class … which is dumb, because it would make me late for all my classes, and how is that helpful? But then those guys realized I had to keep coming back to the office. They were waiting for me."

I wondered if "those guys" meant the ones he mentioned in his nightmares. "Who was waiting for you?"

"Those guys from the thing in the cafeteria. That I got suspended over … and nothing happened to them. Nothing happened to those assholes and they're free to stalk me and follow me to all my classes and shout at me and say shit to me and I just must … what … ignore it? When has ignoring anything ever helped?"

This was the most Jordan had talked about the cafeteria incident since making it clear he didn't want to talk about it. It seemed to me that the school incident had been a trigger for Jordan's other concerns, which included, what I interpreted, as clear signs of trauma.

This was a key point in our relationship; I did not want to pressure Jordan to give more information than he was prepared to give, but I also felt it important to give him the space to discuss it when he was ready. Given that Jordan had brought it up, I decided to gently ask about this day without referencing the cafeteria incident.

"Ignoring things usually doesn't help," I agreed. "Why is it these guys have such an interest in bothering you, do you think?" I asked.

"They keep calling me a … well, they call me slurs, I don't wanna repeat them."

"That's fair, I wouldn't ask you to."

"I know. Thanks. Yeah … like … they bother me because I'm clearly not trying to be a girl looking to hook up with them. I'm a guy who's interested in girls, and they don't think I should be allowed to do either of those things. They want to take that away from me."

Tears began to form at the corner of Jordan's eyes as his voice became more and more angry.

"Take that away from you?" I asked gently.

"Yes." Jordan's jaw tightened and he took a big, shuddering breath, apparently deciding to continue through clenched teeth.

"By grabbing my arms and taking turns shoving their hands down my pants to grope my junk in full view of the entire cafeteria and laughing about it, while the teachers watch and do nothing. They want to do it again."

Jordan gripped the sides of his chair, and his knuckles turned white, nearly shouting.

"I won't let it happen. I'll drop out, I'll get a job, I'll move 10 cities away, it doesn't matter, I'm not letting it happen again!"

Jordan kicked my trash can over and glared at the wall, red-faced as tears escaped his eyes. I waited a moment for Jordan to take a deep breath, looking away from me at the wall. I handed him a tissue …

"I believe you."

Jordan sniffled. "Somebody should." Jordan wiped his face. "Thanks. Sorry for yelling."

"You don't need to be sorry. Yelling is a pretty even-handed response to something like that. You have every right to be mad."

"Yeah. I do." Jordan let out a long sigh, apparently calmer, and met my eyes.

"But no one did anything when it happened, and when I went to a teacher about it, she told the principal and he had me suspended. I didn't start a fight. I let it happen and I told a teacher and they punished me. I told my parents and they pulled me from all my clubs. They all told me to just not talk about it."

I asked Jordan if he felt like he wanted to talk about it now, and he nodded. I encouraged him to tell the story in his own words, without regard for what other people might say or how they had previously contradicted him; this was his space to tell his version of events and know he would be believed.

Jordan said that he'd been reading a book at a lunch table by himself, occasionally sneaking out his phone to message his online friends. Cecilia had just sent him a picture of herself, and one of the four boys had taken his phone and asked if that was his "dyke girlfriend." Jordan was able to wrestle his phone back and put it back in his pocket, but not before another of the boys had grabbed the back of his hooded sweatshirt and dragged him away from the table. At this point, as Jordan said before, one of the boys held his arms in place while the other three reached into his pants, under his underwear, and groped and penetrated his genitals while laughing.

Jordan stated he had a particularly vivid memory of making eye contact with one teacher, and then another while he this was happening, and both teachers simply looked down.

Jordan managed to twist out of the grip of the boy restraining him, grabbed his book and ran down to the literature club teacher's office.

"I tried to tell her what happened, but I couldn't stop shaking. I puked in her garbage can. I managed to explain what had happened, and who did it, and she just said, 'we'll ask the principal.' Like what does that mean? Ask him what? And then she sent me down to his office, and he told me to wait, and he left. I missed fourth period just sitting there in the waiting area, feeling like shit, and when he came back he told me that he'd talked to teachers who had been in the cafeteria and I had started a fight and I was going to be suspended for 3 days, and also, 'Oh, shame on you for trying to get those boys in trouble.' I told him to fuck off, and they made it a week's suspension."

"I would have said the same thing," I said honestly.

Jordan laughed a little. "Yeah, right? It's just ..." Jordan began to cry in earnest as he continued. "I didn't even fight them. I didn't want to hurt anybody, I just wanted it to stop, and that's what happened. Is this how it's gonna be forever? Wherever I go, people can just hurt me however they want and if I try to stop it,

I'll be punished? Just because I'm a guy and they don't think I should be? What is that about? How does that make sense?"

"It doesn't make sense. Jordan, you are entitled to be whoever you are. Even if people want to take that away from you, they can't, because you're always you. But be assured, okay: what happened to you was wrong."

"God, I've been waiting for someone to say that." Jordan took a deep breath, and then another.

"Thank you."

"I can't promise that no one will ever try to hurt you again," I said, "but we will try to get you in circumstances where you are safer."

"Can I get on puberty blockers, too?" He asked, smiling despite the tears. "I'm just saying, I feel like that would help."

"Let's make a plan," I replied.

CASE SUMMARY

During this period, Jordan came in as a transgender youth suspicious of adults, unwilling to talk about a traumatic incident, and defensive about discussing many of the topics affecting his quality of life. By the end of the third session, Jordan was ready and willing to discuss what had happened to him and put to voice the truth of his experience that others previously denied him. This articulation combined with his own stated desires—to seek medical intervention for his transition—indicates he is ready to begin the collaborative process of planning.

QUESTIONS

Now that your reading and study of Jordan's case is complete, please respond to the following questions and tasks to develop a comprehensive plan for Jordan's treatment.

1. What questions did the author leave out of the assessment?
   - What would you have done differently throughout the assessment?
   - Are there questions you would not have asked or pushed for more information on?
2. Based on the case information in this chapter, develop a three-generation genogram (also including important nonfamily members if needed) to represent Jordan's presented life and all who are instrumentally involved. Make any notes and figures on this genogram to aid in developing a wholistic view of this case.
3. Make a list, with supporting evidence, of the main issues in Jordan's life at the time of the interviews. Include a list of the Jordan's personal and

social strengths that may be used as resources in the future pertaining to each of the issues listed.

4. Develop and write a narrative assessment and diagnosis(es) as demonstrated by the information contained in this case. Justify your diagnostic decisions by listing the criteria you believe are met through the interview record. It is inappropriate to base diagnostic decisions on assumptions, only direct evidence provided by your client.

   • If you met Jordan, what additional information would you need to contribute to a more comprehensive narrative assessment and diagnostic decisions?

   • Be sure to place Jordan's personal and social strengths in the narrative assessment, to be used later as part of treatment planning.

5. As discussed in Chapter 1, here is where we initially apply the stages of change developed to assessment client's motivation for change for each diagnosed problem.

   • List each diagnosis you decided upon in the narrative assessment.

   • For each diagnosis, determine what stage of change Jordan is presently in pertaining to his motivation to change that problem. Use Jordan's own words to justify your stage decisions.

   • Use the stages of change during treatment planning.

6. Based on the narrative assessment, develop a written treatment plan to include short- and long-term treatment goals and objectives. Include what methods of treatment and support you will utilize.

   • What treatment theory or combination of theories do you believe best fits Jordan's reality? Defend your decision.

   • What theories or approaches does the latest empirical evidence in the field recommend?

   • Based on the stages of change decisions in Question 5, where will you begin in treatment? Explain and defend your decisions.

   • Pertaining to treating people with co-occurring disorders, what does the current professional literature and practice evidence suggest as the most effective way to proceed when it comes to deciding which issues to treat first?

7. Based on the treatment theory or theories chosen and defended in Question 6, list each intervention you would use in your work with Jordan. Specifically, for each intervention, include the target issue, intervention, and modality (i.e., group therapy) you chose, and the theoretical justification for each.

   • What other options might be available should these interventions prove ineffective?

- What does the latest empirical evidence in the field suggest for each target issue? How does this evidence match with your intervention strategies?
- When developing treatment approaches do not overlook nontraditional approaches and approaches that target multiple systemic levels (i.e., individual, family, community, advocacy, etc.).
- What factors and strategies will you use to build trust and engagement during the intervention phases of your work? How will you assist Jordan as his motivation to change waxes and wanes over the coming weeks and months?
- What if his personal goals do not align with yours? How will you handle this?
- Think about your first session with Jordan as his new therapist. How would you begin, what would your goals be for the session and what would you hope to accomplish?

REFERENCES

Adkins, V., Masters, E., Shumer, D., & Selkie, E. (2018). Exploring transgender adolescents' use of social media for support and health information seeking. *Journal of Adolescent Health, 62*(2). https://doi.org/10.1016/j.jadohealth.2017.11.087

Balsam, K., Beadnell, B., & Molina, Y. (2013). The daily heterosexist experiences questionnaire. *Measurement and Evaluation in Counseling and Development, 46*(1), 3–25.

Basham, K. (2016). Trauma theories and disorders. In J. Berzoff, L. Flanagan, & P. Hertz (Eds.), *Inside out and outside in: Psychodynamic clinical theory and psychopathology in contemporary multicultural contexts* (pp. 481–517). Rowman & Littlefield.

Beckerman, N. L., & Auerbach, C. (2014). PTSD as aftermath for bullied LGBT adolescents: The case for comprehensive assessment. *Social Work in Mental Health, 12*(3), 195–211.

Cramer, R. J., McNiel, D. E., Holley, S. R., Shumway, M., & Boccellari, A. (2012). Mental health in violent crime victims: Does sexual orientation matter? *Law and Human Behavior, 36*(2), 87.

Eckstrand, K. L., & Potter, J. (2017). *Trauma, resilience, and health promotion in LGBT patients: What every healthcare provider should know.* Springer International.

Fallot, R. D., & Harris, M. (2009). Creating cultures of trauma-informed care (CCTIC): A self-assessment and planning protocol. *Community Connections, 2*(2), 1–18.

GLSEN. (2017). *The 2017 National School Climate Survey: The experiences of lesbian, gay, bisexual, transgender, and queer youth in our nation's schools.* Retrieved from: https://www.glsen.org/sites/default/files/GLSEN%202017%20National%20School%20Climate%20Survey%20%28NSCS%29%20-%20Full%20Report.pdf

Graziano, J. N., & Wagner, E. F. (2011). Trauma among lesbians and bisexual girls in the juvenile justice system. *Traumatology, 17*(2), 45–55.

Hales, T. W., Green, S. A., Bissonette, S., Warden, A., Diebold, J., Koury, S. P., & Nochajski, T. H. (2018). Trauma-informed care outcome study. *Research on Social Work Practice, 29(5), 529–539.* https://doi.org/10.1177/1049731518766618

Hicks White, A. A., Pratt, K. J., & Cottrill, C. (2018). The relationship between trauma and weight status among adolescents in eating disorder treatment. *Appetite, 129*, 62–69. https://doi.org/10.1016/j.appet.2018.06.034

Johnson, J. (2004). Fundamentals of substance abuse practice. Thousand Oaks, CA: Wadsworth Brooks Cole.

Klein, A., & Golub, S. (2016). Family rejection as a predictor of suicide attempts and substance misuse among transgender and gender nonconforming adults. *LGBT Health, 3*(3), 193–199. https://doi.org/10.1089/lgbt.2015.0111

McCormick, A., Scheyd, K., & Terrazas, S. (2018). Trauma-informed care and LGBTQ youth: Considerations for advancing practice with youth with trauma experiences. *Families in Society: The Journal of Contemporary Social Services, 99*(2), 160–169. https://doi.org/10.1177/1044389418768550

Mustanski, B., Andrews, R., & Puckett, J. (2016). The effects of cumulative victimization on mental health among lesbian, gay, bisexual, and transgender adolescents and young adults. *American Journal of Public Health, 106*(3), 527.

Narang, P., Sarai, S. K., Aldrin, S., & Lippmann, S. (2018). Suicide among transgender and gender-nonconforming people. *The Primary Care Companion for CNS Disorders, 20*(3). https://doi.org/10.4088/pcc.18nr02273

Richmond, K. A., Burnes, T., & Carroll, K. (2012). Lost in trans-lation: Interpreting systems of trauma for transgender clients. *Traumatology, 18*(1), 45.

Roberts, A., Rosario, M., Corliss, H., Koenen, K., & Austin, S. (2012). Childhood gender nonconformity: A risk indicator for childhood abuse and posttraumatic stress in youth. *Pediatrics, 129*(3), 410.

Robinson, B. A. (2018). Conditional families and lesbian, gay, bisexual, transgender, and queer youth homelessness: Gender, sexuality, family instability, and rejection: Conditional families and LGBTQ youth homelessness. *Journal of Marriage and Family, 80*(2), 383–396. https://doi.org/10.1111/jomf.12466

Russel, S. T., Pollitt, A. M., Li, G., & Grossman, A. H. (2018). Chosen name use is linked to reduced depressive symptoms, suicidal ideation, and suicidal behavior among transgender youth. *Journal of Adolescent Health, 63*(4), 503–505. https://doi.org/10.1016/j.jadohealth.2018.02.003

Schmitz, R. M., & Tyler, K. A. (2018). The complexity of family reactions to identity among homeless and college lesbian, gay, bisexual, transgender, and queer young adults. *Archives of Sexual Behavior, 47*(4), 1195–1207. https://doi.org/10.1007/s10508-017-1014-5

Simons, L., Schrager, S. M., Clark, L. F., Belzer, M., & Olson, J. (2013). Parental support and mental health among transgender adolescents. *Journal of Adolescent Health, 53*(6), 791–793.

Sommers-Flanagan, J. & Sommers-Flanagan, R. (2015). *Counseling and psychotherapy theories in context and practice: skills, strategies, and techniques.* John Wiley & Sons.

Tagay, S., Schlottbohm, E., Reyes-Rodriguez, M. L., Repic, N., & Senf, W. (2014). Eating disorders, trauma, PTSD, and psychosocial resources. *Eating Disorders, 22*(1), 33–49. https://doi.org/10.1080/10640266.2014.857517

Testa, R. J., Rider, G. N., Haug, N. A., & Balsam, K. F. (2017). Gender confirming medical interventions and eating disorder symptoms among transgender individuals. *Health Psychology: Official Journal of the Division of Health Psychology, American Psychological Association, 36*(10), 927–936. https://doi.org/10.1037/hea0000497

Torres, C. G., Renfrew, M., Kenst, K., Tan-McGrory, A., Betancourt, J. R., & López, L. (2015). Improving transgender health by building safe clinical environments that promote existing resilience: Results from a qualitative analysis of providers. *BMC Pediatrics, 15*(1).

Turner, F. (2011). *Social work treatment: Interlocking theoretical approaches.* Oxford University Press.

Urquhart, E. (2016, March 11). Gatekeepers vs. informed consent: Who decides when a trans person can medically transition? *Slate.* Retrieved from https://slate.com/human-interest/2016/03/transgender-patients-and-informed-consent-who-decides-when-transition-treatment-is-appropriate.html

Watson, R. J., Veale, J. F., & Saewyc, E. M. (2017). Disordered eating behaviors among transgender youth: Probability profiles from risk and protective factors. *International Journal of Eating Disorders, 50*(5), 515–522. https://doi.org/10.1002/eat.22627

Wilson, E., Chen, Y., Arayasirikul, S. Raymond, H., & McFarland, W. (2016). The impact of discrimination on the mental health of trans*female youth and the protective effect of parental support. *AIDS and Behavior, 20*(10), 2203–2211.

World Professional Association for Transgender Health (WPATH). (2012). *Standards of Care for the health of transsexual, transgender, and gender nonconforming people,* 7th version. Retrieved from https://www.wpath.org/media/cms/Documents/SOC%20v7/SOC%20V7_English.pdf

CHAPTER 4

The Case of Lauren Barnes

Elizabeth A. Sharda

Client: Lauren Barnes, age 14
Setting: Foster care
Social worker role: Behavior specialist

When I met Lauren Barnes, I was working as a behavior specialist for a non-profit foster care agency. This meant that when kids in foster care were at risk of "breaking placement" due to behaviors, I was sent in to provide services and attempt to preserve the placement. Additional moves often entail adding another layer of trauma and loss to kids who've already experienced plenty of both in their young lives. On top of that, placement stability is one of the metrics by which foster care programs are evaluated, so our goal was to prevent placement breakdown whenever possible. For me, this meant working with both the foster child and the foster parent(s), in hopes of improving the goodness of fit between the child and his or her environment.

As a social worker, I'm always mindful of not only the person and their corresponding needs, problems and strengths, but the person in their environment. Even before meeting Lauren or reading her file, I knew that environment played an important role in her story. She was raised in an environment that included trauma, likely multiple occurrences over time. She was removed from this environment 3 months ago and placed in an entirely new one without warning. What I needed to learn was what Lauren's current environment was like, and how she was coping within it. Then I could determine what the right balance was for intervention, between helping Lauren build skills for dealing with stress in her environment and making changes within the environment to make it less stressful, and ultimately, more trauma informed.

THE REFERRAL

Lauren Barnes was referred to me by her foster care case manager. Because we worked within the same foster care program, this process was relatively straight-forward. Her case manager filled out a one-page referral form, and then we had a conversation about the case so I could determine, with my supervisor, whether Lauren would benefit from behavior specialist services.

Through her case manager, I learned that Lauren was struggling with some challenging behaviors in her foster home and at school. These included verbal aggression at school and home, fighting with peers at school, and generally oppo-sitional behaviors with adults at school and at home. She had been suspended once from school this year for physically fighting with another student. Her foster mother, Deb Schmidt, had called the case manager the day before to say she was at the end of her rope and would be asking for Lauren to be moved if she didn't get help soon. I agreed that Lauren sounded like a good fit for behavior specialist services and agreed to meet with her and the foster parent. Before doing so, I needed to gather more information from the case file.

From the case file, I learned that Lauren had entered foster care approximately 3 months ago. After a short stint (4 days) at the county's temporary residential facility, Lauren was placed in the Schmidt foster home. Deb Schmidt was a single woman in her late 50s who lived in a small town about 10 miles outside the city where the foster care agency was located.

She had a couple children of her own, who were now adults and lived nearby. She was divorced and worked part-time from home. In addition to Lauren, she had two other foster children placed with her, a 7-year-old and a 4-year-old, both boys. In her 2 years of fostering, she had taken mostly younger children, and none as old as Lauren.

I had worked with her on a prior case involving a 5-year-old boy, and together we had developed and implemented a solid behavior plan to address his hitting and spitting. He remained with Deb until being placed with an aunt and uncle. I looked forward to working with Deb again but wondered how she would do with the challenge of a teenager.

Also included in the case file was the family's Child Protective Services (CPS) report and court petition. These documents are often a source of valuable infor-mation about the child's life prior to entering care, specifically, the abuse and neglect that led to their removal. However, they can also be some of the most difficult pieces of reading, as they recount home conditions, series of concerns from teachers and neighbors, injuries and methods for inflicting injuries, and perhaps most difficult, details of sexual abuse. I usually tried to leave this type of reading to the end of the day so that I had space to deal with what I'd taken in.

The times where I could not wait, I had to shove the information to the back of my mind and go on with my day—meeting with foster families, attending staff meetings, and answering phone calls and emails. When this happened, I'd often have flashes of thoughts or images related to what I'd read throughout the day, and sometimes into the night. This was part of the job, part of being in proximity to families' pain. But it wasn't without impact.

Knowing this about myself, I left Lauren's file for late afternoon, when I knew I didn't have any more appointments that day. From the CPS report and court documents, I learned that Lauren and her three siblings were removed from their mother's care for reasons of physical neglect (the home was reportedly piled with trash and smelled of animal urine; there was no food in the home on numerous occasions), medical neglect (Lauren's little sister had missed several appointments for her asthma and as a result did not have her necessary inhaler), and parental substance use (Lauren's mother, Tammy, tested positive for marijuana [prior to its legalization] and was drunk in the middle of the day when she missed a scheduled visit with the CPS worker). I learned that Lauren's father, Joe, was arrested for his third offense of domestic abuse approximately 9 months ago and has been incarcerated since that time. He was recently convicted and sentenced to 2 years in prison.

Lauren was the oldest of Tammy and Joe's four children. She had a brother, Joe Jr. (aka "JJ"), 12; a sister, Trina, 8; and a sister, Tess, who was 5. Trina and Tess were placed in a foster home together. JJ was placed in a local residential facility. Adolescent boys are notoriously difficult to place in foster homes, simply due to the lack of homes willing to take them. On top of this, JJ had run away from home several times before entering foster care, and once had been caught stealing from the corner store. He had a juvenile probation officer and a record. The foster homes willing to take him were limited and were already full when he and his siblings entered care. Thus, JJ was placed in an open residential facility across town from the foster care agency.

Tammy and her children had weekly supervised visits at the agency for 1 hour each Wednesday. The case file noted that Tammy had missed 3 visits thus far, of a possible 10, due to transportation problems. Unfortunately, these visits appeared to be the only time that Lauren and her siblings saw each other. I made a note to ask the case manager about the possibility of regular sibling visits.

Lauren and JJ had been receiving home-based therapy services through the local community mental health agency before they were removed from their mother's care. I placed a call to the therapist named in the case file and received a quick call back. The therapist confirmed that she had worked with Lauren and JJ for about 4 months to address behavioral issues, truancy, and some depressive symptoms in Lauren. She noted that sessions were very inconsistent due to Tammy calling to cancel or the family not being home at the scheduled appointment time. She thought that she had met with Lauren about six times before closing the case due to too many missed sessions.

I asked for her clinical impression of Lauren. She said, "She's mature beyond her years and carries a lot. She did a lot of the parenting of her younger siblings

… cooking … getting them up for school … even the discipline. It's too much for a 14-year-old, the weight of all that. She didn't even have a chance to process the stuff around her dad and his getting arrested. She was just surviving, I think." I thanked her for returning my call, and for the helpful information. My next step was to contact the foster mom, Deb Schmidt.

I called Deb the next morning, after I knew she'd had a chance to get the kids off to school.

"Hi Deb, it's Liz, the agency behavior specialist. I talked to Lauren's case manager about the possibility of working with you and her. She mentioned that Lauren's been having a hard time lately."

"Oh, hi Liz. How've you been? The worker told me she was going to ask you to come out and talk with her. She's a handful. I don't know what to do with her. Everything is a battle, you know. Like the simplest things … I can't ask her to do anything without getting attitude back. Her attitude is the biggest problem. It gets her into trouble at school, too. Every week I have one teacher or another calling or emailing me to say that she was disrupting class or talking back. And did they tell you she got suspended? She's only back at school this week. She was home for 2 days last week. I have trouble dealing with her when she's at school all day, so I really don't know if this is going to work if she keeps getting suspended."

Having worked in this role for about a year already, I had come to expect that initial phone calls to foster parents would entail a fair amount of venting. When it comes to the point at which I'd step in, foster parents were typically at their wits' end. They'd tried everything they knew, tolerated challenging behaviors and emotions for long enough, and were in desperate need of support and relief. Unfortunately, as is often the case in social service systems, the squeaky wheel gets the grease. Foster parents who threaten to have kids removed from their home are the ones who get a swift response, as was the case with Deb and Lauren. Deb was out of ideas. She was out of energy. And she was out of patience. I needed to help her feel heard and understood if I was to get any buy-in from her on the intervention process.

"Ugh. I'm sorry, Deb. That's more stress than you need, to have her home for 2 days, when you're expecting a quiet house and being able to get some work done. And I'm guessing she's not the most pleasant to be around when she's suspended either."

"Lord, no. She just walks around sighing and huffing and eating junk food. I even went up to the school to get the work she was missing, and she didn't touch it."

"You've got enough stress with managing three kids on your own. And I know the other two aren't easy, either! How about I come out to meet with you and Lauren tomorrow?"

"Sure. The sooner the better. She gets home from school on the bus around 3:30."

"Great. How about I come around 3:00 so you and I can talk a bit before she gets home?"

"Sounds good. See you tomorrow." Since I had worked with Deb a few months earlier on a different case, I didn't take the time to explain the behavior specialist role. I'd do that briefly at our meeting the next day, before Lauren arrived home.

QUESTIONS

1. Given what you know about Lauren and her current situation, what issues would you consider as you prepare to meet her for the first time?
2. Because rapport building and engagement seemed to be an issue for Lauren, how would you prepare yourself to be successful in a professional relationship with Lauren?
3. In your study and practice, what are the most important factors in rapport building and client engagement?
4. What percentage of your time do you spend working on and/or practicing your rapport building and client engagement skills? List several ways you can improve your practice engagement skills.
5. It is possible Lauren could fit the description of an involuntary client. How do you approach involuntary and/or mandated clients?
6. The author is serving in the role of behavior specialist in the foster care system. Before proceeding with this case, it might be helpful to research the reciprocal, yet different roles that case managers, therapists, and behavior specialists play in the foster care system. If the titles and roles are different in the state you reside, research what roles and responsibilities may be similar in your state's foster care system.

OUR FIRST MEETING

As a behavior specialist working in a foster care setting, an important consideration for carrying out my job is that all my clients are considered involuntary. Very few child clients in the foster care system are voluntary, with many being pressured by their parents, other adults, or the systems to engage in services.

If you asked them, they'd tell you they prefer that everyone connected to "the system" would just leave them alone. Thankfully, I've experienced this through most of my career in child welfare. I started as a young social worker in a residential treatment facility for girls in the foster care system. Any visions I'd had of grateful kids soaking in all my positive input were long gone. I was used to kids not being thrilled with my presence, my questions, my attention, my "being in their business." I knew it took a lot of work to build rapport with kids in foster care, who have learned from their experience not to trust adults, especially those in "the system."

Therefore, my goals for the initial meeting with Lauren were minimal: engage with the client and explain my role and get enough buy-in for her to agree to a second meeting (even if it wasn't entirely her choice).

I arrived at the Schmidt foster home at about 3:10 PM, unable to kick my habit of running behind schedule most of the time. Deb didn't seem to mind as she let me in the side door off the driveway. Her home was modest—one story with three small bedrooms—but clean and well-kept. She collected cow-themed knick-knacks, and they lined the walls of her kitchen and overflowed into the dining room. "You got a new cow clock!" I remarked, trying to connect with her about something other than her complaints about Lauren.

"Oh yeah," she replied. "Got that one at the flea market last month. You want some coffee?"

"No thanks. I've had too much already today!" I appreciated the offer. I asked if we could sit at the dining room table and talk a bit.

"How did yesterday go? Lauren went back to school. How was that?"

"Not sure. She went right to her room after school and didn't come out the rest of the day. She did come get some dinner later, but then went right back to her room. I asked her to help clean up the dinner dishes, but she gave me an attitude and so I let her off the hook. I know it's not the right thing to do, but I was so tired and didn't need a fight from her. Just easier to do it myself sometimes."

"I get that. She got up alright for school today though?" I was grasping for some minor success, something that was going right, or at least wasn't a source of conflict.

"She did. She didn't talk to me this morning, but she got ready and got on the bus no problem."

"Well that's something."

The rest of the time with Deb, I learned that Lauren responds with opposition whenever she's asked to do something—take a shower, do her homework, complete her weekend chores. I empathized with Deb that this had to be especially hard, because as a single parent she is always the one doing the asking, and always the one getting an oppositional response.

I asked Deb to complete a standard behavioral assessment, which we did for all kids referred for behavior specialist services. She agreed and said she'd bring it to the agency on Wednesday when she dropped Lauren off for her parenting time visit. I also got contact information for one of Lauren's teachers, so she could complete the teacher version of the standard behavior assessment.

While my primary task is to assess and intervene with behaviors in the home, Lauren was also having significant problems at school that were impacting the home environment. Also, it wouldn't hurt to have another source of information on Lauren's current status.

At about 3:30, the door in the kitchen opened and a tall, lanky girl with long brown hair, and round, brown eyes walked into the room. She was simply dressed in a black Michael Jackson T-shirt and black jeans. Her hair was combed and pulled into a simple ponytail at the base of her neck. She dropped her backpack on the dining room floor, as Deb announced, "This is Liz. She's from the agency and she needs to meet with you."

When I saw the look of confusion and then anger on Lauren's face, I knew. Deb hadn't told her I was coming. I tried to interject, but the damage was done.

"What the hell, Deb? You could have at least told me! I'm not talking with anybody. I have a lot of homework and I don't have time for this!"

With this, Lauren grabbed her backpack and stormed down the hall to her room. Immediately, I had a choice to make. On the one hand, I carved out nearly 2 hours from my afternoon to drive out to Deb's home and meet with them. It would really be nice to get the first meeting with Lauren done today. On the other hand, I knew she had been caught off guard by my presence. What I didn't know, and could only guess, was how many times she'd been surprised by visits from social workers, and what the results of these visits had been.

The unexpected presence of a social worker (or someone who looks like a social worker) can trigger a trauma response in foster kids, sending them into fight, flight, or freeze mode. I didn't know where Lauren's mind went when she saw me sitting at the dining room table, but I could bet it wasn't, "She must be here to help me!"

For this reason, I decided to cut my losses and reschedule with Lauren. However, this time I was going to her directly. I wanted to be sure she knew about the meeting, but also that she felt she had some amount of choice in the matter.

I turned to Deb. "Seems like I caught her by surprise. I really like for kids to know I'm coming ... most of them don't like this kind of surprise."

"I know. I tried, but she wasn't even talking to me ... and she was in her room all evening. Whenever I tried talking to her, she was short with me. I hardly even got her to come out to eat dinner."

"I understand. Do you mind if I go knock on her door and try to set up another time to meet with her? Like tomorrow or Friday?"

Deb agreed and I walked down the hall. I knocked on Lauren's door. "What?!"

"Hey Lauren, you mind if I open the door? I'm gonna head back to the agency and just wanted to see if there was a better time for me to come talk with you."

"Fine."

"Lauren, I'm sorry you didn't know I was coming. That's got to be frustrating, coming home thinking you can just relax and then finding out you must talk to me, and nobody even asked you. So, you don't have to today. I'll come back when it's good for you. I'm just here to help figure out how to make things better for you at this foster home. I heard from your case worker and Deb that it's been rough lately. And I want to hear your side. Could I come back tomorrow or Friday?"

"Not Friday. That's the weekend." I wanted to say that I wished my weekends started at 3:00 on Friday, but I remembered being a teenager and saw her point.

"Ok, how about tomorrow? I can come around 4:00. Would that give you time to unwind after school?"

"I guess."

"Ok, I'll see you tomorrow then. Thanks for letting me reschedule, and I like your T-shirt, by the way."

She looked down, and I could see her facial expression lighten, even if only slightly. "Oh, thanks."

OUR FIRST MEETING, TAKE TWO

Before driving out to the Schmidt foster home for the second time in 24 hours, I called Deb to make sure they were there. Deb answered the phone and confirmed that Lauren came home from school on the bus. I packed my work bag with a notepad and a deck of cards, just in case I could talk Lauren into playing a game while we talked and headed out the door. I arrived at the foster home at 4:00, as Lauren and I had scheduled the day before. Deb let me know that Lauren was in her room and that she had reminded her I was coming after she got off the phone with me. I knocked on the door.

"Yeah?"

"Hey Lauren, it's Liz, from the agency. Can I come in?"

"Sure."

I asked Lauren if she preferred to meet there, or somewhere else in the house, or outside. She said she preferred her room. I found a spot on a beanbag in the corner and sat there, while Lauren sat on her bed, her back against the wall. Her hair was styled in a low ponytail, just like yesterday. Today, she had on a white T-shirt with the Rolling Stones logo on it—a set of lips with a big, red tongue sticking out. I decided to start there.

"So, you like the Rolling Stones?"

"Huh?" She looked down at her shirt. "Oh yeah, I guess. They're ok. I like The Beatles more." I must have looked surprised, because she said, "I don't like the music now ... Ariana Grande and Drake and stuff. My friends and I like the old stuff."

"Wow. I have to agree with you about some of the music on the radio ... it all sounds the same to me. But I'm old. What got you into the Beatles?"

"My friends at my old school. We all listen to classic rock."

"Is that what you do for down time after school?"

"Yeah. I usually would go on Instagram and stuff, but SHE won't let me have a cell phone. All I have is this thing I got when I was like 10."

She gestured towards a hot pink iPod on the bed next to her. "I can't watch TV either … at least not what I want to watch. SHE always has some show on for the little kids. I used to watch Maury and stuff after school, but SHE says it's not appropriate." I noticed that Lauren referred to Deb as "SHE" with the emphasis for effect.

"So, things are different here. Different rules. That's a lot of change for you. New school, new house, new rules. That's a lot."

I didn't want to get too deep in this first meeting but wanted to acknowledge the very real fact that she had endured a great deal of change in the last 3 months and was understandably under a lot of stress as a result. "Do you mind if I talk for a few minutes about why I'm here? It won't take long … I don't know what Deb has told you, and I know you were taken off guard when I was here yesterday."

"She said you're coming because I've been having attitude lately and she doesn't know what to do anymore."

"Well, ok, that's her perspective. I know you guys haven't been getting along lately and that's hard on both of you."

I saw my opportunity to clarify some misinformation, and let Lauren know what she could expect from me and our time together. I knew it was important to provide transparency throughout the process, but especially at the engagement stage. Lauren could have been thinking any number of things about me and my role in her life. She may have thought I was going to tell her then and there that she was moving again. I wish I could say that was a completely unrealistic assessment but based on her own experience and the reality of life 'in the system,' it wasn't. Best to give her an idea of what she could anticipate.

"Let me tell you what my job is and then I want to hear from you on how I might be helpful. My job is different than your case worker's job, even though we work together. I don't work with your mom, or your siblings. My job is to work with kids who are having a hard time in their foster homes. I try to figure out what we could change to make things go more smoothly here at your foster home. It's never going to be perfect … but can we make it better for you and Deb, so that you're both less stressed? My goal is to help her understand you better and for you to do what you need to do to not be in trouble so much. Usually I work with kids and foster parents for about 3 or 4 months. Both you and Deb will have work to do—this isn't just about you needing to change—you'll both make changes and maybe learn some new things. I usually meet with kids about once a week, most of the time in their foster home, but sometimes at school or out in the community, like at a park or library or something. I'd like to hear from you about what things are like here. We don't have to do it all today though …We can do something else while we talk. I brought some cards. Do you know how to play the game 'Trash?'"

Lauren agreed to play cards with me, and over the course of about 20 minutes, I learned that she hadn't seen her siblings for 2 weeks, because their mom missed her last parenting time with them. She had never gone that long without seeing them. In fact, she had never gone more than a couple of days before they entered foster care. She seemed worried about them, growing quiet after commenting that her sister, Tess, has asthma.

"Do they tell foster parents about that stuff, like how she's not supposed to run a lot?"

I assured her that foster parents are briefed on all medical conditions, but this didn't seem to help her worry.

"I wonder if we could set up a phone call with Tess and Trina?" I offered.

Lauren visibly brightened for the first time since I'd met her. I agreed to talk to Deb about it and contact the girls' foster home. Lauren deserved to talk to her siblings and may not have even known she could ask. This was one thing I could do to build trust with her, and I had a feeling that the separation from her siblings was a big source of Lauren's distress. We wrapped up our card game and planned to meet the following week. I asked if she preferred to meet at the foster home again, or perhaps at school or a park.

"Could you pick me up from school? I hate the bus."

I had time the following Wednesday, so we penciled it in, and I ran it by Deb before leaving. This would give me a chance to see Lauren outside of the foster home environment, and I could always spend some time touching base with Deb after dropping her off.

QUESTIONS

1. Based on the information given in the first meeting, generate a list of Lauren's initial problems and strengths.
2. What is your initial assessment? Write it down in a concise one paragraph narrative as if you are writing an article abstract of this session.
3. What areas of Lauren's life and history need further exploration in the next session, and how do you plan to gather this information in your next meeting?

SECOND MEETING

On Wednesday afternoon, I picked up Lauren outside her school. My goals for this meeting were to continue building trust and rapport, and to gather some information that might help me understand what was contributing to her difficulties.

We drove to a park about halfway between her school and the foster home. We walked around for a bit, talking about the school day and more about music she likes. We made our way to a picnic table, where she sat opposite me, as I pulled out a pad of paper and a pencil.

"One of the things I like to do when I'm getting to know kids is have them tell me about their families. Would that be ok?"

"I guess. Like what kinda stuff?"

"Well, for starters … who is in your family? And do you mind if I draw a sort of picture to keep everyone straight in my head? It's easier for me to remember that way."

I liked to develop genograms of the kids' families, with them whenever possible. It not only gave me (I'm a visual learner) a method for understanding the complex family structures often inherent in child welfare work. It also gave us an object for our conversation—something tangible to look at and discuss, so I wasn't just peppering kids with questions.

"You're going to draw a picture of my family?"

"Well not really. More of a map. Let's start with you and your siblings."

Lauren proceeded to name the members of her family, correcting me when I misspelled a name, or placed someone in the wrong birth order.

"What are your sisters like?"

"They don't listen. I know they're probably getting in trouble in their foster home because they don't listen to anybody but me."

"They must look up to you."

"I guess. They like how I make mac-n-cheese. I put lots of butter in and a little bit of hot sauce. I let them watch shows on my tablet so I can watch the TV. They like that." I noticed how much older Lauren seemed when talking about her sisters, compared to when she talked about school or chores or the Beatles. I wondered how much of her time was spent worrying about her siblings … Were they listening? Were they getting mac-n-cheese they way they liked it? Were they safe?

I learned that she had a complicated relationship with her dad.

"He's an asshole. He was always mad about something … my mom didn't cook the spaghetti right, or his boss didn't like him, or my sisters had the TV too loud. … I'm glad he's gone. I miss my grandma though. My mom won't let us see her since he got locked up."

I learned that Lauren's paternal grandma lived nearby and would often take Lauren overnight when she was younger. I wondered why she hadn't been considered for placement of Lauren or her siblings and made a mental note to ask her case manager about that.

We talked a bit longer about her family. I learned she gets along with her mom, but her mom's functioning spiraled downward after her dad was arrested. Apparently out of necessity, Lauren seemed to do a lot of the parenting. As the oldest, she had always helped with the younger ones. But in recent years, as her mom dealt with physical and verbal abuse from her dad, it seems that Lauren's role as a caregiver increased beyond what was appropriate for a child of her age. In the months leading to the children's removal, it seemed that it became too much for her to maintain, and her mom was, in many ways, unavailable.

The kids missed school frequently, wore the same clothes for days in a row, and many days, according to the CPS report, didn't eat other than at school. This prompted attention from the school staff, which led to a CPS referral and the ultimate removal of the children.

QUESTIONS

1. Based on this information and what was in first meeting, develop a genogram based on Lauren's family history. What trends and patterns do you see?
2. Does it change your initial assumptions about your developing approach to help Lauren in her present situation?

I thanked Lauren for telling me about her family and had her look over the genogram to ensure that I captured all the important information. We headed back to my car and drove to the foster home. Before we went inside, I asked if it would work for me to pick her up again next Wednesday. She agreed.

Though I also needed to clear this with Deb, Lauren needed to believe she had some control of her situation. Even though she didn't ask to meet with me, or ask to be in foster care for that matter, she could be given the choice about when and where we met rather than being told that it was happening.

Once at the foster home, I sat down with Deb at the dining room table to go over the results of the behavior assessment. I had both Deb's and the teacher's results.

There were some common themes; namely, Lauren scored in the clinical range on the externalizing symptom subscale. This made sense, given her problems with verbal outbursts at home and at school, particularly with authority figures. She also scored in the at-risk range for depression and in the clinical range for withdrawal. These results, though not reported to me at referral, were reflected in what I'd observed in my few short interactions with Lauren.

She spent most of her time in her room, away from Deb and the other kids in the home. She was isolated from her friends and family, having been placed in a foster home separate from her siblings and away from her neighborhood and school. The assessment results made sense to me, and I thought they'd be helpful to review with Deb. I had also brought a two-page handout on traumatic stress in adolescents, hoping that some information on what's behind Lauren's behaviors might increase Deb's empathy and soften her parenting approach a bit.

After going over the assessment results, and my take on them, I asked Deb for her thoughts. "Well, I'm not surprised. Her mouth gets her into trouble. She has no respect for adults." Here was my opportunity to build awareness around trauma and its impact, but I had to proceed with caution if I wanted Deb to stay engaged in this process.

"I've heard the way she talks to you, and you're right, it's disrespectful. My gut response when a kid talks to me that way is to put her in her place ... let her know it is not acceptable. The trouble with kids who've experienced so much trauma is that they don't back down. Many of them will go toe to toe with you, never admitting that they did anything wrong or should act any differently. It's because adults have let them down so much, even hurt them. Why should they respect adults? Add to that the perfectly normal stage that we all went through as teenagers, when adults were all idiots and we knew everything ... and well, it's a recipe for what you've got here with Lauren. It's so hard to remember in the moment. Lots of foster parents have found it's helpful to learn about what trauma does to kids at different ages. Here's some info on adolescents. I thought it sounded a lot like what you're dealing with Lauren." I handed her the information and changed the subject a bit.

"So, when she doesn't do what she's supposed to do ... like take a shower by 8:00 ... what do you do?"

"I knock on her door and tell her if she doesn't get in the shower in 10 minutes, she loses TV for the night."

"That sounds like a fair consequence. She doesn't do what she needs to do, so she doesn't get to do what she wants to do."

"That's what I thought. It worked for my kids when they were her age. But she either acts like she doesn't care, or she blows up, yelling that she doesn't need me to treat her like a little kid. Either way, she usually doesn't shower."

"Hmm ... I know that at her house, she made a lot of the decisions about this kind of stuff, not only for herself but for her siblings, too. Even though she doesn't need to do that here, the change probably feels abrupt to her. I wonder if you talked with her about it ahead of time, maybe that would take some of the pressure out of the moment. Maybe we can come up with a plan for showering that includes her input? Like which days she showers, or what time, and what a consequence should be if she doesn't?"

"Sure. It's worth a try. Anything is better than how it is now." I saw an opportunity for a small, but important win. I got Lauren from her room and explained the idea. I mapped out a rough calendar for the week and asked when she wanted to take her showers. She shared that she has gym class on Monday, Wednesday, Friday and would like to shower those nights. She thought she should be able to shower at 8:00, and not before. Deb agreed to give it a try. We put it on the calendar and posted it on the fridge. I left, crossing my fingers that this attempt to share control with Lauren would bear some fruit, in the form of a calmer household in the coming week.

QUESTIONS

1. Based on the information you have gathered during the first two sessions, what are you clinical impressions of Lauren?

2. Is there enough information to begin making clinical diagnosis(es), if that is appropriate to your role in this case? If so, what would those diagnoses be, complete with case history to justify your ideas. If not, can you begin shaping a "rule-out" diagnosis that requires more information?

3. In terms of treatment planning (behavior planning) based on the information gathered during the sessions and from her extensive case records, what initial step would you take to help her begin making changes, if any?

4. How have your clinical impressions changed since the first session? What factors made them change?

5. What additional information do you need in the next session to become better prepared to help Lauren and her foster mother?

THIRD MEETING

The following Wednesday, I called Deb to check in and find out how the shower plan had been working.

"Well she took her showers."

"That's great! I think I'll take her to McDonald's for a little snack on the way home from school today, if it's ok with you."

"If you want to, but you should also know that she's still had an attitude with me about everything … chores, homework, waking up for school, you name it."

I knew that Lauren was a challenge to live with, but I also had hoped that Deb would take a minute to celebrate the small win before moving on to her list of problem behaviors.

"I do want to celebrate this progress, even as I know there's still a long way to go. We'll pick another issue to tackle next, but as much as I'd like to promise that her attitude will improve … that may take a while."

I picked up Lauren from school and asked her if she'd like to stop at McDonald's for an ice cream or fries to celebrate the showering plan.

"Sure, if you want to."

Not exactly the excitement I'd been anticipating, but I had learned over the years that kids who've lost their trust in adults don't like to show you they care.

It requires vulnerability, and that is a scary thought for them. Better to act like nothing matters than to get your hopes up and have them dashed yet another time. I'd learned that "If you want to" is often the closest I'd get to a hard "Yes!"

Another thing I'd learned is riding in the car influences teenagers—they're much more likely to open on a car ride than most anywhere else. I assume it's because sitting side by side is a lot less intimidating than face-to-face conversation. It's for this reason that I often volunteered to transport kids on my caseload for appointments and pick them up from school. I learned a lot in the car. Such was the case with Lauren on this day.

"We have a McDonalds by our house." I knew she wasn't referring to Deb's house. There were no shops or restaurants within at least a mile. "I went there with Trina and Tess the day before we got taken. My mom gave me $20 and told me to take the little kids there so she could rest. I got a bunch of stuff from the Dollar Menu. I got myself a huge drink and fries and a Flurry. It was great. The next day was when they got us from school. I didn't even get to see my mom until a couple days later. I didn't know where she was or if she knew they got us from school. I didn't know where Trina and Tess were. Nobody told me and I still don't know if they got any of their stuff from our house, like their blankets. JJ was with me … we went to that one place together. I stayed there a couple nights. It was alright. We got to watch a lot of movies. JJ stayed there longer I guess. Miss Deb couldn't take him because she doesn't have enough rooms. I told them he could stay with me, but they said it wasn't allowed."

"Wow, Lauren. That's a lot." I wanted to let her know I was listening, that I valued the weight of what she was telling me, without reacting so strongly that it shut her down.

"Do you think about your brother and sisters a lot?"

"At first I did all the time. I'd wake up thinking that I needed to get the girls ready for school … and then remember. Or I'd be eating something gross that Miss Deb made and wonder what their foster parents are feeding them. Like, do they know Tess won't eat vegetables? Like none."

"You have a lot of questions about your sisters. That makes sense—you did a lot for them and suddenly they're not with you." Silence. "I think it would be a big help to their foster parents if you wrote down some of the stuff you know about them. Like Tess and vegetables. We could give it to them at the next visit."

"If you want to." I took that as a "yes."

"SHE JUMPED OUT OF THE VAN!"

The week after Lauren and I went to McDonald's, I had planned to pick her up from school on Wednesday and head to the foster home for a joint meeting with Deb.

I had gathered enough information and built enough of a rapport with both to begin constructing a treatment plan—a contract between Deb, Lauren, and me about what we were working to change and how. We never got to that meeting though, because on Monday afternoon, I got a voicemail on my office phone. It was Deb, audibly upset, stating, "She jumped out of the van! Liz, she jumped out of my van! You need to get out here. I can't deal with this anymore."

I returned the call to Deb, who reported that Lauren was suspended from school again today for fighting. "When I picked her up, we weren't a mile down the road when she jumped out of the van."

"What? Deb, is she ok?"

"She's fine. I was pulling up to a stop sign. But she refused to get back in. I told her fine, she could walk home if she wanted." Deb followed Lauren from a distance as Lauren walked the final mile home. "Now she won't come inside. She's just been out in the yard this whole time."

"Ok. I have some time now … I'll be there in 20 minutes."

After driving as quickly and safely as I could to the house, I noticed that Lauren was still outside when I arrived.

"Hey, rough day?"

"I'm not going back in the house with that bitch!"

"Sure, we can stay out here. You want to tell me what happened at school?"

"Some girl told everyone my dad's locked up, so I told her to stay out of my business. She just laughed so I had to shut her up. I shoved her into the lockers. Then she came back at me and then we were on the ground and someone pulled her off me. They took me to the office and called HER."

"That sounds horrible. What happened next?" Now was not the time to lecture her about healthy coping skills. She needed me to listen.

"SHE came and got me. She talked to the assistant principle and then said, 'Let's go.' In the car she just started laying into me, like it was my fault this happened. She said, 'You need to control your anger' and 'You can't solve problems this way' and 'You are grounded' … she didn't even ask me what happened … just kept talking and talking and I couldn't take it anymore. When she slowed down for a stop sign, I got out. I could hear her yelling at me to get back in the car, but I couldn't do it … I needed space."

I stayed outside with Lauren for another 30 minutes before she agreed to go inside. I walked her to her room and then tactfully asked Deb to give her some space for the night. No need to shower, no need to do homework. I talked with Deb for a while, reflecting that it must have been scary to have Lauren jump out of the van.

As I was leaving, Deb said, "This just isn't working."

1. How do the developments in this case change your clinical impressions of Lauren and her foster home?
2. How do the developments change your course of action in the immediate and longer term for Lauren and her situation?
3. Explore the pros and cons of leaving Lauren at Deb's foster home and trying to work through the problems versus moving Lauren to another foster placement.
4. What are the policies and practices of the foster care system in the state where you live, and how do these policies and practices apply to this case?
5. Before reading further, given all the information you have gathered and assessed, what would your next steps be regarding Lauren and her foster mother? Justify your decision.

PONDERING A PLACEMENT CHANGE

After Deb stated she did not think it was going to work with Lauren in her home, as I drove back to the office, I thought, "I think I agree with her."

Upon returning to the office, I found my supervisor. We'd talked about Lauren several times before, so she was aware of the struggles between her and Deb. However, our previous conversations always assumed we were working to preserve this placement. For the first time, I was calling into question that assumption. My job was to work with both the child, and those in her environment, to improve the "goodness of fit" and, in turn, improve maladaptive behaviors. I wondered though, if a better "fit" might mean a different foster home. I knew that homes taking teen girls were rare, and those taking teen girls who frequently got suspended for fighting were even rarer. Still, I asked my supervisor about options.

It turned out another foster youth had just moved out of one of our foster homes over the weekend. It was a home that took mostly teen girls and didn't mind taking new placements this soon after another had ended.

The Hill foster home included two parents in their 50s, Dave and Cindy, as well as one 15-year-old girl who had lived there a couple of years and a 12-year-old girl who arrived last month. I had worked with the Hills several times and thought their nurturing, patient style could be a good fit for Lauren. I talked it over with my supervisor and Lauren's case manager. We decided to set up an overnight visit for Lauren at the Hills' to give Lauren and Deb a break from each other and Lauren and the Hills an opportunity to get to know one another. I called Deb to discuss the plan with her, and then I talked with Lauren. She agreed that some space would be good, and we planned for me to pick her up the next day for a visit at the Hills' home.

THE DECISION

The overnight visit went well. The Hills said they were open to her moving in and could take her at any time. I called Lauren to find out how it went, and she reported she liked it there and wished she could stay. We quickly pulled together a family team meeting to decide if this was the path to take. I was at the meeting, as well as Lauren's case manager, the foster care supervisor, Lauren's mom, and Deb Schmidt.

By the end of the meeting, it was clear Deb felt ill-equipped to handle Lauren's behaviors and regretted agreeing to take a teenager in the first place. She was more than open to her moving to a new home. Lauren's mom supported the plan, as did the case manager and her supervisor. It was settled. This was the right choice, even in the wake of the many transitions for Lauren in the last year, and foster care's goal to limit the number of foster home moves.

THE MOVE

I picked up Lauren that Friday afternoon from the Schmidt foster home. She had her few belongings in a couple of duffel bags and one cardboard box. She gave the younger kids a hug and stood looking at the ground as Deb wished her the best in her new place. We loaded up the car and drove the 10 or so miles to the Hill foster home.

Upon our arrival, Dave came out to the car and offered to carry Lauren's bags. "Welcome back, stranger! Long time, no see!" he joked. He walked us inside and upstairs to the room she would share with the 12-year-old girl. "Why don't you put your bags in here? You can come back up when Liz leaves and do some unpacking." We dropped off her things, and walked back down the hall, stopping at a closet. "Here's where we keep the bedsheets and towels. Why don't you pick which ones you want ... everyone gets their own color? Looks like we've got black, pink, blue ..."

"I'll take the black ones." Already I was thankful for the Hills' approach. Something as simple as being able to choose the color of the sheets on the bed can be incredibly impactful for a kid who has very little control over what's happening to and around her.

"Ok, sounds good. Let's head downstairs so we can talk for a bit." Dave led us downstairs, pausing to show us the wall along the staircase where they had hung photos of all the kids who had lived in their home over the last decade. Some were school photos, some were from holiday celebrations, and others were candid snapshots, likely the only images of those kids' brief stints in the home. Lauren didn't comment but looked over the 30 or 40 photos with interest.

Around the kitchen table, Dave and Cindy went over their house rules, and the schedule for a typical day. They asked her questions about food and TV shows and school.

What I remember most, however, is what Dave said about trust. "It's important to have trust. Right now, you have no trust in me, because we only met a few days ago. I don't know much about what you've been through, but I know that adults have let you down. Adults you trusted. So, our job is to earn your trust by doing what we say we'll do and making sure you and the other girls have what you need. That will take time. For now, we'll work on getting to know each other. Friday is pizza night, so it'll be ready at 6:00. Why don't you go get settled in?"

As I left the Hill foster home that afternoon, I thought about the difference a person's environment can make. One of the things I know to be true about trauma-informed care is that a safe, predictable, nurturing environment is critically important. Very little else can be accomplished, clinically speaking, if a psychologically safe environment is not established. Trauma, fundamentally, includes an unsafe, unpredictable, and harmful environment, so healing must include the opposite.

I wasn't naive enough to believe that Lauren's problems were behind her. She had problems with peer relationships, difficulty with authority figures, grief over separation from her siblings, and confusion over what it meant to be a 14-year-old without overwhelming adult responsibilities.

I believed Lauren had a fighting chance in this new environment. She had foster parents who understood the "why" behind her challenging behaviors, which they would undoubtedly soon experience. She was being offered choices, albeit on small things, that would increase her sense of control. There was significant work to be done, and my hope was that this new environment would give us the opportunity to do it.

QUESTIONS

1. Critique the decisions to change placement based on the case evidence and your exploration of the possibility before the last meeting.
2. What new or recurrence of Lauren's issues would you expect to see as she adjusts to her new foster home? What is your plan for handling these issues?
3. Imagine yourself as her therapist, and perform the following tasks based on the information contained in the case:
   - What questions did the author leave out of the assessment?

- What would you have done differently throughout the assessment?
- Are there questions you would not have asked or pushed for more information on?
- Based on the case information in this chapter, develop a three-generation genogram (including important nonfamily members, if needed) to represent Lauren's presented life and all who are instrumentally involved. Make any notes and figures on this genogram to aid in developing a wholistic view of this case.
- Make a list, with supporting evidence, of the main issues in Lauren's life at the time of the interview. Include a list of Lauren's personal and social strengths that may be used as resources in the future pertaining to each of the issues listed.
- Develop and write a narrative assessment and diagnosis(es) as demonstrated by the information contained in this case. Justify your diagnostic decisions by listing the criteria you believe are met through the interview record. It is inappropriate to base diagnostic decisions on assumptions, only direct evidence provided by your client.
- If you met Lauren, what additional information would you need to contribute to a more comprehensive narrative assessment and diagnostic decisions?
- Be sure to place Lauren's personal and social strengths in the narrative assessment, to be used later as part of treatment planning.

4. As discussed in Chapter 1, we apply the stages of change to the client's motivation for change for each diagnosed problem.
- List each diagnosis you decided upon in the narrative assessment.
- For each diagnosis, determine what stage of change Lauren is presently in pertaining to her motivation to change that problem. Please use Lauren's own words to justify your stage decisions.
- Use the stages of change during the next section on treatment planning.

5. Based on the narrative assessment, develop a written treatment plan to include short- and long-term treatment goals and objectives. Include what methods of treatment and support you will utilize.
- What treatment theory or combination of theories do you believe best fits Lauren's reality? Defend your decision.
- What theories or approaches does the latest empirical evidence in the field recommend?
- Based on the stages of change decisions above, where will you begin in treatment? Explain and defend your decisions.

6. Based on the treatment theory or theories chosen and defended above, list each intervention you would use in your work with Lauren. Specifically, for each intervention, include the target issue, intervention and modality (e.g., group therapy) you chose, and the theoretical justification for each.

- What other options might be available should these interventions prove ineffective?
- What does the latest empirical evidence in the field suggest for each target issue? How does this evidence match with your intervention strategies?
- When developing treatment approaches do not overlook nontraditional approaches and approaches that target multiple systemic levels (i.e., individual, family, community, advocacy, etc.).
- What factors and strategies will you use to build trust and engagement during the intervention phases of your work? How will you assist Lauren as her motivation to change waxes and wanes over the coming weeks and months?
- Think about the initial therapy session after the assessment with Lauren. How would you begin, what would your goals be for the session and what would you hope to accomplish?

CHAPTER 5

Gary Greenwell

A Life of Quiet Desperation

Melissa Villarreal

IN THIS CHAPTER, I present a case from my practice career, that exemplifies the many destructive ways childhood sexual trauma can help destroy its victim into adulthood. Meet Gary Greenwell, a 48-year-old White male with a successful family, career, and community reputation. On the surface, aside from a series of health problems, Mr. Greenwell appears to be living a normal middle-class life. He was married for over 20 years to Gail, and they had three adopted children, two of whom had graduated from high school and were now in college. While they were having some behavioral issues with their youngest, his family was the same as so many others. They even took the responsibility of seeking help for their youngest, attending family therapy with me for nearly 1 year before the case circumstances changed … dramatically.

Trauma can be insidious. It can damage and destroy in so many ways, many not obvious to the casual onlooker, or even a well-trained family therapist who knew the Greenwell's for over 1 year. Gary Greenwell's case was interesting, intense, and provided me a learning experience that rivaled any clinical training I ever attended. I challenge you to study the case hard, grow familiar with the literature on trauma-based care, and allow Gary Greenwell to teach you the valuable lessons he taught me that have lasted throughout my career.

CHAPTER PRESENTATION

We present Gary Greenwell's case differently than the cases in previous chapters. In the previous cases, the authors took the readers inside the actual sessions to hear some of the dialogue and understand the process of data collection and motivation, to allow readers to read what the experienced practitioners were thinking and planning as the sessions proceeded. It's almost as if our authors/practitioners were "thinking out loud" during their cases.

In this chapter, instead of being inside the sessions, we present a completed client assessment form that includes all the personal information and data collected during the clinical assessment process. Following assessment protocol, each completed section of this assessment form contains data, along with relevant personal quotes from the client. However, the sections are devoid of "clinical assessment thinking." That is, we have omitted the practitioner's thinking, conclusions, diagnostics, final assessment report, and treatment plan.

It is for the readers to read the case assessment report, and complete each section based on the information contained in the client data. At the end of each section of the assessment form, there is space to write conclusion paragraphs called "Issues to Consider" and "Strengths to Consider." Readers should complete these sections under each assessment dimension before moving to the end-of-chapter tasks.

After completing the issues and strengths sections throughout the chapter, at the end of the case, there are five important areas to be completed either alone, in groups, or as a class. These sections include:

1. **Clinical diagnoses:** Readers will use the client information to make clinical diagnoses. There will most likely be multiple diagnoses, that may include substance use disorders and trauma-based and/or mental health disorders.

2. **Stages of change:** Readers will determine the relevant stage of change for each clinical diagnosis, along with the justification for said change (see Chapter 1 for more on the stages of change).

3. **Narrative assessment:** Readers will write a complete narrative assessment, encompassing all client data, including clinical hypotheses and conclusions. This narrative must me wholistic and be consistent with the clinical diagnoses made earlier.

   We also ask that readers use the client data throughout the case to perform an Adverse Childhood Experience (ACE) screening as part of this narrative assessment. The ACE screening tool is available online from many sources.

4. **Treatment plan:** Using the information from above, in combination with knowledge of treatment modalities, intensities, and methods, readers will develop a treatment plan for Gary moving forward. The treatment plan will include treatment goals, measurable objectives, and a rationale for each section.

5. **High-risk aftercare and intervention plan:** Based on Gary's presentation and life circumstances, here readers decide how his case will be handled in the event of any high-risk activities and behaviors, and how these will be handled by the professionals and through recommendations or referrals for the client.

It is important to remember that all assessment and clinical conclusions, diagnoses, and decision-making must be based on data contained in the case. That is, while it may be appropriate to speculate about issues based on new information learned later in therapy, any documented conclusions must have data to back them up. Conclusions without data represents the practitioner's implicit or explicit bias, out-of-control subjectivity, too much reliance on personal life experience, or simply overconfidence (see Chapter 1). Please take steps to help avoid making clinical decisions based on practitioner life experience, beliefs, attitudes, and thoughts. This exercise is good practice about an issue that professionals must be aware of throughout their clinical careers.

Gary Greenwell is an interesting case for study. Good luck with this case.

CLINICAL ASSESSMENT FORM

Guide for use: Each dimension requires data, narrative, and a short summary of the relevant issues and strengths to consider in the final assessment.

Client name: Gary Greenwell   **Date of first contact:** 00/00/00

Practitioner: **Date completed:**

Dimension 1: Client Description, Presenting Problem, and Context of Referral

A. Brief Description of Client

Gary Greenwell is a 48-year-old White male, dressed appropriately in a business suit and glasses. He appeared well-kept and clean but looked physically tired and appeared older than his 48 years. He made eye contact while shaking hands. Gary appears to be an outgoing person, who greets people warmly and appears friendly and open. He speaks in a loud voice, louder than the environment would require.

Gary is not a new client. He had attended family therapy with his wife and youngest son with this therapist for more than 1 year prior to this appointment. They began attending family therapy because of his adopted son David's behavioral problems. David had experienced troubles in school, was fighting with peers, and using alcohol and other drugs as a 17-year-old adolescent. He also acted-out at home with his parents and siblings, sometimes becoming violent against property, and twice had threatened physical violence against his father, Gary. David reportedly had broken doors and walls during fits of anger and was nearing the point of being removed from high school.

Gary is a former mortician and funeral director, who now works as an insurance salesman in a local community. He is married to his wife Gail of 20 years. In addition to David (17 years old), he has two other adopted children, Marie (19 years old) and Carlie (18 years old).

This is his first appointment for individual therapy. Gary called for an individual appointment earlier this week, claiming he had some "personal" things he wanted to discuss in a private session. My assumption was he wanted to talk about his son David, who had been his almost singular focus for the last year. Beyond the "personal" reference, Gary gave no indication about the nature of his need for an individual appointment. The assessment period and all the information that follows was gathered over two 1-hour sessions covering 3 weeks.

B. Chief Complaint and Symptoms by Client and Others Present

Having known Gary as a family therapy client for over 1 year, I expected him to immediately start complaining about David. David had been "a handful" over the last 2 years, using alcohol, marijuana, stimulants, and acting out at home and school, including physical fighting in school. He had been suspended several times.

When asked about the purpose of the meeting, Gary suddenly became sullen and monotone, as if a switch had been thrown. He said that last week at a gathering of his wife's family, he had "stumbled" upon some "memories" and it would "drive me crazy" to do nothing about it. "I've been fighting these memories all of my adult life, so maybe now is the time to talk about them … if I can, that is."

Gary reported that at the gathering and after a few drinks, he was prompted by a conversation between his wife and sisters-in-law about sexual abuse they had experienced as children, Gary said he sat back in his chair, and in his usual loud voice, said, "If you ladies think you had it bad … my father and all his friends used to rape me nearly every night until I was 15 years old."

Aside from stunning his wife of 20 years (who had never heard this before) and her family, his memories and that he had said anything about his past stunned him as well. He claims to have "not thought about it," remembered it, or talked about it since his father's death many years before. However, Gary claims to have a long history of "bad dreams" and "scary images" most of his life. "I need help … my head is exploding now that it's out in the open … why did I have to bring it up?"

Gary went on to tell his story. Beginning when he was 5 years old, he claims his father began sexually abusing him at night, "every night as I remember," in his bedroom, and sometimes during the day outside in the garage or back barn. He said his dad, a cattle farmer, was a mean drunk, whose breath "stank," and he always smelled bad, "sort of like cow shit," Gary said.

Every night at about the same time, after his mother had passed out from drinking, he could hear the floor and stairs creaking, and the next thing he knew his father was in his room, throwing him around on the bed and raping him anally and orally until he was finished and satisfied. Gary spent nearly every night, he said, crying and hurting, both physically and psychologically, from the abuse. "I got to point where I didn't want to go to bed … and If I did I wished my father would somehow die before it was my time … to this day I have scars on my anus from that time." At the time, he says he did not realize he was being abused. Gary said he just knew "it hurt and made me feel bad and hate the old man."

His father used to say to him, "you don't tell your mother, or she will die … that's a promise." So, he kept the secret for nearly 5 years. Gary was raped multiple times per day until, at around age 10, when he finally worked up the courage to tell his mother that dad was "hurting" him every day. His mother, who was very submissive and a heavy drinker, said, as best as Gary can recollect, "Oh, your father has his funny ideas … but he would never hurt you unless you had it coming. Now go to bed and never speak of it again."

Gary claims that his mother died, in her sleep, from too much vodka 2 weeks later. "I've hated and resented women ever since," he said. "My mother was use-less … hell … she probably didn't want him to stop on me, cause she didn't want to deal with that asshole. … She abandoned me to be alone with that pervert for 5 more years … how could she die on me like that?"

That she died as his father predicted made him even more frightened and passive to his father's desires. "It's a big part of why I haven't ever told anyone. I know it sounds crazy … but I didn't want anyone else to die 'cause I told them about this."

Gary said that after his mother died "on me," his father and the sexual abuse got "out of control." Not long after her death, Gary said his drunken father began having his male friends over, and each one would get their "turn" raping him, to do "whatever they wanted to me." That is, his father allowed his friends to rape Gary in their home. According to Gary, sometimes five and six times per night. "It would last until they all left or passed out," he said

Other nights, his dad would take him to the bar, and have his male friends go to the car to have sex with him. "I'm not sure if they were paying him … but I believe they were," he said. "I wasn't a human son to that man. I was a play toy for him and his perverted friends … I didn't exist to any of them outside of my ability to 'get them off' however they wanted it."

Gary said that although this torture was happening every day, he continued in school. He learned that if he became funny and "outgoing" and always smiled and was compliant, nobody would ever suspect something bad was happening to him. So, I became this happy guy who laughed a lot and made friends … on the surface. "I learned it worked … and I didn't want anyone else to die cause of my problems."

At the age of 15, Gary's father died in a drunken driving accident. "I was free," he said. My mother's parents took me in, and I lived with them until I graduated high school and left to be on my own. "I never told them, or anyone about what happened. I didn't want them to die." He went on, "I know it's ridiculous to believe that crap, but I did, so I kept it all to myself … I just wanted to be normal and have a normal life."

Gary claims he never, in the last 33 years, mentioned a word to anyone about his past, until the family gathering last week. "I heard these women whining and crying about their pity party ... they were going on and on about victim this and victim that ... so I just let them have it. I let them hear what a real victim had done to them." He says he wanted them to know just what abuse was ... not realizing he was "opening a can of worms that was better left closed."

When he finished confessing to her family, Gary says his wife was "horrified and furious with me for bringing it up and ruining the party." He says, everyone in attendance fell silent ... "that's one way to break up a party," he sighed. Gary said his wife "didn't want to talk to me about it ... just like a woman to not even care enough to help her husband." She told him to talk to a shrink, not her. "She seemed mad at me for not telling her, instead of feeling sorry for me ... that's all I've come to expect from women in my life ... it's all about them, all the time" he said.

Gary claims he immediately began having more frequent and vivid nightmares, many of them included snakes, apparently a consistent theme in his life (more below). He says he's always been afraid of snakes, but his terror dreams lately have all included him being attacked by large, dangerous, and terrifying snakes. "I don't even want to sleep, because I know what's coming in my dreams." Gary claims that whenever he gets even a little sexually aroused, even when trying to masturbate, he sees "horrifying" images of snakes and "smells" his father and loses any interest. "I have no idea what the snake thing is ... but this fear and the visions have been with me my whole adult life, as far as I can remember."

It seems Gary has thought about his childhood most of his life, not just since he revealed his story at that gathering. He says he's always had periods of "vivid memories," especially when he would hear stories of sexual abuse and rape or even think about being sexual himself. Gary claims that for most of his life he would, often in bed or just before falling asleep, have "periods" where he could smell the "cow shit" and feel his father attacking him, and smell his "stinky" breath. He says any creaking sounds in his house usually trigger these "real" feelings.

Gary claims he was good at excusing off his dreams, night terrors (after waking in full sweat and screaming), irritability and anger, his lack of sleep, and his desire to be alone. He said that a few drinks, along with his "mood pills" seem to help him find an "even keel."

He also said he became especially good at explaining to his wife why sex was impossible for him, especially early in their marriage. "I just told her I had a rare medical condition that stopped me from ever being able to have sex," he said. "She seemed to accept that as an excuse ... at least after a while." Even when they did try getting sexual early in their marriage, he says the "snakes would attack" and that would end it.

As he was telling his story, Gary fell into what appeared to be a trance. That is, calm, monotone, and distanced, so different than his usual social presentation. He had a lost look in eyes, almost as if he was unaware he was still in my office. His recollections transported him back, where it appeared the only way to deal with it was to be emotionally distanced from it.

As he spoke he slowly curled up into a near-fetal position in the deep corner of the oversized couch in my office. At least twice during this conversation, or monologue, he stopped and said, "I can't believe I'm talking about this." Then he would continue.

During the discussion, Gary never cried, or became angry, except when he talked about his mother. "You know what?" he asked. "I think that bitch killed herself instead of doing something to help HER OWN SON! Can you believe that shit? Since that day I knew to never count on a woman to help."

When asked, given all that has happened to him and his feelings about women, why he chose to marry and have a family, Gary became sad.

"I just wanted to be normal … I just wanted everyone to think there was nothing wrong with me … or bad about me," he said. I met Gail in college, and she was nice enough. She wanted children and to be married, so we hit it off as friends."

He said he felt some pressure to be intimate, even if not sexually, and was able to "play the game." His desire to be "normal" led to marriage, "why she wanted to marry me as distant as I always was is beyond me … hell maybe she has issues, too, … we never talked about it"

Their lack of a sex life, ostensibly because Gary had a medical condition, led to them adopting three children. "I was able to get lost in my work and children, and community involvement … we reached a point where we had a good life together, just like two roommates with a common mission, our kids."

When asked about what it is like for him to have a life without intimacy, physical or emotional, he bristled. "I loved my father and mother as their son … and look what that brought me. Trust me, I can do without it … all those damn self-help books got it wrong. Intimacy and love almost killed me … and who knows, maybe it did kill me inside … or might still, who knows?"

After all that's happened in the last 2 weeks to reveal his lifetime of secrets, Gary decided he needed professional help more than his son. Even his wife told him to go "see a shrink." Before calling me, Gary said he tried another therapist, "a so-called expert in abuse" for one session. He said she "creeped him out" by sitting too close and challenging him on his "discomfort" around women. When that did not work, and his "memories" kept getting worse, he thought of me, mainly because we already had a good relationship, and he "liked my style." He did not think that my being a female therapist would be an issue, "because I know you so well."

Issues to Consider (based on client data):

Strengths to Consider (based on client data):

Dimension 2: Treatment History

A. Substance Abuse Treatment

Gary reports having attended outpatient therapy once before "many years ago" because he was caught drinking and driving (5 years earlier). He also said he attended Alcoholics Anonymous meetings for the 1 year he was on probation. He reports that his son David was presently in therapy for alcohol and drug use (with this therapist). He claims his father was a "raging drunk" who "obviously" never received help.

Gary reports no additional substance abuse therapy or classes for anyone in his family, except the family therapy he and Gail had made David attend in my office.

B. Client Attitude Toward Treatment

Presently, Gary seems to have a favorable opinion of therapy, both for himself and his son. However, he claims he "hated" his previous, court-mandated therapy for drunken driving, and would "never set foot" in another AA meeting. He called it "useless," but he needed to comply to satisfy the judge and his probation officer.

C. Mental Health Treatment

Gary recounted his previously mentioned single session with a "local expert in abuse" 1 week prior to this meeting. He says he mentioned he had always "disliked" and "distrusted" women, since his mother refused to help him after he told her about "what dad and is drinking buddies" did to me. Soon after her refusal to help, she died suddenly. Gary said he told the therapist her death felt like she "abandoned" him and left him to years of even worse abuse.

According to Gary, after he said this, the female therapist got up from her chair, walked across the room and sat on the couch near him, and asked him, "Does this make you uncomfortable?" He claimed he told her to "Get the fuck away from me!" He says he proceeded to get up and leave the session immediately.

This is the only mental health therapy Gary claims he or anyone in his family has attended, until today. "Given what I told you … I wanted to stay away from therapists for myself … I didn't want all this to come out."

D. Attitudes About Previous Treatment(s)

Clearly, Gary had a negative attitude about therapy pertaining to his issues resulting from years of abuse as a child, given his remarks about his one encounter prior to this meeting. He claims, however, that he is comfortable seeing me (a female therapist, who identifies as female). Because of our previous relationship, I have a valuable entrée into rapport-building and client engagement.

Issues to Consider (based on client data):

Strengths to Consider (based on client data):

Dimension 3: Substance Use History

A. Lifetime Substance Use History (Complete Table. Explain in Narrative)

SUBSTANCE	FREQUENCY	DOSE (AVG.)	AGE FIRST USE	AGE LAST USE	ROUTE OF ADMIN.	OVER-DOSE
Alcohol	Daily	3–4 whiskeys/day	16	48	Drink	None
Nicotine (cigarettes)	Daily	2 packs/day	16	48	Smoke	None
Benzodi-azepine (prescribed)	3 × daily	20 mg × 3	26	48	Oral	None

B. Drugs Used in Previous 30 Days

Gary reports drinking at least three to four "normal size" drinks of whiskey and water per day. When asked, he claims he had four to five drinks per day for the last 3 days, a slight increase since he revealed his past abuse. His "normal size" drinks are about 1.5 oz whiskey and water over ice. Gary claims the last 3 days have not been normal days. Gary says he likes to "get drunk" on weekends, mostly staying at home instead of driving to be with friends. "Ever since I got arrested, I just drink at home," He says he can drink most of a fifth of whiskey on Saturdays, Sundays, and holidays. "It helps me relax."

Gary also takes a well-known benzodiazepine three times per day at 20 mg per dose. This medicine has been prescribed by his family doctor for "mood upheavals" since Gary was approximately 26 years old (22 years).

C. Top Three Drugs of Choice

Gary reports using alcohol, cigarettes, and his benzodiazepine as the only drugs he uses. He reports never trying "street" drugs at any time in his life.

D. Drug Mixing

Gary mixes, and has mixed benzodiazepines and four or more shots of liquor daily, and has for 20+ years. He mixes more heavily on weekends and holidays when his alcohol intake increases, according to Gary. He reports no incidence of overdose.

E. Longest Period of Abstinence

Gary reports not going a day without drinking for as long as he can remember. He also added that it's not an issue for him to not have at least one drink per day, because he does not now, nor has he ever had, what he would call an alcohol problem. Gary brought up "drinking problem" in this context, as it was not, at any time during the session, suggested he may have a substance use disorder.

F. Narrative

Gary reports drinking four or five shots of liquor per day since he was 16 years old. He also reports that his alcohol use has increased "some" since he revealed his childhood sexual abuse to his wife and extended family a week ago. He says he drinks up to a fifth per day on weekends and holidays, because he likes to get drunk when he is home.

He was arrested for drunken driving 5 years earlier (reported BAL = .14) and attended mandated AA meetings and therapy during that time. He claimed that experience was a waste of his time, because he did not then, nor does he presently, have any issues with alcohol. Gary says he has always had trouble managing his anxiety, especially at night, and having a "few drinks" helps him relax and cope with these issues.

Gary was prescribed a well-known benzodiazepine to help with his anxious moods, by his family doctor. He has been taking this without a pause for the past 22 years (since he was 26 years old). He also says that without this medication he would be "impossible to live with" and would never get any sleep or be able to relax.

When asked about any issues taking both a benzodiazepine (a depressant) and four to five shots of liquor (also a depressant) together, Gary stated he has not noticed. That is, when asked, Gary does not report any memory of passing out, or alcoholic blackouts, or any signs of slowed respiratory function needing medical attention. When prodded, he did report many nights where he "got really drunk" on the same number of drinks he would normally have, and that sometimes was confusing. He stated that the night he revealed his past to his wife and extended family was one night where he had only a couple drinks, but was heavily intoxicated, although he had eaten a full meal.

Gary comes from a horrific childhood, caused mainly by his biological father he claims was a "roaring and nasty" drunk his whole life. He claims that his father died from a drunken driving accident, where his father was the drunk person. He also claims his mother was a heavy, yet quiet drinker. He blames his mother's alcoholism on his father. According to Gary, one night his mother drank a fifth of vodka, went to sleep, and died.

Gary reports never using any "street" drugs at any time in his life.

Issues to Consider (based on client data):

Strengths to Consider (based on client data):

Dimension 4: Medical History

Gary reported a long and serious medical history during the assessment. He reported having three open heart surgeries over the last 20 years, the first being when he was about 27 years old. He has had stents and two bypass surgeries. Gary also claims that he is scheduled to be assessed for a pacemaker. He also reports lifelong hypertension, resulting in high blood pressure that he takes medication to handle.

Gary also reports having two surgeries for gastric ulcers, the last one being 6 months prior. He claims to have a "naturally occurring" high acidity that causes his ulcers. "But, my anxiety probably doesn't help my gut," he stated.

In addition, Gary reports a lifetime of erectile dysfunction, a problem that is so "profound" that he has never been able to have intercourse with his wife of 20 years. "Why do you think our kids are adopted?" he asked with a chuckle that sounded sad more than funny. He has had two surgeries, including having a permanent penile implant. He has since had it removed.

He began trying to find a "cure" for this, long before present day sildenafil. "It's too late for that to work on me ... the surgeries over the years have ruined any hope at this point for me and an erection." Gary says he does not care, "being unable has saved me a lot of grief and fear."

He had the implant removed because it would show through his clothing and was embarrassing. He claims his impotence is no problem for him, because he finds the idea of sexual intercourse with women, even his wife whom he loves, "unappealing ... I never really wanted to have sex with her ... I did the surgeries just to make her think I cared about that."

He is currently under medical care from his family doctor, a cardiac doctor, and a gastrointestinal doctor. "Thank God for health insurance," he laughed.

Issues to Consider (based on client data):

Strengths to Consider (based on client data):

Dimension 5: Basic Needs and Vocational Pursuits

Gary is employed as an insurance salesman at a local insurance agency. He has been a salesman for 15 years. Prior to that, he attended college to become a licensed mortician and funeral home director.

He owned a local funeral home for several years and served as the mortician, director, and grief counselor. He says he left the profession to go into insurance because he grew "weary being up to my neck in death" every day. He says the work, especially planning funerals with newly grieving families and performing grief counseling, "wore me down."

He says he also left that business to enter the insurance field because it provided him and his growing family (at the time) with much better income potential. Gary claims to earn an annual salary in the "near 200 grand" and that his family is comfortable.

Gary claims his income, and the family's conservative money management approach, provides them a comfortable existence. They own a home in an upper-middle-class bedroom community near the local large city in the Midwest. He claims he is setting himself for retirement and hopes to retire "early," perhaps before he turns 60 years old, 12 years from now.

When asked how he likes his insurance career, he claims he enjoys meeting and talking to people, but "selling insurance isn't the meaningful career being a mortician was." He says he looks back at that time and believes he was "being helpful and making a contribution" to "hurting" people during their difficult times. He says that he fantasizes about returning to his profession. "I want to feel like I'm contributing by helping people with their pain and grief." He also added, "Let's face it, I'm not shooting for satisfaction ... I am hoping just to keep going. Insurance keeps me going financially."

Issues to Consider (based on client data):

Strengths to Consider (based on client data):

Dimension 6: Psychological and Emotional Functioning

The following information was gathered during a two-session assessment period after Gary requested individual therapy, as a mental health screening.

A. General Appearance

1. **Physical appearance:** Gary presented as a professional male in clean, casual attire, appropriate to the meeting. He is 48 years old yet appears much older than his stated age. His hair is prematurely gray, and he has deep skin lines and dark eye circles. He appeared to this clinician to be at least in his early 60s. His weight appears normal for a man his age. That is, he does not appear overweight or unhealthy.

2. **Attitude:** Generally, Gary presented as a cooperative, open, polite, and frank person in the assessment sessions. Perhaps because we have a pre-existing therapeutic relationship, in the assessment phase Gary seemed willing to discuss highly personal information in a blunt manner (i.e., see medical history).

When discussing his past sexual abuse history and his feelings/attitudes about women (including his wife), Gary became sullen, angry, and resentful. Particularly regarding his father and abuse, Gary also became detached yet remained open to provide details when asked.

B. Behavioral Functioning

1. **Motor activity:** Gary as an excitable, almost hyperactive male during the assessment phase. He did not calm his motor activity during the sessions, until and only when he was discussing his childhood sexual abuse (see above). He used quick, staccato-like gestures, moved his hands quickly, and appeared restless.

2. **Gait:** His excitable motor activity was belied by the slowness of his gait. When walking, he moved slowly, was mildly stooped, leading at one point during the medical history discussion to ask about back problems.

He walked like an older person who appeared to be in pain, or worried he might stumble or fall, which he did not.

3. **Speech:** He generally speaks loudly, excitedly, and rapidly in most conversations. When he begins discussing serious personal issues, especially his father, mother, and wife, he demonstrates a noticeable change in speech patterns. But for the most part, he could be so loud and fast in his "normal" conversation that he was difficult to listen to and follow. He laughed loudly and it often seemed to this therapist that his signs of happiness through laughter were forced. It was as if he was in a near constant state of excitement or anxiety.

C. Emotional Functioning

1. **Mood:** Gary discussed many years of "mood problems," claiming he suffered most of his life with "intense" anxiety and an inability to relax, settle, sit still, and/or sleep. He said he is easy to anger and irritable most days. While he denied any significant bouts of depressed feelings, he did discuss how he would feel "blue" and "melancholy" when he thought about his parents and sometimes when he wonders about his choices in life, especially his choice to get married and have a family.
During these periods, he claims that he could sit still and quiet for hours but was always able to "get myself going" after a period of "feeling sorry for myself." He has been taking medication (benzodiazepine) for many years to manage his "moods."

2. **Affect:** Gary seeks to present an upbeat and happy affect during many casual conversations. However, when he begins discussing serious personal matters his affect changes from "upbeat" to sad, monotone, detached, and flat. He does exhibit the tendency to detach from his childhood abuse experience, when his affect flattens, and he describes the issues as if he was recounting someone else's story. He gets even more sullen and sad when he discusses his wife and children, at one point saying he "had no business" marrying and having a family because of his inability to "love." He later denied this statement. Notably, at no point during any discussions, including his recounting of his childhood abuse, was Gary able to cry, or even become choked up. He discusses it as if he is talking about someone else, and not him.

D. Thought Process

For the most part, Gary's thought process was normal, organized, consistent, and appropriate. He did not demonstrate any significant issues. He appears to be an intelligent, well-spoken, and well-read male, who completes his thoughts and stories.

In his original recounting of his childhood abuse, he demonstrated some incoherence, flights of ideas, magical thinking, and became distractible. However, this type of thinking was not apparent at any time other than that first recounting of his deeply held childhood secrets.

E. Thought Content

Given Gary's difficult history with sexual abuse, his marriage, and his long-held, and now revealed secrets, along with having to cope with nightmares, night terrors, and flashbacks, he appears remarkably appropriate in his thoughts.

Gary does express deep sadness, along with guilt and shame over many things. It appears that Gary believes there was something about him personally that led to his treatment by his father and his mother "dying on me." He did say his mother told him his father "wouldn't hurt him unless he had it coming."

He also expresses guilt and confusion about his life after—marrying and having children, the utter lack of emotion and intimacy in his life, and his attitude toward love and intimacy. Moreover, he harbors a deep resentment, often sounding like anger, toward women in general, and his mother and wife specifically. His intense shame and sense of abandonment leaves him looking for confirmatory reasons to mistrust and be angry toward women in his life, past and present.

F. Perceptions

Gary reports experiencing multiple dreams about his abuse, occurring since childhood. These dreams have intensified in the last weeks since he revealed his abuse secrets. He also reports vivid fantasies in dreams and sexual interactions pertaining to being attacked by "vicious snakes."

Gary also reported experiencing tactile flashbacks, in that he claims at times he can hear his father coming toward his room, smell the "cow shit" odor he described his father having when he was a child, and the smell of his father's bad breath. Gary also suggested that in some dreams and/or flashbacks, he can feel his father throwing him around and being physical with him. He did not say that he reexperienced any rape sensations.

G. Cognitive Functions

1. **Consciousness:** Gary presents as an alert, almost hyperalert consciousness. He has trouble relaxing, sitting still, and falling asleep. Without his daily alcohol and benzodiazepine intake, Gary claims it is hard for him to sleep.
2. **Orientation:** Gary presents as normal in terms of time, place, and person orientation.
3. **Memory:** Gary presents with a highly accurate memory or past and present events. Given the fleeting and changing nature of memory, it appears

that Gary is fully aware of many, if not all the details from his childhood abuse and his present life.

4. **Attention/concentration:** Gary presents as having normal attention and concentration. He has no apparent impairments or deficits.

H. Insight

Gary appears to have normal insight. He seems to grasp when his beliefs do not seem to be rational (i.e., keeping secrets so nobody else would die, etc.) and now overtly understands and recognizes that he has significant problems encompassing his life since he revealed his childhood secrets.

I. Judgment

Gary presents as an adult male with normal judgement. One could argue that keeping his secrets from his wife and family demonstrates otherwise, but given his upbringing and understanding what his childhood taught him about trust versus/ mistrust and intimacy, his judgment is normal within his life experience.

Mental Status Impressions

(Include issues, symptoms, possible diagnoses, and personal/social strengths)

Dimension 7: Family History and Structure

Gary is the only son of his father and mother. He is 48 years old at the time of this series of assessment interviews. His mother stayed at home during his childhood, while his father was a cattle farmer. Both of his parents, according to Gary, had severe alcohol disorders. His father subjected Gary to what can only be termed as horrific sexual abuse from the time Gary was 5 years old until his death in a drunken driving accident when Gary was 15 years old. The details of this abuse is described earlier.

Gary's father had threatened that if he told his mother about the abuse, his mother would die. After 5 years of abuse, when Gary was 10 years old, he told his mother about it. According to Gary, she denied that this would happen, that if it was happening it was not abuse and he had it coming to him, that his father had "funny ideas," and that he should never speak of it again. Within 2 weeks, according to Gary's account, she drank a fifth of vodka, went to bed and died in her sleep. Gary claims he has been angry with her over her failure to believe him, protect him, and for abandoning him during that time.

Gary did not mention his paternal grandparents, so it is unclear if he knew them, or if they were alive during his lifetime. He did say he went to live with his maternal grandparents after his father's death from the age of 15 until he graduated high school and left to be on his own at age 17. He did not discuss his relationship with his grandparents, even when prompted.

Gary met his future wife during college, and they began dating. Despite his unwillingness to share intimacy with her, they were soon married. Over the first 3 years of their marriage, they adopted two daughters and a son. Gary says his wife came to accept his unwillingness to have sex, because he claimed to have a long-term medical condition that stopped him from having erections, or from keeping erections long enough to have intercourse. According to Gary, in their 20 years of marriage, they never had intercourse.

Gary claims they have a "good" marriage. He compares it to long-term room-mates who have found ways to work together to raise children and take care of daily life and existence. Gary claims they have rarely had disagreements, and that despite the "unusual" marriage, she has been willing to put up with his extreme moods, irritability, and sometimes explosive anger. He said he has never abused her, always being able to leave when he loses his temper.

Gary says his first two children were "easy to raise," in that they posed no problems, graduated from high school, and have gone off to college. However, their third child David presented significant challenges during his teen years. David was known to act out physically in school and home, challenge his father to fights, use drugs and alcohol, and was near "flunking out" of high school. Gary and Gail had been in family therapy with David under this therapist's care for nearly 1 year, before Gary presented for individual therapy.

Unprompted, Gary stated that he has lived his adult life as a father "terrified" he would be a "pervert" like his father and the other men of his childhood. He saw a story on a national talk show that he said claimed that children who were abused, grow up to be abusers as adults. "That has scared the crap out of me … I could never do that to my kids … or any kids." He said if I did not believe him, I was welcome to ask his wife, kids, or anybody who knows him.

Gary said he was unsure what his abuse revelations would do to his marriage and family. He claims his wife reacted badly to hearing about it, and refused to discuss it with him, demanding he see a "shrink." According to Gary, they had yet to tell their adolescent children about Gary's childhood.

Issues to Consider (based on client data):

Strengths to Consider (based on client data):

Dimension 8: Social Relational and Culture

Gary presented as a White male, who claims that while his wife is a practicing Catholic, he has never been inclined to practice religion of any type. He now says that there "cannot be a God who would let this happen to a child, and if there is … I don't want anything to do with him."

Gary says one of his ways of dealing with his past, of getting outside himself and his memories while giving the appearance he was normal, was to become social and happy. He became a person who wanted to be with people, and he seemed to enjoy it, or at least appear to be enjoying it. He said he "craves" people, meeting people, and being involved in his community.

In both of his careers (mortician/funeral home director and insurance sales), Gary has been able to present a welcoming and friendly presence by working with the public. He also told me that being out and involved in public gave him reason to stop thinking about his past, and helped him to avoid bad memories and flashbacks.

Gary was involved in several local community groups and charitable causes. He raised money for both child abuse causes and adopted children programs. He was the leader of two different support groups for parent with difficult children.

Before revealing his abuse, Gary had adopted a community reputation as a champion of parents supporting a "tough love" approach to troubled teens. He spent most of his time outside of his profession, working toward these issues for himself and on behalf of others. As Gary said, "Over the last few years, because of my troubles with David, I've thrown myself into trying to help families with teen problems." He claims he likes the "support group" environment and believes it can be a source of support and strength for people in trouble."

Gary says he finds being "normal" in his reputation and appearance is "difficult" and it "wears me out sometimes." However, even though it's difficult to hide my moods it is "better than being a lonely drunk living alone until I killed myself … like that bitch of a mother I had."

Gary says amongst his social relationships, he believes he has "a couple of people" who would be sources of support in the future, but worried that most of his friends, customers, and colleagues would "abandon me" if they knew his past. Hence, Gary stated he hopes to be able to keep his past a secret so not to alienate any of the people in his life, or in their life as a couple/family.

Pertaining to his legal history, Gary was arrested and convicted of drunken driving 5 years earlier. When arrested, he registered a blood alcohol level (BAL) of .14, nearly twice the legal limit. He claims he was not "drunk" that evening, and he had not drunk any more than normal. He had been at a work function. He was stopped and arrested on the way home. As part of his sentence, Gary was mandated to substance abuse counseling (which he attended) and spent nearly 1 year attending AA under the direction of the court. He claims he found those services "unhelpful" because he had simply made a mistake and did not have a "drinking problem." See substance use history above.

Issues to Consider (based on client data):

Strengths to Consider (based on client data):

CASE SUMMARY

Gary Greenwell presents as a troubled male with a tragic childhood. The information contained in the case was gathered over a two-session assessment period. Having known him as his family's therapist for the previous year helped with issues of early rapport and client engagement. However, I found Gary to be forthright, bordering on blunt when he described his childhood abuse, relationships, and sexual history.

Now its time for you, the readers, to make sense of Gary's case. Throughout the case history, I presented only the client data, avoiding drawing any conclusions or connections as one does during an assessment. At the end of each Dimension, you are asked to summarize the presented data under "Issues and Strengths to Consider." In addition, you are asked to write a summary and concluding narrative following his mental health screening.

When those tasks are completed, please continue below to develop a comprehensive assessment based on clinical diagnoses, his current stages of change, and complete narrative assessment, treatment plan, and emergency response plan.

> *The challenge of this exercise is to assume Gary will be your client beginning with the next session and that you will have to present your full assessment and treatment plan to your supervisor before beginning with Gary.*

Gary is an interesting man. Good luck with your work.

COMPREHENSIVE ASSESSMENT

1. Diagnoses (DSM-5 diagnoses; substance use and mental health):

2. Stages of change (each treatable problem; include justification):

3. Comprehensive narrative assessment (use the client data to perform an ACE assessment as part of narrative):

4. Treatment plan:
Client: Gary Greenwell
Practitioner:

Treatment recommendation:

    A.   Modality:
    B.   Program name:
    C.   Type and frequency of services:

    D.   Other supportive services and activities:

Rationale for treatment recommendation:

Treatment goals:
Goal 1:
Objectives:
    A.
    B.
    C.

Goal 2:
Objectives:
    A.
    B.
    C.

Goal 3:

Objectives:

    A.

    B.

    C

Goal 4:

Objectives:

    A.

    B.

    C.

Rationale for plan:

5. High-risk after care and intervention plan:

    A.   Identified high-risk situations:

    B.   Developed strategies to cope with high-risk situations:

    C.   Social support:

    D.   24-hour crisis/safety plan:

CHAPTER 6

Suzie Burnett

Job Jeopardy and Trauma

Salvador Lopez-Arias

THIS CHAPTER PRESENTS an interesting case of an adult woman, the client Suzie Burnett, who was mandated into an assessment by her employer after several instances of verbal and physical altercations between the client and her coworkers. Instead of being immediately terminated from her employer of 15 years, the employer was forced by the employee's union contract to refer her for an assessment, and possible treatment. Known as a job-jeopardy referral, this assessment is critical to Suzie Burnett's employment future.

In cases such as this, practitioners must become and remain aware of their own biases, beliefs, and attitudes about their client, recognizing the power that is ascribed by an employer to professional practice and expertise. Even more than in some other circumstances, it is the ethical and moral responsibility to be as objective as humanly possible, to avoid and counteract one's own personal beliefs about a client's lifestyle and beliefs, and to ensure that the recommendations are best for the client, and not just suit the practitioner's belief system.

As you will learn, Suzie Burnett is a self-identified lesbian woman in a long-term relationship with her partner. Ms. Burnett is undergoing hormone therapy in hopes of physically transitioning to a male gender identity, with possible surgery in her future. In addition, as you will learn, Ms. Burnett has a long history of trauma-related issues dating back many years, and may compound these issues with a quick temper, fighting spirit, and possible substance use disorders.

In this chapter, instead of presenting the individual sessions as in earlier chapters, we present a completed client assessment form that includes all the personal information and data collected during the assessment process. In this case, the information was collected over two sessions. Following assessment protocol, each completed section of this assessment form contains data, along with relevant personal quotes from the client. However, the sections are devoid of "clinical assessment thinking." That is, we have omitted the practitioner's thinking, conclusions, diagnostics, final assessment report, and treatment plan.

It is for the readers to read the case assessment report and then to complete each section based on the information contained in the client data. At the end of each section of the assessment form, there is place to write conclusion paragraphs called "Issues to Consider" and "Strengths to Consider." Readers should complete these sections under each assessment dimension before moving to the end-of-chapter tasks.

After completing the Issue and Strengths sections throughout the chapter, at the end of the case, there are five important areas to be completed either alone, in groups, or as a class. These sections include:

1. **Clinical diagnoses:** Readers will use the client information to make clinical diagnoses. There will be at least one substance use disorder and at least one mental health disorder. There may, in fact, be more.

2. **Stages of change:** Readers will determine the relevant stage of change for each clinical diagnosis, along with the justification for said change (see Chapter 1 for more on the stages of change).

3. **Narrative assessment:** Readers will write a complete narrative assessment, encompassing all client data, including clinical hypotheses and conclusions. This narrative must be wholistic and be consistent with the clinical diagnoses made earlier.

4. **Treatment plan:** Using the information from above, in combination with knowledge of treatment modalities, intensities, and methods, readers will develop a treatment plan for Suzie moving forward. The treatment plan will include treatment goals, measurable objectives, and a rationale for each section.

5. **High-risk aftercare and intervention plan:** Based on Suzie's presentation and life circumstances, readers will here decide how this case will be handled in the event of any high-risk activities and behaviors, and how these will be handled by the professionals and through recommendations or referrals for the client.

It is important to remember that all assessment and clinical conclusions, diagnoses, and decision-making must be based on data contained in the case. That is, while it may be appropriate to speculate about issues based on new information learned later in therapy, any documented conclusions must have data to back it up. Conclusions without data represents the practitioner's implicit or explicit bias, out-of-control subjectivity, too much reliance on personal life experience, or simply overconfidence. Please take steps to help avoid making clinical decisions based on practitioner life experience, beliefs, attitudes, and thoughts. This exercise is good practice about an issue that professionals must be aware of throughout their clinical careers.

The author, Dr. Salvador Lopez-Arias, presents an interesting and instructive case for study. Suzie Burnett lives a complicated and complex life that brings with it a complex clinical presentation.

Good luck assessing and managing this case.

SUBSTANCE ABUSE ASSESSMENT/CASE HISTORY FORMAT

Client name: Suzan Burnett   **Date of first contact:** 00/00/0000

Practitioner: **Date completed:** 00/00/0000

Dimension 1: Client Description, Presenting Problem, and Context of Referral

A. Brief Description of Client

Suzan Burnett presents as a 45-year-old White lesbian female dressed in traditionally male attire (i.e., suit with tie), with short hair parted on the left. Suzan asked that she be addressed as "Suzie" and noted that she identifies as a lesbian female who is currently transitioning into a male by means of hormone treatments. Suzie was raised in a rural, socially and religiously conservative area. She currently resides in a bedroom community close to a midsize Midwestern city with her partner Samantha of 20 years. Suzie graduated from a local community college with an associate's degree in auto mechanics. Suzie is currently employed (for 15 years) at a large international manufacturing company. Suzie considers herself a spiritual person but notes that she has not always identified with a religious faith.

B. Chief Complaint and Symptoms Reported by Client

Unlike most mandated clients, from the start Suzie was forthcoming regarding the reason for this visit and on many, but not all, details of her life. "I got into trouble at work and they told me I have a drinking problem and I need an assessment and probably treatment," she stated.

When asked about the incident at work, she said, "I have had many quarrels, and a few shoving matches with several coworkers over the years, and we had another recently." After being reported, management required me to submit to urinalysis and breathalyzer test. It turns out Suzie tested positive for alcohol and marijuana. She claims they threatened to fire her, but the employee's union said they needed to refer her first for an assessment and possible treatment. "My coworkers hate me ... they call me all kinds of derogatory names 'cause of my identity ... and

I don't think my employer appreciates my identity either." When asked how she concluded she is disliked, she claimed, "They are constantly talking shit. They call me a dyke, and stuff like that ... even worse."

Suzie said she intends to comply with her employer's requirement to seek an assessment and possibly treatment, because she is currently working towards a promotion from production line attendant to a "troubleshooter and mechanic" and would like to remain employed at this company, despite her statement that her employer does not like her gender identity.

She claims that the problems with her coworkers started years ago, long before she "came out" as a lesbian and before the hormone therapy began. She claims they thought she "looked like a lesbian, and acted very manly, so they started calling me names based on my looks." I never actually told them anything until just a couple years ago ... it was none of their business, but I lost it one day and let it slip out."

Suzie confirmed she has filed several formal complaints of hostile work environment with management, but nothing came of it. She claims that discrimination is at the root of why her complaints go unheard, and why management has refused to promote her.

Suzie reports drinking nearly every day of the week, consuming approximately 6 to 12 cans of beer per day. She claims she had drunk the day of the incident. "Do I drink before work? Do I drive myself? ... Yes, who doesn't. ... Do you?"

Suzie claimed that she was "fine." Regarding treatment, she said, "I don't have a problem ... I don't need it. I drink for the same reasons that everyone else does ... to forget problems, cut loose ... you know."

Aside from employment, Suzie briefly explained her ongoing emotional state, "I've always felt even ... depressed at times ... never really happy. Often I find myself feeling very little joy or happiness." Suzie has never been prescribed medications to address these concerns and appears uncertain about whether they would be helpful (see below under Mental Health for more detail).

Furthermore, Suzie reports problems with her concentration. She explained, "The majority of time it is hard for me to focus." She confirmed that despite her ongoing struggle with concentration, she has not discussed this with a doctor before today.

C. Context of the Referral: Precipitating Events, Facts, and Dates

Suzie was referred for an assessment and treatment by her employer. As previously mentioned, Suzie explained she intends to comply with her employer's requirement to seek treatment because she is currently working toward a promotion.

As stated above, she reports having ongoing physical altercations and "quarrels" with her coworkers over the time of her employment. She says they treated her badly for years, but adamantly states her desire to transition is what set her coworkers against her, leading to fights.

Issues to Consider (based on client data):

Strengths to Consider (based on client data):

Dimension 2: Treatment History

A. Substance Abuse Treatment

Suzie reports she has not received any prior substance abuse treatment. She also reports her family does not have a history of substance abuse treatment. She said, "Some should because they drink all the time and can't handle their drinking." Earlier in the assessment Suzie noted, "My family doesn't believe in therapy or treatment. Neither do I."

B. Attitude Toward Substance Abuse Treatment

When asked about her need for treatment, Suzie responded, "No, I don't have a problem, and I don't need it." She explained her attitude mirrored that of her family: "They [family] don't believe in therapy or treatment, neither do I. But, I'm here because work made me come here ... I really don't need any help. I need you to fill this shit out and send it to Human Resources."

She appeared to become angry, the more I probed her substance use.

C. Mental Health Treatment

Suzie denied ever attending or needing mental health treatment. "I mean ... like I said before, sometimes I've felt depressed ... but mostly I feel even ... I don't get excited a lot ... never really happy.... I do feel sad at times, and occasionally have trouble coming back to even ... but I don't need therapy for it."

Suzie reported that her family has not undergone any mental health treatment but explained she sees many mental health concerns, especially with her parents. She noted, "My dad is crazy … angry … never happy." In addition, "My mom should be getting help for living with him. She is unhappy, depressed, constantly just runs around trying to please him."

Suzie also said she first attempted suicide at age 17, by means of overdosing on alcohol. She claimed she tried killing herself because her father forbade her from speaking with or seeing Samantha. Suzie was hospitalized as a result but notes she did not receive any treatment while admitted because she did not have medical coverage.

At age 27, Suzie attempted suicide again. This time by overdosing on a popular benzodiazepine. Her reason this time was because Samantha accepted a job in Texas and moved. Suzie was hospitalized and had her stomach pumped, but she did not participate in therapy.

Suzie meets regularly with a doctor concerning her hormone medications but has not spoken to a mental health professional, until this assessment session.

D. Attitudes About Previous Treatment(s)
She does not believe in therapy or treatment. See above under substance use treatment.

Issues to Consider (based on client data):

Strengths to Consider (based on client data):

Dimension 3: Substance Use History

A. Lifetime Substance Use History (Complete Table. Explain in Narrative)

SUBSTANCE	FREQUEN-CY	DOSE (AVG.)	AGE FIRST USE	AGE LAST USE	ROUTE OF ADMIN.	OVER-DOSE
Alcohol	4–5 days/week	6–12 pack of beer	15	45	Oral	Yes
Opioid painkiller	Once	Unknown	21	21	Oral	No
Marijuana	2–3 times/week	1–2 joints or edibles	15	45	Smoke	No
Ecstasy	About two times in the past	1–2 pills, unknown dosage	20s	20s	Oral	No
Mushrooms	About two times in the past	Unknown	20s	20s	Oral	No
Benzodiaze-pine	Once	½ to 1 bottle	27	27	Oral	Yes

B. Drugs Used in Previous 30 Days

Suzie reports using marijuana and alcohol within the previous 30 days, often conjointly. As illustrated on the above table, Suzie reports drinking between 6 and 12 cans of beer, 4 to 5 days per week. She also smokes and eats marijuana two to three times per week. Suzie did not report any other drug use within the previous 30 days.

C. Top Three Drugs of Choice

Suzie's two primary drugs of choice are alcohol and marijuana. Suzie did not report regularly using or favoring any other substance.

D. Drug Mixing

Suzie reported using both alcohol and marijuana during the time that she attempted suicide (by ingesting a benzodiazepine at age 27). This combination resulted in Suzie passing out in her back yard and a subsequent hospitalization. When asked about current mixing of substances Suzie explained, "Yeah, but it's not like I need my joint lit and have a beer in hand. But it happens sometimes."

E. Longest Period of Abstinence

About 10 years ago Suzie abstained from drugs and alcohol for 10 days because she promised Samantha she would quit. Suzie reported feeling sick with vomiting, having the shakes, chills and a fever, but did not interpret these symptoms as withdrawal. Suzie reported, "I was sick during that time, I had the flu."

F. Substance Use Narrative

Suzie reported she began using alcohol and marijuana around the age of 15. Although Suzie did not note a definitive reason for starting use at that age, she reported that her maternal grandmother, whom she was very close with, died during the same year.

She said she currently drinks alcohol "Almost every day … about four or five times per week." Suzie reported that the average dose is about one 6- or 12-pack of beer per day. Suzie said stated she usually starts drinking when she gets home from work in the late afternoon. She claims she drinks throughout the day to relax on weekends. She explained that although she drinks for longer periods on the weekends, her consumption rarely exceeds 12 beers per day. She also stated that she does not get "drunk" on these amounts, and that it takes her "at least twice that amount" to get intoxicated. She claims she rarely drinks to intoxication, with the last time occurring the previous Saturday.

Suzie reiterated that she does not "believe in treatment" and does not feel as though she has a "problem." Suzie explained, "I drink for the same reasons that everyone else does. To forget problems, cut loose, and relax … I mean … it's not like I need it or anything."

Suzie's alcohol use led to her being required by her employer to attend this assessment and possibly treatment. In addition, at age 17, Suzie attempted to "drink [herself] to death."

At the age of 21, Suzie received a driving under the influence (DUI) charge but was not required to attend treatment, despite a blood alcohol level (BAL) of .13. Suzie said she often drives under the influence, because she likes to have "a nip" in the morning before work. She claims it "gets me ready for the bullshit at work."

At age 27, Suzie attempted suicide, by overdosing on a benzodiazepine with alcohol that she borrowed from a friend. Suzie claimed that she has only taken a benzodiazepine on that one day.

Aside from alcohol, marijuana is the only other substance that Suzie reports using within the past 30 days. She began smoking marijuana around age 15 and reports that she currently smokes about two to three times per week with an average dose of about one joint per sitting. Suzie also ingests marijuana at times, that she and Samantha "eat a brownie" every now and again.

In addition to alcohol, marijuana, and a one-time use of Xanax, Suzie said she also tried ecstasy and mushrooms while in her 20s. She could not recall the number of times she used these substances but estimated one to two times for each. She said she did not like how these substances made her "trip" and "feel out of control" and does not have a desire to use them again in the future. She also said she took a friend's opioid painkiller once when she was 21 years old, trying to knock out a headache.

Throughout the assessment Suzie remained willing to discuss her and her family's past and present alcohol and substance use and suicide attempts. Suzie reports that her and her family members have not received any treatment for substances abuse in the past and noted, "They [my family] don't believe in therapy or treatment and neither do I."

Issues to Consider (based on client data):

Strengths to Consider (based on client data):

Dimension 4: Medical History

A. Injuries and Health Issues
None reported.

B. Health Treatment and Current and Past Medication
Suzie is currently undergoing hormone treatment for the purpose of transitioning to becoming male. These medications are taken daily. Suzie hopes to have a gender reassignment surgery in the future. Another area of concern is that Suzie has not shared with the doctor who is supervising her hormone treatment that she is drinking alcohol on a regular basis. Suzie has two prior hospitalizations due to attempted suicides by overdose (once with alcohol and once with borrowed Xanax).

Issues to Consider (based on client data):

Strengths to Consider (based on client data):

Dimension 5: Vocation and Basic Needs

It appears Suzie is currently meeting her basic needs for clothing, food, and shelter and a safe community environment. Both Suzie and Samantha are employed, and Suzie reported their income meets and exceeds their basic needs. Samantha and Suzie own a home, and both have access to safe and reliable transportation.

Suzie's employment is currently at-risk due to a recent altercation between Suzie and some coworkers. The consequences of the altercation led to her referral for an assessment and possible treatment. Suzie's job is presently in jeopardy.

Issues to Consider (based on client data):

Strengths to Consider (based on client data):

Dimension 6: Family History and Structure

A. Family Relational History

Suzie is one of five children born to parents Joseph and Mary Burnett. Suzie has two older brothers named John and James, each married with children. She also has two younger sisters named Mary and Sarah who are married but do not have children.

Suzie and her siblings were raised Christian. About her family, Suzie said, "I've been disowned by my family because I am not a rigid ass like they are." When asked what she meant by "rigid ass" Suzie said, "Conservative, religious, never leave their little town where they're from. When they do they're afraid they'll get robbed or mugged."

Suzie "came out" about her sexual identity to her family in her mid-20s and attributes much of her stress regarding her lesbian lifestyle to the tension this caused between her and her parents and siblings. When she announced she was undergoing her transition, both hormonally and surgically, her relationship with the family was nearly severed. Aside from recent negative dynamics, Suzie reports always feeling like "the lost child."

She said she still speaks with her mom occasionally. However, Suzie said she is "angry" at her mom for always "walking on eggshells" around her father. Suzie explained, "My dad is crazy. He is always angry, never happy. He is an ass." She claims her father used to hit her mother when Suzie was young. She further stated how difficult it was for her to see her mother being beaten, but she was powerless to stop it. "I'm sure he beats her to this day."

When asked if her father abused others in the family, she said, "He'd always whoop us with a belt or strap or his hands and fists whenever something happened he didn't like." Suzie then disclosed her father also sexually abused her as a child. "He touched me sexually a few times," but would not further elaborate at this moment. When queried further regarding the sexual abuse, she became angry and stated, "what the hell does this have to do with the assessment for my job?"

After some discussion about the importance of addressing abuse as part of the assessment, and my role in exploring how her abuse experiences may affect her well-being, she acquiesced and slowly shared more details of her sexual abuse by her father, and others (see below). As a child, Suzie always wanted to hang around with her father and brothers. She was not allowed to do so, because "I was a girl, I had to stay inside." Today, Suzie says she has "fallen out of the family." It appears most of her siblings have built homes on portions of the family acreage, creating a Burnett family compound, as such. Suzie is the only child that moved away, largely because, "I'm not like them ... I don't pray as they do ... and I certainly don't love the way they do. They will never accept who I am, who I love, and how I feel inside."

B. Family Educational History

Suzie's mom completed high school and her dad dropped out of high school. All of Suzie's siblings obtained their bachelor's degrees. Suzie obtained her associates degree in auto mechanics from an undisclosed community college. Samantha also completed a liberal arts degree.

C. Family Legal History

Suzie reported that based on the little that she knows about them, her two older brothers, John and James, each have a DUI charge on their record. When asked to elaborate on these charges Suzie stated, "I don't know their business." Suzie received a DUI charge when she was caught driving while impaired at age 21.

D. Family History of Domestic Violence/Abuse/Neglect/Trauma

Suzie reported a long history of witnessing domestic violence during her child-hood, particularly her father beating her mother regularly. Suzie described her father as, "always angry, never happy, and took it out on mom, and the rest of us." She explained her father would "whoop" her and her siblings often and would also physically abuse her mother in front of her and her siblings. Suzie said, "He should have gone to anger management ... or jail for all he did." Suzie also reported her siblings and mother were abused mentally. Father would scream, yell, and belittle them daily, "for the littlest things ... he was a cruel man ... but what were we all to do?"

Suzie also claims her father abused her sexually, from about age "5 or 6" to age 10. She claims, "there was some touching by my father, that led to him forcing me to touch his penis, often until he climaxed." She says he never forced intercourse or oral sex, just hand stimulation, while he fondled her vagina. She claims the sexual abuse suddenly stopped by the time she was 10, and she never spoke of it out of fear of being punished.

Suzie also noted that her siblings were also "touched" by their father. She knows because she said she saw her father with a younger sister, but the siblings "never spoke of it." She does not know if her mother was sexually abused.

As the assessment progressed, Suzie also revealed she was sexually abused by two of her older cousins from age 5 until she was 13 years old. "It would always begin with games such as hide and seek ... they would hide with her and force themselves on her ... including intercourse and later, forced oral sex."

Suzie claims she revealed this abuse to one of her older brothers, who told her to tell mother. When she told her mother, her mother refused to believe her and "did nothing about it." She was not allowed to play outside or be with kids outside the family for a long time. However, mother did allow her cousins to continue coming to the house to play.

Suzie claims that her brothers regularly physically abuse their wives and kids, "like it was at home." She partially attributes this to their collective experiences with domestic violence as children.

When asked if there was any abuse in her relationship with Samantha, Suzie reported she "pushed Sam around often" during high school and college but noted, "that is in the past."

E. Family History of Mental Health and Substance Abuse Issues

Suzie reported her father is "always angry" and "never happy." She attributes many of these traits to his upbringing. Suzie also claims her father had an extremely abusive father and that her mother suffered from depression that was never addressed. Suzie's paternal grandmother ended up completing suicide. Her father's unaddressed mental health issues left Suzie and her siblings as well as their mother at risk of physical, emotional, and sexual abuse.

Suzie said her mother "isn't happy" either and she is always "walking on eggshells around her husband." Suzie expressed frustration and said, "She's in that relationship still because she thinks she's supposed to be."

Suzie claimed her father and brother's drink "all the time" and "heavily on occasion." Furthermore, Suzie noted her father and brothers are physically and emotionally abusive towards their wives and children.

"They don't believe in therapy or treatment, and neither do I. Where were all those therapists and social workers when we were having problems ... being abused, beaten, and raped? I knew many of my friends experienced the same thing we did, and they went to therapy and nothing changed for them."

Issues to Consider (based on client data):

Strengths to Consider (based on client data):

Dimension 7: Community/Macro Context

A. Local Community

Suzie and Samantha currently own a home. Suzie said that although they live in the "Bible Belt" with "rigid and segregated" areas, Samantha and she feel comfortable where they live. "People mind their business and we keep away from everyone." Suzie said she is happy to be in a more urban area, different from the rural setting in which she grew up. She likes "more diversity" and more "things to do."

Suzie said that Sam and she often visit local businesses and their group of friends often go out to dinner or go to the beach. When discussing their relationship with their friends she explained, "We just like to do normal things that other couples like to do." She claims they have a regular and small group of friends that provide them with support, comfort, and fun, and that they are engaged in their local community on different levels.

Issues to Consider (based on client data):

Strengths to Consider (based on client data):

B. Cultural/Spiritual Context (Racial and Gender Identity, Discrimination)

As previously noted, Suzie identifies as a 45-year-old White female lesbian who is currently undergoing hormone treatments in preparation for a gender transition to male. Suzie presents as a female dressed in generally masculine clothing, including a suit with a tie and close-cropped hair.

She recalls having issues with people for years because she identifies as a lesbian in a relationship with another woman. However, she says her treatment by others, especially her coworkers, got worse after she began her transition.

According to Suzie, "My coworkers have a hard time accepting who I am. I am currently taking hormone medications and they don't agree with my sexual identity of that I want to change my gender. ... They don't get it ... it's who I am inside ... I've always known I was male, stuck inside a female body. My decision to transition was the easiest decision of my life."

Suzie has also faced oppression from her family who have reportedly "disowned" her. Suzie attributes this to her not being "rigid" like them and her lack of participation in what she calls their conservative Christian views. In addition, her family will never accept her as a lesbian or male; "no chance of that happening," she chuckled.

Suzie came out to her family in her mid-20s and reports "feeling better about myself" since then.

In the community where they live (neighbors, etc.) she reports feeling "marginalized" because many in her neighborhood are traditional and conservative. "I do not feel totally accepted because we [Samantha and I] are usually the minority," but claims her "circle of friends" helps offset these feelings.

She claims that much of the negativity in her family and at work, and in the media, about her sexual identity and transition effort is offset by her local community of friends and loved ones. She claims they treat her "like anybody else," and this includes friends in the LGBTQA+ community and her many cisgender friends.

Suzie claims that they do not practice any form of organized religion or faith tradition. She says they are more "spiritual" in their beliefs and worldview. She was unable to explain what her spirituality encompasses.

Issues to Consider (based on client data):

Strengths to Consider (based on client data):

C. Social-Relational Patterns (With Significant Other, Colleagues, and Friends)
Suzie and Samantha met in high school and have been together for 20 years. Suzie reported they hope to adopt children, but this worries her (see below). Suzie describes Samantha as "loving, supportive, intelligent, kind, and nurturing."

Suzie does not currently have much interaction with her parents and siblings. She reports she always felt like the "lost child" as she was not the eldest or the youngest. Suzie had trouble connecting with her family for all the reasons stated above. Suzie reports that she and her mother occasionally talk on the phone but that she "is not close" to her mother. "I feel both sorry for my mother because of her life with that man, but I'm also angry with her because she just took it and didn't help me when I needed it about my cousins." She claims she cannot remember the last time that she spoke to any of her siblings, or her father.

Suzie spoke in depth about her feelings toward her maternal grandmother, Ruth. Suzie explained, "I could tell her anything and we would just talk for hours. She was always there for me, no matter what. She was a great person." Ruth passed away when Suzie was 15. Suzie says that even today, her grandmother appears during my darkest hours to comfort me."

Issues to Consider (based on client data):

Strengths to Consider (based on client data):

Dimension 8: Psychological and Emotional Functioning
Mental Status Screening (check all that apply):

A. General appearance:

1. Physical appearance: X neat   X clean   X appropriate
2. Attitude: __X_cooperative X__suspicious __X_frank
                         __X_hostile   X_resentful   _X irritable
                         X__indifferent X_defensive   __X_tense

B. Behavioral functioning:

1. Motor activity: _X__normal
2. Gait: _X__normal
3. Posture: _X__normal   __X rigid

C. Speech:

__X_normal   X_hesitant   X__threatening

D. Emotional functioning:

1. Mood: _X__euphoric   __X_depressed
2. Affect: X__flat

E. Thought process:

__X_appropriate

F. Thought content:

_X__appropriate   X__suicidal (remote)

G. Perceptions:

Hallucinations: _X__auditory   _X__visual

H. Cognitive functions:

1. Consciousness: __X_alert
2. Orientation: _X__normal
3. Memory: _X__normal
4. Attention/concentration: _X__normal

**I. General knowledge
(estimated):**   __X_average

**J. Intellectual function
(estimated):**   X_average

K. Insight: ___good   _X__fair   ___poor

L. Judgment: ___good   ___fair   __X_poor

[See Narrative for explanation.]

M. Developmental History:

Motor:	_X_good	___fair	___poor
Language:	_X_good	___fair	___poor
Cognitive:	_X_good	___fair	___poor
Learning disability:	___yes	_X_no	___unknown
Disability:	___ADD	___ADHD	___EBD

Medication use: Prescription hormone treatments

Summarize the mental status impressions (potential mood, anxiety, thought, or personality disorders; results of any screening tools; suicidal or homicidal thoughts or history).

Throughout this assessment, Suzie's appearance was neat, clean, and appropriate. Suzie remained cooperative and frank when answering most questions. Toward the middle of the first session Suzie appeared to become irritable, suddenly asking, "How long is this going to take?" Once her question was addressed Suzie returned to a more cooperative state.

At times Suzie's tone changed and she became suspicious, tense, and defensive when asked multiple questions concerning the nature of her and Samantha's relationship and whether she feels she has "a problem" with alcohol and substance use. Her defensiveness was also apparent when asked about her mental health.

Suzie presented as indifferent regarding therapy and treatment. At one point she explained that her family does not believe in treatment or therapy, but at another time disclosed that she believes her father could use "some help" with his drinking and her mother could use "help because of living with him [her father]." Finally, Suzie appeared hostile and resentful when discussing her relationship with her parents and siblings who have disowned her.

Suzie reported no concerns with motor activity but reports a history of altercations with her coworkers that began years ago. Suzie notes that her coworkers "have a hard time accepting who I am" and when confronted she begins "pushing," "arguing," and "fighting." Although she knows she is quick to anger and at times, according to Samantha, she could be at fault, Suzie says she must defend herself at all cost.

Suzie reports having a "bad temper." She says she first realized she could defend herself in her early teenage years, "I stopped taking shit from people. I know I have a short fuse, but it is always justified and only toward people who deserve it." She reports her temper and aggression have increased since she began hormone therapy (testosterone). Suzie's gait appeared normal, but her posture fluctuated between normal and rigid depending on the topic being discussed.

Suzie's speech remained normal for most of the assessment but became hesitant and and/or threatening when discussing her strained relationship with her parents and siblings and the interactions with her coworkers. Suzie hesitated before answering questions concerning childhood abuse, but finally relented and discussed her history.

Suzie's emotional functioning appeared steady at a level between euphoric and depressed. She reported feeling "even." When asked to expand on what "even" meant, she said, "I don't get excited much. I feel depressed at times but I've never felt really happy." When asked if she ever felt happy as a child, she responded that most of the time she was afraid of her father.

Additionally, she shared that she has always, since childhood and continuing today, felt like something bad was going to happen to her or that she was going to do something that would lead to being in trouble. She also said she becomes "sad" or irritable during the days when she could not sleep because of nightmares.

She claims she has consistent nightmares about monsters trying to hurt her, monsters getting on top of her and not allowing her to breathe, and of her father abusing her or her mother. She also reported that sometimes she would also dream about her cousins hurting her, or of her desire to hurt them.

In addition to the nightmares, Suzie also reported a sense of general worry/dread/anxiety and overall feeling sad or flat. She refused to discuss how, if at all, she believed her history of abuse (physical, mental, and sexual) affect her today.

Suzie also reported wanting to have a child for many years, but experienced an overpowering fear that she would become a parent "like my father," or that she could not protect her own child from being sexually abused.

Although Suzie was apprehensive in sharing her childhood, and at times she became angry and defensive, overall she appeared honest and forthright in sharing her history and present life. She reported everyday symptoms including a lost interest in normal activities and relationships, hopelessness, low self-esteem, low appetite, low energy, sleep changes, feeling jumpy, being easily irritated and angered, and poor concentration. She ascribed the cause of these symptoms to her stress at work.

Suzie appeared calm and collected when discussing her feelings towards Samantha and their friends. When discussing her current work environment and her past experiences with her family there appeared to be a shift from calm and collected to reserved and hesitant. This change was apparent by changes in Suzie's posture and speech. Changes in emotional functioning/mood were also detected by changes in Suzie's affect. Suzie's affect remained flat for a majority of the assessment but grew blunted at times.

Suzie reported a history of suicidal ideation and attempts. During our first session, Suzie asked, "Doesn't everyone consider ending their life? I've considered it over the years. But I love Sam." During the second session Suzie disclosed information about a second suicide attempt at the age of 27 that was triggered by Samantha moving to Texas. When asked again about a psychological evaluation or treatment, she stated that she refused services.

When asked if she ever hears or sees things that others do not see or hear, Suzie explained, "I used to see my [maternal] grandmother. She came at my darkest hour in my sleep." Suzie said no one else in her family saw her maternal grandmother after her death and said that she doesn't "visit" her anymore.

Suzie's level of cognitive functioning appears normal. She presented as alert with normal orientation. Suzie did not report any concerns with cognitive functioning and reported that she was always "developmentally ahead of everyone else" in motor, language, and cognitive functioning.

Furthermore, Suzie reported she graduated from high school early and was happy to discuss her accomplishment of graduating from a local community college with an associate degree in auto mechanics. These are indicators of average general knowledge and intellectual functioning.

Suzie is currently trying to obtain a promotion to become a mechanic at her employer. Suzie reports having trouble with concentrating and making decisions.

Suzie's insight appears to be fair and her judgment poor. Suzie's father used substances and often abused his wife and Suzie and her siblings at times. These experiences shaped Suzie's perception of wrong and right and have led her to choices such as using substances, operating while impaired, and hitting Samantha during an isolated incident.

The only medications that Suzie reports taking daily are her hormones treatment medication. When asked about the psychological evaluations and counseling sessions that normally are included with gender transition, she reported she just tells the psychologist what they need to hear to continue her treatment. Suzie said her hormone treatments are monitored closely and has weekly blood draws and visits with her physician.

Issues to Consider (based on client data):

Strengths to Consider (based on client data):

CASE WRAP-UP

Now it is the reader's turn to create a plan for ongoing therapy with Suzie Burnett. As noted in the case, Suzie presents with multiple complex issues in her life and history.

Perhaps the most useful and instructive approach to this case is to assume Suzie is being referred to you for therapy. As the new therapist on the case, your task is to complete all the sections of the assessment (each issues and strengths to consider summary) before progressing to the questions and tasks listed below.

To further enhance the learning experience, when you have completed the assessment and treatment plan, present this case to a colleague, instructor, or supervisor for feedback. Learning how to organize a case presentation like this one will be a valuable skill across your human service career.

QUESTIONS AND FINAL ASSESSMENT TASKS

1. What questions did the author leave out of the assessment?

    - What would you have done differently throughout the assessment?
    - Are there questions you would not have asked or that you would have pushed for more information on?

2. Based on the case information in this chapter, develop a three-generation genogram (also including important nonfamily members, if needed) to represent Suzie's presented life and all who are instrumentally involved. Make any notes and figures on this genogram to aid in developing a wholistic view of this case.

3. Make a list, with supporting evidence, of the main issues in Suzie's life at the time of the interview. Include a list of the Suzie's personal and social strengths that may be used as resources in the future pertaining to each of the issues listed.

4. Develop and write a narrative assessment and diagnosis(es) as demonstrated by the information contained in this case. Justify your diagnostic decisions by listing the criteria you believe are met through the interview record. It is inappropriate to base diagnostic decisions on assumptions, only direct evidence provided by your client.

    - When you "meet" Suzie, what additional information would you need to contribute to a more comprehensive narrative assessment and diagnostic decisions?

- Be sure to place Suzie's personal and social strengths in the narrative assessment, to be used later as part of treatment planning.

5. As discussed in Chapter 1, here is where we initially apply the stages of change developed to assess a client's motivation for change for each diagnosed and/or treatable problem.

   - List each diagnosis you decided upon based on the narrative assessment for both substance use and mental health disorders.
   - For each diagnosis listed, determine what stage of change Suzie is presently in pertaining to her motivation to change that problem. Use Suzie's own words to justify your stage decisions.
   - Use the stages of change during the next section on treatment planning.

6. Based on the narrative assessment, develop a written treatment plan to include short- and long-term treatment goals and objectives. What methods of treatment and support will you utilize?

   - What treatment theory, or combination of theories, do you believe best fits Suzie's reality? Defend your decision.
   - What theories or approaches does the latest empirical evidence in the field recommend?
   - Based on the stages of change decisions in Question 5, where will you begin in treatment? Explain and defend your decisions.
   - Pertaining to treating people with co-occurring disorders, what does the current professional literature and practice evidence suggest as the most effective way to proceed when it comes to deciding which issues to treat first?

7. Based on the treatment theory or theories chosen and defended above, list each intervention you would use in your work with Suzie. Specifically, for each intervention, include the target issue, intervention, and modality (e.g., group therapy) you chose, and the theoretical justification for each.

   - What other options might be available should these interventions prove ineffective?
   - What does the latest empirical evidence in the field suggest for each target issue? How does this evidence match with your intervention strategies?
   - When developing treatment approaches, do not overlook nontraditional approaches and approaches that target multiple systemic levels (i.e., individual, family, community, advocacy, etc.).
   - What factors and strategies will you use to build trust and engagement during the intervention phases of your work? How will you assist

Suzie as her motivation to change waxes and wanes over the coming weeks and months?

- What if Suzie's personal goals do not align with your own? For instance, if she says she wants to focus her sessions on healthier communication with Samantha rather than issues surrounding her mental health or substance use?
- Think about the initial therapy session after the assessment with Suzie. How would you begin, what would your goals be for the session and what would you hope to accomplish?

HIGH-RISK AFTER CARE AND INTERVENTION PLAN

Identified high-risk situations:

Developed strategies to cope with high-risk situations:

Social support:

24-hour crisis/safety plan:

CHAPTER 7

Best Practices in Trauma and Trauma-Informed Care

Jerry L. Johnson and Glen A. Brookhouse

INTRODUCTION

After presenting theory and practice methods, the Guiding Practice Principles in Chapter 1, and five different cases involving real-life clients struggling with trauma and, in some cases co-occurring substance use disorders, this chapter brings the contents of the text together. Here, we examine the professional literature regarding trauma and trauma-informed care to present current best practices in the field. We rely on the latest theory, practice literature, research, and evaluation to examine this burgeoning practice area.

Trauma has been an important topic for behavioral health for many years, dating back to Freud's work on "hysteria" and early understanding of the symptoms that victims experience in after being confronted with traumatic experiences (Basham, 2016). In recent years, assessing, diagnosing, and treating clients suffering from trauma exposure has become a major area of practice and study in the behavioral health professions.

There is general agreement in the professions on how behavioral health programs working with trauma-exposed clients must prepare to increase the odds of treatment success. That is, programs should prepare to serve not only clients, but also deal with the stress, secondary trauma, and other issues practitioners often experience as a function of working with trauma. Failure to address these issues may further traumatize clients and harm the staff members who work with them (Bloom & Farragher, 2011).

Hence, trauma-informed care (TIC) has emerged as best practice when addressing trauma in the lives of children and adults. Trauma-informed care is multifaceted, in that it recognizes the pervasiveness of trauma while making a commitment to identifying and addressing trauma in treatment by understanding the connections between presenting problems and a person's trauma history (Hodas, 2006). TIC becomes an individual practitioner's and organization's worldview, a central part of its mission in terms of practice, policy, and internal staff support (see further discussion later).

DEFINING TRAUMA

Over the years, trauma has been defined in many ways. Our goal is to present common definitions on which to build the remainder of this discussion. In practice, clients will present with single-event trauma reactions, multiple trauma–based experiences (complex trauma, see below), trauma-based issues that are not diagnosable, and trauma reactions often as co-occurring disorders in addition to substance use and/or other disorders.

We define trauma as exposure to experiences (single or multiple, toward self or others) that cause intense physical and psychological stress reactions outside a person's control and normal abilities to cope. These events and reactions overwhelm people's ability to handle the stress caused by the experience or integrate the realities and emotions generated by the experience.

Hence, traumatic experiences are unexpected; people are unprepared for the events or experiences, and there is/was nothing they could do to stop it from happening to self or others (Johnson, 2004). Similarly, Horowitz (1989) defined trauma as a sudden and forceful event that overwhelms a person's ability to respond, recognizing that a trauma need not involve actual physical harm to oneself; an event can be traumatic if it contradicts one's worldview and overpowers one's ability to cope.

Our working definition is consistent with SAMSHA (2012), which defines trauma as resulting from an event, series of events, or set of circumstances experienced by people as physically or emotionally harmful or threatening. These events and resulting experiences have lasting adverse effects on people's functioning and physical, social, emotional, or spiritual well-being.

As stated above, people may present for therapy reacting to a single specific traumatic event, whereas others, especially those seeking mental health or substance abuse services, have been exposed to multiple or chronic traumatic events across their lifetime. According to the DSM-5 (APA, 2013) trauma occurs when a person experiences or is exposed "to actual or threatened death, serious injury, or sexual violence" (p. 271). Further, the DSM-5 classifies a person having experienced trauma if:

1. He, she, or they directly experiences a traumatic event;
2. She, he, or they witnesses a traumatic event in person;
3. They, she, or he learns that a traumatic event (with actual or threat of death either accidental or violent) occurred to a close family member or close friend;

4. He, she, or they experiences first-hand repeated or extreme exposure to aversive details or traumatic events- not through television or movies; and/or,

5. They, she, or he re-experience events through spontaneous memories; avoidance of events and/or people; negative cognitions and mood; and hypervigilance, aggression, self-destructive behavior, and insomnia.

Terr (1999) developed definitions of type I and type II trauma to better understand its nature. Type I trauma refers to single catastrophic events. These events include natural disasters; violent acts on a person; witnessing injury or death; handling of body parts or dangerous combat duties; accidents or diagnosis of a life-threatening illness; and loss due to refugee or immigrant status.

Type II trauma refers to individual, chronic, repetitive exposure to abuse or violence, most notable domestic violence, physical assault, and/or sexual abuse and assault. A person can have both type I and type II trauma as well as other mental health disorders and/or substance use disorders. Type I and II trauma histories are present in both children and adults.

However, trauma is not limited to diagnostic criteria; that is, many practitioners have stopped considering trauma-related symptoms as indicators of mental disorders. Instead, they consider trauma-based symptoms as a normal part of human survival instincts or as "adaptive mental processes involved in the assimilation and integration of new information with intense survival emphasis which exposure to the trauma has provided" (Turnbull, 1998, p. 88). These normal adaptive processes only become pathological if they are inhibited in some way (Turnbull, 1998) or if they are left unacknowledged and untreated (Scott, 1990).

In our practice, we agree with Turnbull (1998) and recommend practitioners try to avoid any language or labels that pathologize victims. In our view, they are simply trying to adapt and survive in life circumstances and environments they cannot control (more on this later under "Best Practices").

PREVALENCE OF TRAUMA

Trauma exposure is common but varies across different demographic groups. It is especially high among clients receiving behavioral health services (SAMHSA, 2014). In years past, many believed trauma was uncommon. However, the first National Comorbidity Study (NCS), a national survey designed to study the prevalence and effects of mental health disorders in the United States, established how prevalent trauma experiences were (Kessler et.al., 1995).

In this study, 60% of men and 51% of women reported experiencing at least one traumatic experience in their lifetime (Kessler, 2000; Kessler et al., 1995, 1999).

The most common traumatic experience reported was witnessing someone being badly injured or killed (cited by 36% of men and 15% of women). The second most common was being involved in a fire, flood, or other natural disaster (cited by 19% of men and 15% of women). The third most common trauma was a life-threatening accident/assault, such as from an automobile accident, a gunshot, or a fall (cited by 25% of men and 14% of women).

The NCS also discovered it was common for individuals to have experienced multiple traumatic events (Kessler, 2000). Among men, 15% reported two traumatic events, 10% reported three, and 10% reported four or more. Among women, 14% reported two traumatic events, 5% reported three, and 6% reported four or more.

The National Epidemiologic Survey on Alcohol and Related Conditions (NESARC), assessed the prevalence of posttraumatic stress disorder (PTSD) and trauma exposure during a large-scale series of interviews (Pietrzak et al., 2011). Researchers asked over 34,000 respondents about 27 different types of potentially traumatic events.

In this study, the most commonly reported traumatic events were serious illness or injury to someone close (affecting 48% of those who did not have PTSD symptoms and 67% of those with PTSD), unexpected death of someone close (affecting 42% of those without PTSD and 66% of those with PTSD), and seeing someone badly injured or killed (affecting 24% of those without PTSD and 43% of those with PTSD) (Pietrzak et al., 2011).

According to the same data, 72% witnessed trauma, 31% experienced a trauma resulting from injury, and 17% experienced a trauma that was purely psychological in nature, like being threatened with a weapon (El-Gabalawy, 2012).

PREVALENCE OF PTSD AND OTHER TRAUMATIC STRESS REACTIONS

PTSD can happen to anyone. Developing PTSD is not a sign of personal weakness. Many factors increase the likelihood a person will develop PTSD, many of which are not under a person's control. For example, if someone was directly exposed to a trauma or injured, they are more likely to develop PTSD. As stated below, women are more likely to experience sexual assault and sexual abuse in both childhood and adulthood, increasing the likelihood of developing PTSD. Meanwhile, men are more likely than women to experience a traumatic event in their lifetimes (i.e., accidents, physical assault, combat, disaster, or to witness death or injury), but are less likely to develop PTSD.

While everyone who experiences trauma can develop PTSD, there are differences between people. As with trauma, rates of PTSD vary across different demographic groups. The DSM-5 (APA, 2013) estimates that the prevalence of PTSD in the U.S. adult population is about 8%, but studies of populations at high risk for PTSD (e.g., combat veterans, survivors of natural disasters) have found PTSD rates ranging from 3% to 58%, depending on the group and the experienced trauma (SAMHSA, 2014).

The NCS found a lifetime rate of PTSD for Americans ages 15 to 54 of 8%. Women (10%) were more than twice as likely as men (5%) to be diagnosed with PTSD during their lives (Kessler et al., 1995). In a follow-up to the NCS (the NCS-R), the lifetime prevalence of PTSD was 7%, again with much higher rates for women (10%) than for men, at 4% (Kessler et al., 2005; NCS, 2006).

GENDER COMPARISONS

Research consistently finds that women are more likely than men to develop PTSD during their lives (Pietrzak et al., 2011). Women were nearly twice as likely as men to have a lifetime PTSD diagnosis, with 9% of women and 4% of men meeting those criteria. Women were also more likely to meet criteria for a partial PTSD during their lives (9% compared to 4.5%). The NCS also found that women ages 15 to 54 were twice as likely as men (10% vs. 5%) in that age range to develop PTSD at some point during their lives (Kessler et al., 1995).

In a different analysis, Kessler (2000) discovered that a larger percentage of women who were exposed to trauma (20%) developed PTSD than men (8%). Women were significantly more likely to develop PTSD than men if they experienced a sexual assault, a physical attack, a trauma to a loved one, or threat with a weapon. It also appears that women are more likely to be diagnosed with PTSD after experiencing traumatic events than men (Olff et. al., 2007), which could lead to higher lifetime prevalence. Other research suggests that childhood abuse histories are significantly related to PTSD diagnoses for women (Brewin et al., 2000), but not for men in the same way.

According to data from the Trauma Recovery Project, women were more likely to develop prolonged PTSD (lasting for at least 18 months) and had significantly worse quality of life ratings as a result of prolonged PTSD (Holbrook et al., 2002) than men. Additionally, studies indicate that women with PTSD are more likely to have co-occurring mood disorders but less likely to have co-occurring substance use disorders than men (McLean & Anderson, 2009; McLean et al., 2011; Olff et al., 2007).

Women are much more likely to experience intimate partner violence and sexual assault, in both childhood and adulthood, than men (Pratchett et al., 2010). Multiple studies indicate that approximately 20% to 22% of women experience intimate partner violence, while upwards of 25% of all women are victims of sexual assault at some point in their life, compared to 1.4% of men. More than half (51%) of female victims of rape reported the perpetrator as an intimate partner, while 41% reported the perpetrator as an acquaintance; for male victims, more than half (52%) reported being raped by an acquaintance and 15% by a stranger (Black et. al., 2011).

Women more often seek treatment for behavioral health disorders (McLean & Anderson, 2009). Accordingly, women are approximately 34% more likely to seek treatment for PTSD than men (Roberts et al., 2011). Therefore, women are also more likely to be diagnosed with PTSD than men. This could help account for the higher PTSD rates for women in surveys. But there may be other reasons, too. For instance, women experience specific types of trauma with a much higher risk of developing PTSD. That is, because women are more prone to experience rape, sexual assault, and sexual abuse as a child, they may have higher incidences of PTSD. One study found the effects of sexual assault so damaging that 94% of female victims developed PTSD symptoms within the first 2 weeks of the incident (Chivers-Wilson, 2006).

Pratchett et al. (2010) claim that women's cognitive appraisals of trauma may differ from those of men. Hence, interpersonal violence may be perceived as a greater threat to women's core identity. Others have found that the incidence of PTSD is higher in communities that stress traditional gender roles (men having more social power than women) because women in this type of culture feel more emotionally vulnerable (Chivers-Wilson, 2006).

Women may also be affected differently than men by resilience factors, like social support. Research conducted with victims of violent crime found that negative responses (disbelief, defensive response to accusations, etc.) from others can lead to lower-level satisfaction with social support (Pratchett et al., 2010). This reportedly has a greater effect on women than on men. Therefore, women's main coping strategy against stress reactions (social support) can double as a factor that increases susceptibility to PTSD.

Most agree that men and women cope with stress differently (Chivers-Wilson, 2006). A recent study found that instead of a "fight-or-flight" response to stressful or threatening situations, women apparently used a "tend and befriend" strategy. Tending involves taking care of people around them, whereas befriending is the process of reaching out to people around them to find relief from distress. Considering women's reliance on social support during problematic times (e.g., traumatic events), they can be viewed as more vulnerable to experiencing PTSD symptoms if their social network does not give the support they need or if they feel rejected and abandoned (Andrews et al., 2003).

LGBTQA+ AND STRESS RESPONSES

LGBTQA+ people experience trauma at a much higher rate than their hetero-sexual, cisgender, and gender-conforming counterparts (Graziano & Wagner,

2011; McCormick et al., 2018), including bullying (Beckerman & Auerbach, 2014; McCormick et al., 2018) and sexual assault (Cramer et al., 2012; McCormick et al., 2018; Roberts et al., 2010). Balsam et al. (2013) found that LGBTQA+ individuals were significantly more likely than cisgender siblings to report psychological and physical abuse by parents/caretakers during childhood and to report more childhood sexual abuse. This level of victimization places LGBTQA+ persons at a greater risk for depression and PTSD (Mustanski et al., 2016).

Gender-nonconforming youth (youth whose gender expression does not conform to the gender they were assigned at birth) specifically have a greater lifetime risk of PTSD (Kersting et al., 2003; Roberts et al., 2012). Thus, while it is appropriate to incorporate trauma-informed care approaches to avoid retraumatization (i.e., a re-experiencing of the trauma) for any set of clients, this is especially relevant for LGBTQA+ clients.

Additionally, LGBTQA+ clients are at increased risk of experiencing minority stress. Minority stress is the enduring, chronic stress experienced by social minorities in stigmatizing environments due to social attitudes, including experiences of violence and discrimination (Balsam et al., 2013; Eckstrand & Potter, 2017). In an Internet survey of LGBTQA+ adults, approximately 20% reported being the victim of hate crimes involving physical violence or damage to property (Herek, 2009). At present, nearly 25% of all LGBTQA+ persons in the United States are victims of violent crimes each year, with over 30% occurring in a person's home (Roberts et al., 2011).

The same holds true for adolescents. Research conducted with LGBTQA+ youth (ages 15 to 19) found that 80% had experienced verbal victimization, 11% physical victimization, and 8% sexual victimization outside the home because of their sexual orientation or atypical gender behavior. Physical victimization is significantly associated with PTSD (D'Augelli et al., 2006). Research has indicated that the daily, repeated experiences of minority stress result in a higher likelihood of mental illness (Balsam et al., 2013). This being the case, minority stress can also exacerbate or compound any other trauma an LGBTQA+ person faces.

RACIAL, CULTURAL, AND ETHNIC GROUPS

Rates of trauma exposure among some cultural, ethnic, and racial groups are higher than the U.S. average. To what extent this reflects socioeconomic and geographic factors is not clear, as other data indicate that people in urban areas and those with lower incomes are at greater risk for certain types of trauma (Roberts et al., 2011).

Researchers have found that PTSD rates vary considerably among diverse cultures and that rates are high among people exposed to significant trauma, regardless of their culture of origin (Marques et al., 2011). White Americans were significantly more likely to have trauma exposure during their lives compared with members of other ethnic and racial groups, with 84% of White Americans, 76% of African Americans, 66% of Asian Americans, and 68% of Latinos reporting some type of trauma exposure during their lives (Roberts et al., 2011).

However, this did not hold true for every type of trauma. African Americans and Latinos were significantly more likely than White Americans to have been exposed to childhood maltreatment, with the largest difference being the increased likelihood of witnessing domestic violence. African Americans were significantly more likely than White Americans to have been violently assaulted. Asian Americans, who had significantly lower levels of exposure than White Americans to many kinds of trauma, were significantly more likely to have been exposed to war-related trauma (mostly as the result of being unarmed civilians in a combat zone) and to be refugees from a region where combat was occurring.

Among certain subpopulations of major ethnic and racial groups, trauma exposure may be even more common. Goldmann et al. (2011) found that 87% of African Americans in Detroit reported at least one type of trauma during their lives; 51% reported experiencing assaultive violence, 65% reported another type of injury or shocking experience (e.g., witnessing someone being seriously injured or killed), and 64% reported learning about trauma from a loved one.

Of those who reported at least one trauma, 17% likely developed PTSD at some point during their lives, with a higher rate of likely PTSD for individuals experiencing certain types of trauma (e.g., 33% of those who had been raped and 31% of those who had been badly beaten had a lifetime PTSD diagnosis). African American men were significantly more likely than White American men to have PTSD at some point during their lives, but this was not the case for African American women (Roberts, Kitchner, et al., 2010).

Asnaani et al., (2010) found that White Americans and African Americans were more likely than Asian Americans or Latino Americans to have PTSD at some point during their lives. Latino Americans were also significantly more likely than Asian Americans to have the disorder.

Lilly and Graham-Bermann (2009) evaluated PTSD symptoms in 120 mothers with low incomes who were victims of intimate partner violence. The women in the study experienced multiple traumas in the prior year. The authors found that African American women had significantly fewer PTSD symptoms (as assessed with the Posttraumatic Stress Scale for Family Violence) than did the White American women, even though African American women had experienced more severe violence than the White American women.

Research has also found that the relationship of different types of childhood abuse to PTSD symptoms varies by cultural group. For example, emotional abuse in childhood had a significantly stronger relationship to PTSD and other anxiety symptoms for African Americans compared with White Americans, and physical abuse in childhood had a significantly stronger relationship to PTSD and other anxiety symptoms for Latinos than for White Americans (Balsam et al., 2010).

VETERANS

People who have served in the armed forces, in addition to exposure to combat-related trauma, also have high rates of exposure to other types of trauma before, during, and after their service. Veterans have high rates of motor vehicle accidents, especially while driving military vehicles (Bell et al., 2000; Rossen et al., 2011) and of unintentional injuries related to activities such as exercising and training (Jones & Knapik, 1999; Wilkinson et al., 2011).

According to the Veteran's Administration, National Center for PTSD, the number of veterans experiencing PTSD depends on which conflict they participated in. For example:

- **Operations Iraqi Freedom (OIF) and Enduring Freedom (OEF):** About 11 to 20 out of every 100 veterans (11–20%) who served in OIF or OEF have PTSD annually.
- **Gulf War (Desert Storm):** About 12 out of every 100 Gulf War Veterans (or 12%) have PTSD annually.
- **Vietnam War:** About 15 out of every 100 Vietnam Veterans (or 15%) were currently diagnosed with PTSD at the time of the most recent study in the late 1980s, the National Vietnam Veterans Readjustment Study (NVVRS). It is estimated that about 30 out of every 100 (or 30%) of Vietnam Veterans have had PTSD in their lifetime.

More alarming, female veterans report high rates of sexual assault and rape, mostly occurring during their military service. Surveys of female veterans receiving U.S. Department of Veterans Affairs (VA) services reported anywhere between 23% and 28% were victims of sexual assault, including forcible rape, while in the military (Booth et al., 2011; Hankin et al., 1999; Skinner et al., 2000; Sadler et al., 2003). Others, (Suris et al., 2007) found that 33% of female veterans reported a sexual assault while in the military.

Among women who had served in a combat or war zone, rape was most often cited (by 36%) as the worst trauma they had ever experienced, including combat. Kang et al. (2005) interviewed Gulf War veterans with and without current PTSD symptoms and found that sexual trauma (defined as sexual harassment and/or assault) was more common among female veterans who had PTSD than among female veterans who did not. Hence, the authors determined that sexual trauma (either harassment or assault) was associated with greater risk for PTSD than combat exposure. Sexual trauma occurring during a woman's military service more likely results in the development of PTSD than does sexual trauma experienced before or after leaving the military (Himmelfarb et al., 2006).

SPECIFIC TRAUMA DEFINITIONS

Complex Trauma

People experience complex trauma when they have been repeatedly exposed to the same type of trauma or have experienced multiple types of trauma (van der Kolk et al., 1996). People experiencing complex trauma will typically require more intensive and extensive treatment, as well as possible adaptations to standard treatment (Cloitre et al., 2011).

Complex trauma often involves multiple traumatic events (occurring simultaneously or sequentially) and multiple forms of trauma (e.g., experiencing emotional abuse, sexual abuse, and physical abuse). Children who experience complex trauma, for example, those who experience sustained, repeated abuse, typically have significant problems with emotional dysregulation and a lack of healthy coping mechanisms. This increases the risk of being the victim of further traumatic experiences. These issues are seen in both children and adults who experienced complex trauma as children.

Herman (1992) highlighted the inadequacy of existing PTSD diagnostic criteria for people with complex trauma experiences. The author pointed out that standard PTSD diagnostic criteria were based on symptoms experienced by people who had survived relatively time-limited traumatic experiences (e.g., combat veterans, survivors of rape). Herman suggested that many individuals with a history of prolonged and repeated trauma (as opposed to trauma that is time limited or related to a single traumatic event) present with clinical characteristics that "transcend simple PTSD" (p. 379); these characteristics include physical symptoms that may appear more "complex, diffuse, and tenacious" (p. 379). They also present as people whose sense of identity is negatively affected in a way that often inhibits their ability to form relationships with others, and a propensity for vulnerability to further harm, by self or others.

Herman (1992) also proposed changes to the DSM to include a new term for this trauma-related constellation of symptoms, complex posttraumatic stress disorder (complex PTSD). To date, these changes and terminology have not been included in the DSM, including the DSM-5 (APA, 2013). Although some believe (Jackson et al., 2010) that the inclusion of "associated features and disorders" into the DSM-IV (APA, 2000) and now DSM-5 (APA, 2013) covers symptoms of complex PTSD (e.g., problems with affect regulation, impaired relationships), we agree with Herman that complex PTSD should be considered equally important and directly related to multiple traumatic experiences as its own category, given the complexities and difficulties people with complex PTSD symptoms present in behavioral health settings.

Moreover, complex trauma presents with added features, often including additional symptoms and disturbances in their ability to self-regulate beyond those seen in PTSD. These include enhanced difficulties with emotional regulation, difficulties in one's capacity for relationships, problems with attention or consciousness (e.g., dissociative experiences), a disturbed belief system, and/or somatic complaints or disorganization (Briere & Scott, 2012; Cloitre et al., 2011; van der Kolk et al., 1996). Additionally, complex trauma is typically experienced interpersonally and often involves situations where the traumatized person cannot escape from the traumatic experiences because they are constrained physically, socially, or psychologically. The interpersonal issues inherent in complex PTSD will present barriers to practitioners trying to create a safe and trusting therapeutic relationship with clients in treatment.

ACUTE STRESS DISORDER (ASD)

According to the DSM-5 (APA, 2013), acute stress disorder (ASD) involves a traumatic stress reaction within 1 month of trauma exposure. These symptoms must last at least 3 days and include at least nine symptoms from any of the five categories included in the diagnostic criteria, including intrusion, negative mood, dissociation, avoidance, and arousal (APA, 2013).

Specifically, these symptoms may include flashbacks, nightmares, low mood, negative thoughts, detachment from reality (derealization), distancing from oneself and one's experiences (depersonalization), avoidance of anything that might be associated with the trauma, numbing of emotions, feeling on edge and irritable, and possibly experiencing guilt and a sense of shame about what happened during the trauma or about the fact that they are experiencing such distress and can't get over it. A person does not need to exhibit all these symptoms in order to be diagnosed with ASD, and each person's experience and symptoms will be unique. When acute stress symptoms continue, they can significantly impair an individual's ability to function at work, in relationships, socially, and even with their everyday self-care and regular tasks at home.

Although there is significant overlap between the symptoms of ASD and PTSD, what distinguishes ASD and PTSD is the timing of symptoms relative to trauma exposure (Roberts et al., 2010). ASD can, and often does, develop into PTSD if the symptoms extend beyond 1 month. When ignored, ASD can be like an ignored fresh wound on someone's arm that escalates into a serious infection without treatment. ASD should be immediately treated for the best outcome. Although it will not necessarily progress to PTSD, it certainly can without early intervention and treatment (Cardeña & Carlson, 2011).

PTSD DEFINED

PTSD is a traumatic stress reaction that develops in response to a significant trauma. It is classified as a mental health disorder in the DSM-5 (APA, 2013). For clinical professionals, the definition of psychological trauma is tied to the diagnostic criteria for PTSD, which first appeared in the DSM-III (APA, 1980). However, over the years, the diagnostic criteria have undergone significant changes.

According to the Mayo Clinic (2018), PTSD is triggered by a terrifying, or traumatic event or events—either experiencing it or witnessing it. Symptoms of PTSD may include flashbacks, nightmares, and severe anxiety, as well as uncontrollable thoughts about the event.

Many people who go through traumatic events may experience temporary difficulty adjusting and coping, but with time and good self-care they usually get better. However, if their symptoms get worse, last longer than 1 month (see ASD above), and interfere with day-to-day functioning, the person may have developed PTSD. The symptoms of PTSD can last for months and years and may be based on complex and multiple traumas (see above). PTSD symptoms may start within 1 month of a traumatic event, but sometimes will not appear until years after the event. The symptoms cause significant problems in social or work situations and in relationships, and often interfere with a person's ability to perform daily tasks.

PTSD symptoms are generally grouped into four types: intrusive memories, avoidance, negative changes in thinking and mood, and changes in physical and emotional reactions. Symptoms can vary over time and vary from person to person.

Intrusive Memories

Symptoms of intrusive memories may include recurrent, unwanted distressing memories of the traumatic event or events (i.e., reliving the traumatic event as if it were happening again [flashbacks]); upsetting dreams or nightmares about the traumatic event; and/or severe emotional distress or physical reactions to something that reminds them of the traumatic event.

Avoidance

Symptoms of avoidance may include trying to avoid thinking or talking about the traumatic event and/or avoiding places, activities, or people that remind them of the traumatic event.

Negative Changes in Thinking and Mood

Symptoms of negative changes in thinking and mood may include negative thoughts about oneself, other people, or the world; hopelessness about the future; memory problems, including not remembering important aspects of the traumatic event; difficulty maintaining close relationships; feeling detached from family and friends; lack of interest in activities once enjoyed; difficulty experiencing positive emotions; and/or feeling emotionally numb.

Changes in Physical and Emotional Reactions

Symptoms of changes in physical and emotional reactions (also called arousal symptoms) may include being easily startled or frightened; always being on guard for danger; self-destructive behavior, such as drinking too much or driving too fast; trouble sleeping; trouble concentrating; irritability, angry outbursts, or aggressive behavior; and/or overwhelming guilt or shame.

In children 6 years old and younger, signs and symptoms of PTSD may also include re-enacting the traumatic event or aspects of the traumatic event through play and/or frightening dreams that may or may not include aspects of the traumatic event.

Intensity of PTSD Symptoms

PTSD symptoms can vary in intensity over time. These symptoms may increase in intensity when the person is under stress, and especially when they experience any reminder of their traumatic event or events. For example, a combat veteran may relive combat experiences upon hearing a car backfire, or a sexual assault victim may relive aspects of their assault when they see and advertisement on television for sexual assault services or a news report about a sexual assault. The intensity of PTSD symptoms often come and go, depending on the person and the life experiences and the stimuli they encounter each day.

Because people with PTSD may not be aware of their issues with trauma, the likelihood of events triggering traumatic stress reactions in daily life exists. Hence, it is important for practitioners to obtain a complete trauma event history with every client, regardless of the purposes of a clinical visit, intention of a referral, or specific specialty of the practitioner and/or agency. For example, a study by Clark and Power (2005) found that experiencing trauma during a natural disaster can activate, trigger, or complicate symptoms from previous traumatic experiences and/or PTSD.

This was especially true for victims of physical or sexual abuse. Hales et al. (2019), found that gathering a trauma history for all clients helps to "recognize the pervasiveness of trauma and its effects" and "actively avoid re-traumatization" (p. 529). In addition, Muskett (2014) noted the indiscriminate application of coercive practices in inpatient settings. Hence, the simple act of being admitted to an inpatient mental health facility can be traumatic for clients with preexisting histories of trauma, depending on how they are treated by staff. Muskett (2014) reported on a series of earlier Adverse Childhood Experiences (ACE) studies and found that up to 90% of people seeking treatment for serious and enduring personality disorders, substance abuse, and mental illness, such as eating disorders, anxiety, and depressive disorders, and those in contact with the criminal justice system, were exposed to significant emotional, physical and or sexual abuse in childhood.

TRAUMA AND CO-OCCURRING DISORDERS

The SAMHSA (2005) defines co-occurring disorders as the presence of at least one mental health disorder coexisting with at least one substance use disorder, as defined by the DSM-5 (APA, 2013). The presence of co-occurring disorders in behavioral health clients is well known. Studies conducted in substance abuse programs typically report that 50% to 75% of clients have some type of co-occurring mental health disorder. Studies of mental health caseloads reported that 25% to 60% had co-occurring substance use disorders (Johnson, 2004). Related specifically to trauma, substance use disorders are the most common co-occurring disorders with PTSD, followed by mood disorders, various anxiety disorders, eating disorders, and personality disorders (SAMHSA, 2014).

Research suggests that the norm for people with PTSD is to have at least one co-occurring behavioral health disorder; 88% of men and 79% of women with PTSD have at least one other diagnosis, and 59% of men with PTSD and 44% of women have three or more diagnoses (Kessler et al., 1995). Kessler (2000) also presented NCS data indicating that a prior PTSD diagnosis significantly increased the risk of subsequently developing a substance use disorder, major depression, dysthymia, mania, generalized anxiety disorder (GAD), panic disorder, social phobia, simple phobias, and/or agoraphobia.

Moreover, certain types of trauma appear to be associated with increased substance use, regardless of whether use results in a substance use disorder. Survey data from New York indicate that in the 6 months after the 9/11 attack, there was a 30.8% increase in the use of cigarettes, marijuana, and/or alcohol among the general population (Vlahov et al., 2004). Other studies similarly indicate a rise in alcohol consumption, binge drinking, illicit drug use, and/or smoking in communities after natural disasters (Adams & Adams, 1984; Lutz et al., 1995; Office of Applied Studies, 2008).

Data from the Multisite Adult Drug Court Evaluation of inmates who were not incarcerated and used illicit drugs indicated that experiencing a physical or sexual assault was associated with a significant increase substance use in the year following the assault, even after controlling for other factors related to drug use

(Zweig et al., 2012). These authors also found that the relationship between assaultive trauma and PTSD was often mediated by depressive symptoms. Similarly, in a large longitudinal study of violence and women, experiences of physical and/or sexual assault were associated with a significant increase in the likelihood of substance abuse in the following year (Kilpatrick et al., 1997). The use of illicit drugs, but not the abuse of alcohol alone, was also associated with a significant increase in the likelihood of being assaulted in the following year.

The assessment and treatment of clients with co-occurring mental health and substance use disorders presents unique challenges to practitioners compared to clients with either a mental health or substance use disorder alone. Not only do the symptoms of each disorder(s) interact to make assessment and diagnoses difficult at best, but the intensity of each issue also interacts to make treatment retention and success a challenge.

The first step is often the most difficult: to determine if co-occurring substance use and PTSD or other trauma-based disorders exist. This is often difficult because the effects of many drugs mimic a mental health disorder, and vice versa, making it hard to discriminate between PTSD and other traumatic stress reaction and the normal effects of substance use (Johnson, 2004).

Ideally, to accurately assess mental health disorders practitioners need clients to have experienced a period of substance use abstinence of at least a month or more (Flynn & Brown, 2008), some say 90 days is the optimal time for the most accurate results (Johnson, 2004). This period of abstinence allows clinicians to avoid confusing client presenting symptoms with the normal effects of substance use (Hasin et al., 1998; Quello et al., 2005; SAMHSA, 2005). However, practitioners are rarely able to have this clinical luxury.

Knowing whether substance abuse or PTSD came first informs whether a causal relationship exists, but learning this requires thorough assessment of clients and access to complete data on PTSD; substance use, abuse, and dependence; and the onset of each. The relationship between PTSD and substance use disorders is thought to be bidirectional and cyclical: substance use increases trauma risk, and exposure to trauma escalates substance use to manage trauma-related symptoms. Three other causal pathways described by Chilcoat and Breslau (1998) further explain the relationship between PTSD and substance use disorders:

1. The self-medication hypothesis suggests that clients with PTSD use substances to manage PTSD symptoms (e.g., intrusive memories, physical arousal). Substances such as alcohol, cocaine, benzodiazepines, opioids, and amphetamines are frequently used in attempts to relieve or numb emotional pain or to forget an event.

2. The high-risk hypothesis states that substance use places people in high-risk situations that increase their chances of being exposed to events that lead to PTSD.

3. The susceptibility hypothesis suggests that people who use substances are more susceptible to developing PTSD after exposure to trauma than people who do not. Increased vulnerability may result from failure to develop effective stress management strategies, changes in brain chemistry, or damage to neurophysiological systems due to extensive substance use.

Practitioners must be aware that the presence of other disorders, especially substance use disorders, typically worsens and prolongs the course of PTSD and complicates clinical assessment, diagnosis, and treatment. Persons presenting for treatment with substance use and trauma-based co-occurring disorders are more susceptible to relapse (of each condition), exacerbation of the symptoms and behaviors related to each disorder, and that clients with PTSD, and especially complex trauma will often experience more emergencies, have higher risk or new trauma exposure, and more frequent short-term hospitalizations than others (Johnson & Brookhouse, 2020).

Given the prevalence of traumatic events in clients who present for substance abuse treatment, practitioners should assess all substance abuse clients for possible trauma-related disorders. Studies indicate that the patterns of substance use differ between women and men and that histories of trauma often proceed co-occurring disorders for women (McHugo et al., 2005). However, Farro et al. (2011) found an equalization of rates for the risk of PTSD resulting from substance use in men and women. Further, McHugo et al. (2005) reported that women experiencing co-occurring disorders that include trauma usually encounter inappropriate, inadequate, and uncoordinated services in contemporary treatment systems. Hutchison and Bressi (2018) suggest that trauma and its effects, along with substance use, disproportionately affect communities of color and low-income communities. African Americans often face the dual problems of being more likely to experience trauma and co-occurring substance use and less likely to seek services.

Gender-specific studies have indicated the prominence of physical and sexual abuse among women who are substance abusers, upwards of 55% to 99% according to some research (Najavits et al., 1997). A large study called Women, Co-occurring Disorders, and Violence Study (WCDVS) found that 85% of women experienced physical abuse in adulthood and 60% reported childhood sexual abuse. Repeated exposure incidence averaged 16 to 31 times in a lifetime, with an average of four stressful events in the past 6 months (McHugo et al., 2005). The relationship between violence and co-occurring disorders is "multi-directional and complex" and substance use is one way of coping (McHugo et al., 2005, p. 92).

Results of the WCDVS demonstrated that services for women with co-occurring disorders and a history of interpersonal violence are more effective when they are gender specific, trauma informed, and integrated (McHugo et al., 2005). A second report from the WCDVS (Morrissey et al., 2005) concluded that services integrated to include trauma, mental health, and substance abuse treatment had more favorable results with mental health improvement, lessening of substance use problem severity, and a reduction in PTSD symptoms.

For a more in-depth review of the research and best practices related to clinical work with people experiencing co-occurring disorders, including trauma-based reactions, see Johnson and Brookhouse (2020). Also see the book *Substance Use and Mental Health Practice: A Casebook in Co-Occurring Disorders* by Johnson and Grant (2020) as a recommended companion volume to this book.

BEST PRACTICES IN TRAUMA-INFORMED CARE

What Is Trauma-Informed Care?

As a practice perspective, trauma-informed care (TIC) involves treatment approaches and methods that account for a person's trauma history as a significant part of any assessment, treatment planning, and treatment efforts. It promotes the type of environment that does no harm, always striving to ensure that the clinical process does not subject clients to further traumatizing experiences or reactivate past traumatic experiences.

Hence, TIC involves practitioners developing strong, trusting, and safe therapeutic relationships, in the context of being culturally responsive (Johnson, 2004; Johnson & Grant, 2020); understanding the role of violence and abuse; respecting the client's autonomy; emphasizing client strengths; encouraging resilience through positive social support; and avoiding incidences of retraumatization (Hutchison & Bressi, 2018; Johnson & Grant, 2020; McHugo et al., 2005).

The loss of trust, social isolation, re-experiencing trauma through spontaneous memories and flashbacks, avoidance, negative cognitions and mood, and arousal, including hypervigilance, aggression, self-destructive behavior, and insomnia, can make it difficult for practitioners to establish a working professional relationship with trauma-exposed clients. This becomes especially difficult when a client's trauma exposure and symptoms co-occur with substance use disorders, a common occurrence in practice (Johnson, 2004; Johnson & Grant, 2020).

At its core, TIC includes understanding the impact trauma has on individuals and families, with an understanding of the various dimensions of recovery; recognizing the signs and symptoms of trauma in clients and fellow providers; integrating the knowledge of trauma into agency methods, policies, and practices; and continued quality improvement through training and supervision (SAMHSA, 2012). Others propose the need to understand how traumatic experiences negatively affect behavioral health in multiple ways and commit to universal trauma screening and staff education and training regarding trauma and its effects (Farro et al., 2011; Harris & Fallot, 2001; SAMSHA, 2015).

Elliott et al. (2005) conducted a study that identified 10 principles of trauma-informed care. These principles are as follows:

Principle 1: Trauma-informed services recognize the impact of violence and victimization on development and coping strategies.

Principle 2: Trauma-informed services identify recovery from trauma as a primary goal.

Principle 3: Trauma-informed services employ an empowerment model.

Principle 4: Trauma-informed services strive to maximize a client's choices and control over recovery.

Principle 5: Trauma-informed services are based in a relational collaboration.

Principle 6: Trauma-informed services create an atmosphere that is respectful of survivors' need for safety, respect, and acceptance.

Principle 7: Trauma-informed services emphasize client's strengths, highlighting adaptations over symptoms and resilience over pathology.

Principle 8: The goal of trauma-informed services is to minimize the possibilities of retraumatization.

Principle 9: Trauma-informed services strive to be culturally competent and to understand each client in the context of their life experiences and cultural background.

Principle 10: Trauma-informed agencies solicit consumer input and involve consumers in designing and evaluating services.

Najavits (2017) defines TIC as "a treatment in which staff are trained to understand trauma. The goal is compassionate care (no harsh confrontation or coercion) and strong attention to trauma (evaluating all clients for trauma and providing trauma services)" (p.67). Leitch (2017) concluded that by using nonclinical, skills-based approaches, clients and care givers can learn to assess the state of trauma and use practical skills to promote self-regulation and deepen resilience.

In a longitudinal study, Hales et al. (2019) tested five hypotheses surrounding the impact of TIC on organizational climate, procedures, staff and resident satisfaction, and client retention. Results demonstrated that staff members reported an overall increase in a sense of safety, trustworthiness, choice, collaboration and empowerment; moderate changes in policies, procedures, and practices; and an increase in overall staff satisfaction. Clients reported a significant increase in client satisfaction rates at discharge and a significant decrease in unplanned client discharge and/or dropout.

Trauma-informed care is designed for healing. It is not limited to professional mental health settings, but applies to multiple systems and settings, including those in community organizations. Thus, for children and adults, TIC is necessary in residential settings, outpatient settings, schools, foster care, and community-based programs, including community-based clubhouses and other organizations designed to be nonclinical supports.

In an evaluation by Azeem et al. (2011) of a TIC-based adolescent residential treatment program, evaluators considered environmental changes, staff training, and purposeful client–staff partnerships. Azeem et al. (2011) "found that TIC was related to a marked decrease in the use of seclusion and restraints among youth residents" (p. 530). Muskett (2014) also found that "seclusion and restraints are acute catalysts for re-traumatization among both adult and adolescent clients in psychiatric inpatient settings" (p. 530).

Given that clients with mental health problems and significant trauma histories also often abuse substances, including prescription medication, TIC requires cross-system coordination and the working knowledge, values, and skills to help people with co-occurring disorders across different settings and systems of care (i.e., mental health, substance use, child welfare, veterans' services, etc.).

Trauma-Informed Care in Practice

As stated earlier but worth repeating here, TIC involves treatment approaches and methods that account for a person's trauma history as a significant part of any assessment, treatment planning, and intervention planning. It promotes an environment that provides client safety and ensures that clients are not retraumatized (SAMSHA, 2014). TIC-based practitioners understand the impact trauma has on individuals and families by recognizing the signs and symptoms of trauma in clients and fellow providers, understanding of the various dimensions of recovery, and seeking new knowledge and skills to improve practice.

The foundation of TIC rests on practitioners developing therapeutic relationships with clients based on trust, respect, and compassion; respect for client autonomy; an emphasis on client strengths (Hutchison & Bressi, 2018; McHugo et al., 2005); use of existing social support resources; and/or enabling clients to create social support networks to build resilience and provide acceptance and sense of belonging (Johnson & Grant, 2020).

SETTING THE STAGE: BUILDING THE THERAPEUTIC RELATIONSHIP

To remain consistent with the Advanced Multiple Systems (AMS) approach and our Guiding Practice Principles described in Chapter 1, an examination of best practices with clients experiencing trauma begins where all other therapy begins: with solid client engagement.

First, practitioners must focus on build trusting, respectful, and supportive relationships. Successful TIC is built on this foundation. Before treatment models or interventions can work, clients must have an investment in the therapeutic relationship as something they value. Review Chapter 1 on client engagement for details.

Second, practitioners should always keep the First Practice Principle in front of mind. In Chapter 1, we discussed the importance of the First Practice Principle to help clients be successful at developing long-term connections to helpful and supportive systems, including therapists. As a reminder, the First Practice Principle states: *Healthy outcomes (and lives) are directly related to people's connections to helpful, supportive systems, across a lifetime.*

Third, behavioral health professionals must employ culturally respectful approaches, models and methods. See Chapter 1 for the importance and value of being culturally appropriate in all therapeutic contacts.

Fourth, clients with trauma exposure and those with co-occurring disorders must have an accurate and comprehensive assessment that includes a trauma history. Professionals must acquire training in trauma, the impacts of trauma, the signs and symptoms of traumatic stress reactions, substance use, mental health, and different modalities (e.g., group and family therapy) for best-practice treatment to occur. Moreover, an accurate and comprehensive screening and assessment of a client's trauma history and presenting symptoms in the context of their life and possible co-occurring disorders is a must (Johnson & Grant, 2020).

Briere (2002) suggested that all screening and assessment should elicit information about the client's psychological functioning prior to the trauma; the exact nature of the traumatic event(s), including type, duration, frequency, and severity; social and family support available after the trauma; co-occurring behavioral health problems; and posttraumatic response, including PTSD symptoms. In addition, practitioners must assess factors such as the client's current safety level (e.g., is the client at risk for further trauma), current psychological stability (e.g., is client currently experiencing acute psychological distress, limiting their ability for inquiries about traumatic experiences), and the client's readiness for treatment (Briere & Scott, 2012).

Perhaps more than others, people presenting for therapy with trauma histories require that the therapeutic relationship receive special attention. In addition to other aspects of client engagement, there are two critical goals for client engagement with trauma clients: establish client safety and avoid retraumatization (SAMHSA, 2014).

ESTABLISH CLIENT SAFETY

Beyond identifying trauma-related symptoms and collecting additional client data, the initial objective of a TIC-aware practitioner is to establish a relationship and treatment that promotes client safety. Safety is the first goal of treatment. Establishing safety is important early in TIC and is a recurrent need throughout the clinical process. In the context of TIC, safety has several meanings:

1. *Clients must have a sense of safety from trauma symptoms.* Practitioners must learn what factors in the client's daily experience of trauma makes the feel unsafe, even with a therapist. Perhaps they live with recurring intrusive nightmares; painful memories; feelings of sadness, anger, shame, guilt, or being overwhelmed; or feelings of being out of control or dominated. These issues, often outside the immediate control of clients entering treatment, can make daily living seem unsafe. Clients may indicate their lack of safety through statements like, "I can't control my feelings," "I just space out and disconnect for no reason," or, "I'm afraid to go to sleep because of the nightmares." The intense feelings that accompany trauma can also make clients feel unsafe.

   In addition, clients may report feeling fine one moment but suddenly becoming immobilized by depression the next moment. Clients with histories of trauma may experience panicky feelings of being trapped or abandoned. An early effort in trauma treatment is to help clients gain control over their symptoms (and label them as such) by developing new coping skills and learning to stay grounded when flooded with feelings or memories.

2. *Safety in the environment.* A client's environment, either at home, in the community, or in a treatment setting, can have devastating effects on their sense of safety. Trauma reactions can be triggered by sudden loud sounds (e.g., door slamming, raised voices), tension between people, certain smells, a "feeling in the air," or casual touches. Clients can feel vulnerable when discussing their trauma and/or life history in therapy, leading them to an overwhelming sense of physical vulnerability and feeling unsafe.

   Sudden or inadequately explained treatment transitions, like moving from one level of treatment to another or changing therapists, can also evoke feelings of danger, abandonment, or instability. Early in treatment, trauma survivors generally value routine and predictability. Practitioners must recognize their need for structure and predictability and respond appropriately.

3. *Preventing a recurrence of trauma.* People with histories of trauma and co-occurring substance abuse are more likely to engage in high-risk behaviors and experience subsequent traumas. Early treatment must focus on helping clients stop using unsafe coping mechanisms, such as substance abuse, self-harm, and other self-destructive behaviors, and replacing them with safe and healthy coping strategies. These clients will also present and experience more crises and emergencies than others, especially clients with co-occurring trauma and substance use disorders.

To begin planning for these probabilities, always attend to the basics first. That is, attend to your client's most immediate crisis first, before moving into treatment. Look for potential emotional, psychological, or physical issues early in your relationship to ensure your client has their needs met by the appropriate professional. After these issues have been stabilized and addressed, formal treatment planning to address their trauma and other disorders can begin. Think of this as a "practice hierarchy of needs" that encompasses, food, clothing, shelter, health, and safety. Without these issues stabilized, it is difficult to get clients to work on their other issues in good faith.

Early in clinical contact the focus should be on relapse prevention. Relapse, of both trauma reactions and especially substance use, is common and will exacerbate a client's tendency to experience crises and make them susceptible to becoming victims of further traumas. Therefore, practitioners should focus on heading off potential relapses early in treatment. Although this may appear to be a treatment strategy, early focus on relapse prevention is mainly a safety strategy.

As discussed earlier, a substance relapse can have devastating effects on a person with co-occurring disorders, including medication/substance interactions leading to overdoses, exacerbation of traumatic stress reactions, other mental health symptoms, treatment dropout, and increased potential for further trauma. Moreover, practitioners can use the same tactics to discuss potential trauma relapses (i.e., stop taking medications, ignoring newly learned coping skills to manage symptoms, etc.) as they do with substance use relapses. Here is a simple guide to relapse prevention (Johnson, 2004; Johnson & Brookhouse, 2020):

1. *Determine high-risk situations.* Help clients determine what circumstances place them at high-risk for relapse of any kind. This involves identifying triggers in the environment and in the client's way of thinking that begins the process of being overwhelmed and reacting in unsafe ways.

2. *Develop strategies to cope with high-risk situations.* Once identified, clients must develop coping strategies. Group treatment is helpful in this step, as clients can share experiences and strategies in a supportive and helpful manner. However, one can be just as successful during individual therapy, too. Focus on teaching client's alternative ways to handle high-risk situations by giving homework that forces clients to practice these responses.

3. *Social support is critical.* Help clients engage and remain in positive social support networks such as trauma-based support/recovery groups, AA or NA, church, groups of supportive friends, and/or family. Group treatment is helpful in this area; it exposes clients to a new, supportive networks. Family treatment can also be helpful in this regard, depending upon the relationship of a client's family to their past trauma exposure.

4. *Make a discussion about relapse part of treatment.* The goal of relapse prevention is to: (1) keep the amount and duration of the relapse contained;

(2) lengthen the time between relapses; (3) help clients place relapses into a positive context; and (4) retain clients in treatment after relapses occur. To accomplish these goals, it is appropriate to begin discussing the probability of relapse early in treatment, along with efforts to reframe a relapse as a normal and regular part of the recovery process (i.e., two steps forward, one-step back). It is vital that the practitioner not give clients the impression that a relapse signals failure, loss of all that has been gained, or a disappointment to the practitioner or anyone else. If clients come to accept relapses as a normal part of the process, the four goals can be met with minimal damage to the client's sense of self, level of self-efficacy, or physical and emotional safety.

5. *Develop a safety plan.* Work with your clients to identify what steps they can and will take should they find themselves nearing relapse, in a relapse, of in unsafe social situations.

Helping clients learn to protect themselves is a central goal of treatment, often by encouraging the development of a safety plan. SAMHSA (2014) suggests encouraging clients to read *Seeking Safety: A Treatment Manual for PTSD and Substance Abuse* (Najavits, 2002). This menu-based manual covers a variety of treatment topics, including safety.

AVOIDING RETRAUMATIZATION

To help clients feel safe, practitioners must avoid triggering a client's trauma symptoms or using methods or behaving in ways that trigger a client's relapse. Making this more difficult, practitioners can unintentionally trigger retraumatizing reactions by doing their job well. For example, a clinician's empathic questioning about their client's history can seem to the client like the interest shown by a perpetrator many years before. Direct confrontation about behaviors related to substance use can be seen, by someone who has been repeatedly physically assaulted, as provocation building up to assault. Efforts to help clients limit destructive behaviors can be interpreted as efforts to control and dominate. Intrusive shaming or insensitive behavior demonstrated by another client in a group setting can threaten a trauma survivor whose boundaries have been disregarded in the past. Each of these examples, and more, can make treatment feel dangerous, not safe (SAMHSA, 2014).

To minimize the possibility of triggering a trauma reaction during therapy, practitioners should strive to be sensitive to their client's needs, avoiding any behaviors or practices that might trigger memories of the trauma. For example, practitioners should not ignore a client's symptoms or demands when they act out in response to trauma memories; these clients are not "seeking attention." They need the practitioner's attention and should receive it immediately.

Practitioners should never disrespectfully challenge reports of abuse or other traumatic events or discount a client's report of a traumatic event. They should avoid direct confrontation methods of any type in therapy (Johnson, 2004). For sure, they should avoid any unwanted or unapproved physical touch—even the slightest touch can be a trigger. Finally, the practitioner should listen for clues about the client's specific triggers. An important step in client recovery is helping them identify their cues, with a goal of better understanding their reactions and behaviors, all part of relapse prevention methods discussed earlier.

In our practice, we believe that, "Words matter." That is, as a therapist, once a therapeutic relationship develops, our words and how we talk to and about our clients, their problems, and their future, matters deeply. As such, avoid retraumatizing clients with therapeutic talk, negative labeling, by focusing too much on the details of traumatic events before they initiate, and ever saying anything that resembles, "your life would have been so much better had 'X' not happened."

Here we discuss these briefly one at a time:

1. *Avoid focusing on negative labels and descriptions that pathologize clients or make them feel like they are dealing with insurmountable issues.* Instead of focusing on the "disorder" part of their trauma diagnosis and their traumatic experiences, the practitioner should focus on the resilience and strength of survival and endurance. Review the discussion in Chapter 1 about the power of hope, or lack thereof, for a better tomorrow. Without hope, clients will not find the motivation and resilience to endure what can be a difficult road to recovery.

2. *Avoid focusing too much on detailed, gritty descriptions of traumatic events.* Too often, therapists and counselors want or require a detailed account of what happened to clients. Allowing clients to discuss their trauma is important, but not beyond the bounds of where they are comfortable going, on their timeline, not ours.

   Therapy cannot change what happened to people in the past; it can only change the meaning people have attached to the traumatic events, and how those events continue to affect their lives today and in the future. The focus should be on the client's constructed meaning of their traumatic events (e.g., definition of self, others, relationships, family, the world, etc.) rather than on what happened to them in retraumatizing detail. There is a time and place for detail during treatment (e.g., exposure therapy, EMDR, etc.), but getting to that point takes time, preparation, and client safety.

3. What almost all clients want out of life is to believe they have a chance to live a "normal" life, free from their trauma-induced symptoms. This hope, often generated by a therapist or counselor during treatment, can

be the primary foundation for successful recovery. Therefore, the practitioner should avoid initiating any conversation about how "great" or "wonderful" a person's life would have been had something traumatic not happened. The practitioner should be prepared to challenge (gently) this notion when clients mention it, and ensure, as a practitioner, to never say anything like this.

It is impossible to know what someone's life "would have been," because it is speculative. This type of thinking by clients, and these comments, although well-intentioned by practitioners, can destroy a client's hope for a better life. Instead, the key is to help clients know that they are not alone in their struggles. That is, no matter how awful a person's experience with trauma is presently, there are people living happy, productive, and normal lives who have also experienced significant trauma. And, that they, too, with a lot of hard work, can be among that group.

BEST PRACTICE: TREATMENT METHODS

According to the practice and evaluation literature, the most commonly employed treatment methods in TIC for trauma with co-occurring substance use and/or mental health disorders include cognitive behavioral therapy (CBT), trauma-informed cognitive behavioral therapy (TI-CBT), eye movement desensitization and reprocessing (EMDR), and exposure therapy.

Cognitive Behavioral Therapies

Most PTSD, trauma-based, and substance use disorder treatment models include elements of cognitive behavioral therapy (CBT). CBT integrates cognitive and behavioral theories by incorporating two ideas: first, that cognitions (or thoughts) mediate between situational demands and one's attempts to respond to them effectively. Second, that behavioral change influences acceptance of altered cognitions about oneself or a situation and establishment of newly learned cognitive–behavioral interaction patterns.

In practice, CBT explores and teaches a wide range of coping strategies. There are many different varieties of CBT, including those for use with people who abuse substances, people who experience anxiety, people with PTSD or personality disorders, children and adolescents, individuals involved in the criminal justice system, and many others.

CBT also includes various techniques, coping skills, and approaches, such as dialectical behavior therapy (DBT) (Linehan, 1993), Seeking Safety (Najavits, 2002), and mindfulness (Segal et al., 2002). Traditional CBT prioritizes symptom reduction or resolution, but recent CBT approaches also emphasize the quality of the therapeutic relationship, a particularly important dynamic in trauma treatment (Jackson et al., 2009).

CBT has been deemed as effective in the treatment of trauma, and has been widely and effectively used in the treatment of substance use. A full review of efficacy research on CBT for PTSD is provided by Rothbaum et al. (2000), Najavits et al. (2009), and O'Donnell and Cook (2006). Readers are encouraged to review this literature.

McGovern et al. (2009, 2011) reported that CBT was effective in reducing the symptoms of PTSD. In a study of co-occurring disorders and PTSD, McGovern et al. (2011) demonstrated that CBT treatments reduced PTSD symptoms significantly, with 27% of participants measuring positive for PTSD at intake, but only 20% remaining PTSD positive at the 3-month follow-up. According to the authors, this represents a significant reduction in PTSD symptoms when CBT was integrated with traditional substance use therapy (McGovern et al., 2011).

Trauma-informed cognitive behavioral therapy (TI-CBT) is the integration of TIC practices into CBT treatments. Gatz and colleagues (2007) found that women who received TI-CBT through the *Seeking Safety* manual (Najavits, 2002) reported significantly better treatment retention over 3 months and greater improvement on posttraumatic stress symptoms and coping skills. Gatz and colleagues (2007) further found that symptom improvement regarding distress and substance use problem severity were partially mediated by gains in coping skills. Morrissey et al. (2005) found that TI-CBT led to greater improvement on both posttraumatic stress and mental health symptoms for women compared to a non–TI-CBT treatment group.

Cognitive processing therapy (CPT), another offshoot of CBT, is a manualized 12-session treatment approach administered in either a group or individual setting (Resick & Schnicke, 1992, 1993). CPT was developed for rape survivors and combines elements of existing treatments for PTSD, specifically exposure therapy and cognitive therapy. The exposure therapy component consists of clients writing a detailed account of their trauma, including thoughts, sensations, and emotions they experienced during the event. The client then reads the narrative aloud during a session and at home. The cognitive therapy aspect uses six key PTSD themes identified by McCann and Pearlman (1990): safety, trust, power, control, esteem, and intimacy. Clients are guided to identify cognitive distortions in these areas, such as maladaptive beliefs.

Results from efficacy studies for treating PTSD related to interpersonal violence (Resick, 2001; Resick et al., 2002) support the use of CPT. CPT and prolonged exposure therapy models are reported effective in treating PTSD and depression in rape survivors. CPT was also reported superior in reducing guilt (Nishith et al., 2002; Resick et al., 2002, 2003). CPT has shown positive outcomes with refugees when administered in the refugees' native language (Schulz et al., 2006) and with veterans (Monson et al., 2006) for reducing PTSD symptoms. However, CPT has not been studied with PTSD and co-occurring disorders such as substance use, homelessness, current domestic violence, serious and persistent mental illness, or suicidality.

Exposure Therapy

Exposure therapy is just as it sounds. Through organized interventions that consider the risks of retraumatization and concern for client safety, clients are exposed to their trauma, trauma reactions, and feelings as a way of reducing symptoms and the control symptoms have in client's lives. In exposure therapy for PTSD, clients are asked to directly describe and explore trauma-related memories, objects, emotions, or places, verbally, through journals, or in person. These interventions evoke intense emotional responses (e.g., sadness, anxiety, disassociation, etc.), but eventually desensitize clients through repeated encounters with traumatic material. In its simplest form, exposure occurs when clients are asked to describe their traumatic memories in session and is best used when clients are fearful and avoidant of certain people, places, or situations.

It was developed to help people confront their fears and avoidant situations and seems most effective in those narrow circumstances. When people are fearful, they tend to avoid the feared objects, activities, or situations. Although this avoidance might help reduce feelings of fear in the short term, over the long term it can make them even more fearful. In these cases, exposure therapy, when planned and monitored in a safe environment, can help break the pattern of avoidance and fear. Practitioners create a safe environment in which to "expose" individuals to the things they fear and avoid.

The exposure to the feared objects, activities, or situations in a safe environment helps reduce fear and decrease avoidance. Exposure therapy was found to produce significantly larger reductions in avoidance and re-experience of symptoms; tended to be faster at reducing avoidance; and yielded a greater proportion of participants who no longer met criteria for PTSD after treatment (Foa et al., 2005). The effectiveness of exposure therapy has been firmly established (Rothbaum et al., 2000); however, adverse reactions to exposure therapy have also been noted. Some individuals who have experienced trauma exhibit an exacerbation of symptoms during or following exposure treatments.

Careful monitoring of the pace and appropriateness of exposure-based interventions is necessary to prevent retraumatization. Skilled practitioners use grounding techniques, mindfulness techniques, and at-home journaling to help clients manage the often-intense reactions to exposure techniques. During sessions, clients must have ample time to process their memories and integrate cognition and affect, so sessions often last longer than usual, and practitioners are encouraged to allow session to continue until the processing is complete. For simple cases, exposure can work in as few as 9 sessions; more complex cases may require 20 or more sessions (Foa et al., 2007).

Exposure therapy is recommended when the prominent trauma symptoms are intrusive thoughts, flashbacks, or trauma-related fears, panic, and avoidance. However, practitioners should exercise caution when using exposure with clients who have not found mental health symptom stability or maintained abstinence from substance use disorders (SAMHSA, 2014).

Practitioners of exposure therapy need comprehensive training and supervision to master its techniques (Foa et al., 2007); a counselor unskilled in the methods of this treatment model can not only fail to help their clients, but also cause symptoms to worsen. Moreover, routine use of exposure has consistently excluded high-complexity clients such as those with substance dependence, homelessness, current domestic violence, serious and persistent mental illness, or suicidality. The only trial of exposure therapy with a substance dependence sample found that it underperformed standard substance abuse treatment on most variables (Mills et al., 2006).

Eye Movement Desensitization and Reprocessing (EMDR)

EMDR is one of the most widely used therapies for trauma and PTSD (Shapiro, 2001). Over the years, the treatment protocols of EMDR have evolved into sophisticated ideas requiring training and clinical supervision. The goal of this therapy is to process the experiences that are causing problems and distress. EMDR is an integrative treatment model that includes principles from many theoretical perspectives, including psychodynamic, behavioral, cognitive, person centered, and physiological or body centered (Sommers-Flanagan & Sommers-Flanagan, 2015). It has been found to be a "sophisticated and structured approach that has a strong cognitive treatment component" and "helpful in addressing and reducing troubling trauma symptoms in adults and adolescents" (Sommers-Flanagan & Sommers-Flanagan, 2015, p. 485).

EMDR consists of an eight-phase treatment plan. The phases include (1) client history and treatment planning; (2) preparation (client engagement); (3) assessment, which identifies the target memory; (4) desensitization, the action phase that incorporates the target memory and eye movement and other sensory exercises designed to shift the client's focused attention from the memory to the present; (5) installation, in which the therapist attempts to increase positive cognition; (6) body scan; (7) closure, which returns the client to a state of equilibrium; and (8) reevaluation and assessment of further target memories of the client (Menon & Jayan, 2010). EMDR values the development of resource installation (i.e., calming procedures) and engages in exposure work to desensitize clients to traumatic material, using external tracking techniques across the visual field to assist in processing distressing material.

A comparison study conducted by Taylor et al. (2003) examined EMDR, relaxation training, and prolonged exposure therapy. This study found EMDR and relaxation training to be equal in speed and efficacy. It is an effective treatment for PTSD (Seidler & Wagner, 2006) and is accepted as an evidence-based practice by the U.S. Department of Veterans Affairs (VA), the Royal College of Psychiatrists, and the International Society for Traumatic Stress Studies (Najavits, 2007). Numerous clinical reviews support its effectiveness (Mills et al., 2006). Thus far, there is no study examining the use of EMDR with clients in substance abuse treatment or with treatments outside the trauma field.

CONCLUSION

To close, we return to Chapter 1. There, we presented a one-paragraph statement about our Core Beliefs of practice. These beliefs apply to clients suffering from traumatic histories and traumatic stress reactions, alone or in conjunction with co-occurring disorders, including substance use and/or other mental health disorders. Our Core Beliefs, repeated below, encapsulate all we have learned about practice excellence over the decades, across the behavioral health profession.

Core Beliefs

Clients do not change because of models, methods, or interventions alone. They change because they are helped into a trusting and respectful therapeutic relationship based on enhancing their dignity as human beings, have hope they can change for the better, and the motivation to endure the process of change. All of this is accomplished in the context of helpful and supportive systems of support to build personal resilience.

REFERENCES

Adams, P. R., & Adams, G. R. (1984). Mount Saint Helens' ashfall: Evidence for a disaster stress reaction. *American Psychologist, 39,* 252–260.

American Psychiatric Association. (1980). *Diagnostic and statistical manual of mental disorders* (3rd ed.). Author.

American Psychiatric Association. (2000). *Diagnostic and statistical manual of mental disorders* (4th ed.). Author.

American Psychiatric Association. (2013). *Diagnostic and statistical manual of mental disorders* (5th ed.). Author.

Andrews, B., Brewin, C. R., & Rose, S. (2003). Gender, social support, and PTSD in victims of violent crime. *Journal of Traumatic Stress, 16,* 421–427.

Asnaani, A., Richey, J. A., Dimaite, R., Hinton, D. E., & Hofmann, S. G. (2010). A cross-ethnic comparison of lifetime prevalence rates of anxiety disorders. *Journal of Nervous and Mental Disease, 198*, 551–555.

Azeem, M. W., Aujla, A., Rammerth, M., Binsfeld, G., & Jones, R. B. (2011). Effectiveness of six core strategies based on trauma informed care in reducing seclusions and restraints at a child and adolescent psychiatric hospital. *Journal of Child and Adolescent Psychiatric Nursing, 24*(1), 11–15.

Balsam, K., Beadnell, B., & Molina, Y. (2013). The daily heterosexist experiences questionnaire. *Measurement and Evaluation in Counseling and Development, 46*(1), 3–25.

Balsam, K. F., Lehavot, K., Beadnell, B., & Circo, E. (2010). Childhood abuse and mental health indicators among ethnically diverse lesbian, gay, and bisexual adults. *Journal of Consulting and Clinical Psychology, 78*, 459–468.

Basham, K. (2016). *Inside out and outside in* (4th ed). Rowan & Littlefield.

Beckerman, N. L., & Auerbach, C. (2014). PTSD as aftermath for bullied LGBT adolescents: The case for comprehensive assessment. *Social Work in Mental Health, 12*(3), 195–211.

Bell, N. S., Amoroso, P. J., Yore, M. M., Smith, G. S., & Jones, B. H. (2000). Self-reported risk-taking behaviors and hospitalization for motor vehicle injury among active duty army personnel. *American Journal of Preventive Medicine, 18*, 85–95.

Black, M. C., Basile, K. C., Breiding, M. J., Smith, S. G., Walters, M. L., Merrick, M. T., Chen, J., & Stevens, M. R. (2011). *The National Intimate Partner and Sexual Violence Survey: 2010 summary report.* Centers for Disease Control and Prevention. Available from: https://www.cdc.gov/violenceprevention/pdf/NISVS_Report2010-a.pdf

Bloom, S. L., & Farragher, B. (2011). *Destroying sanctuary: The crisis in human service delivery systems.* Oxford University Press.

Booth, B. M., Mengeling, M., Torner, J., & Sadler, A. G. (2011). Rape, sex partnership, and substance use consequences in women veterans. *Journal of Traumatic Stress, 24*, 287–294.

Brewin, C. R., Andrews, B., & Valentine, J. D. (2000). Meta-analysis of risk factors for posttraumatic stress disorder in trauma-exposed adults. *Journal of Consulting and Clinical Psychology, 68*, 748–766.

Briere, J. (2002). *Detailed assessment of posttraumatic stress: Professional manual.* Psychological Assessment Resources.

Briere, J., & Scott, C. (2012). *Principles of trauma therapy: A guide to symptoms, evaluation, and treatment* (2nd ed.). Sage.

Cardeña, E., & Carlson, E. (2011). Acute stress disorder revisited. *Annual Review of Clinical Psychology, 7*, 245–267.

Chilcoat, H. D. & Breslau, N. (1998). Investigations of causal pathways between PTSD and drug use disorders. *Addictive Behaviors, 23*, 827–840.

Chivers-Wilson, K. A. (2006). Sexual assault and posttraumatic stress disorder: A review of the biological and sociological factors and treatments. *McGill Journal of Medicine*, 9(2), 111–118.

Clark, H. W., & Power, A. K. (2005). Women, co-occurring disorders, and violence study: A case for trauma-informed care. *Journal of Substance Abuse Treatment*, 28(2), 145–146.

Cloitre, M., Courtois, C. A., Charuvastra, A., Carapezza, R., Stolbach, B. C., & Green, B. L. (2011). Treatment of complex PTSD: Results of the ISTSS expert clinician survey on best practices. *Journal of Traumatic Stress*, 24(6), 615–627.

Cramer, R. J., McNiel, D. E., Holley, S. R., Shumway, M., & Boccellari, A. (2012). Mental health in violent crime victims: Does sexual orientation matter? *Law and Human Behavior*, 36(2), 87.

D'Augelli, A. R., Grossman, A. H., & Starks, M. T. (2006). Childhood gender atypicality, victimization, and PTSD among lesbian, gay, and bisexual youth. *Journal of Interpersonal Violence*, 21, 1462–1482.

Eckstrand, K. L., & Potter, J. (2017). *Trauma, resilience, and health promotion in LGBT patients: What every healthcare provider should know.* Springer International.

El-Gabalawy, R. (2012). *Association between traumatic experiences and physical health conditions in a nationally representative sample.* Anxiety and Depression Association of America

Farro, S. A., Clark, C., & Hopkins Eyles, C. (2011). Assessing trauma-informed care readiness in behavioral health: An organizational case study. *Journal of Dual Diagnosis*, 7(4), 228–241.

Flynn, P. M., & Brown, B. S. (2008). Co-occurring disorders in substance abuse treatment: Issues and prospects. *Substance Abuse Treatment*, 34(1), 36–47.

Foa, E. B., Hembree, E. A., Cahill, S. P., Rauch, S. A., Riggs, D. S., Feeny, N. C., & Yadin, E. (2005). Randomized trial of prolonged exposure for posttraumatic stress disorder with and without cognitive restructuring: Outcome at academic and community clinics. *Journal of Consulting and Clinical Psychology*, 73, 953–964.

Foa, E. B., Hembree, E. A., & Rothbaum, B. O. (2007). *Prolonged exposure therapy for PTSD: Emotional processing of traumatic experiences: Therapist guide.* Oxford University Press.

Gatz, M., Brown, V., Hennigan, K., Rechberger, E., O'Keefe, M., Rose, T., & Bjelajac, P. (2007). Effectiveness of an integrated, trauma-informed approach to treating women with co-occurring disorders and histories of trauma: The Los Angeles site experience. *Journal of Community Psychology*, 35(7), 863–878.

Goldmann, E., Aiello, A., Uddin, M., Delva, J., Koenen, K., Gant, L. M., & Galea, S. (2011). Pervasive exposure to violence and posttraumatic stress disorder in a predominantly African American Urban Community: The Detroit Neighborhood Health Study. *Journal of Traumatic Stress*, 24(6), 747–751.

Graziano, J. N., & Wagner, E. F. (2011). Trauma among lesbians and bisexual girls in the juvenile justice system. *Traumatology, 17*(2), 45–55.

Hales, T. W., Green, S. A., Bissonette, S., Warden, A., Diebold, J., Koury, S. P., & Nochajski, T. H. (2019). Trauma-informed care outcome study. *Research on Social Work Practice, 29*(5), 529–539.

Hankin, C. S., Skinner, K. M., Sullivan, L. M., Miller, D. R., Frayne, S., & Tripp, T. J. (1999). Prevalence of depressive and alcohol abuse symptoms among women VA outpatients who report experiencing sexual assault while in the military. *Journal of Traumatic Stress, 12,* 601–612.

Harris, M. & Fallot, R. D. (2001). Designing trauma-informed addictions services. In M. Harris & R. D. Fallot (Eds.), *Using trauma theory to design service systems* (pp. 57–73). Jossey-Bass.

Hasin, D., Trautman, K., & Endicott, J. (1998). Psychiatric research interview for substance and mental disorders: Phenomenologically based diagnosis in patients who abuse alcohol or drugs. *Psychopharmacology Bulletin, 34,* 3–8.

Herek, G. M. (2009). Hate crimes and stigma-related experiences among sexual minority adults in the United States: Prevalence estimates from a national probability sample. *Journal of Interpersonal Violence, 24,* 54–74.

Herman, J. L. (1992). *Trauma and recovery.* Basic Books.

Himmelfarb, N., Yaeger, D., & Mintz, J. (2006). Posttraumatic stress disorder in female veterans with military and civilian sexual trauma. *Journal of Traumatic Stress, 19,* 837–846.

Hodas, G. R. (2006). *Responding to childhood trauma: The promise of trauma informed care.* Pennsylvania Office of Mental Health and Substance Abuse Services.

Holbrook, T. L., Hoyt, D. B., Stein, M. B., & Sieber, W. J. (2002). Gender differences in long-term posttraumatic stress disorder outcomes after major trauma: Women are at higher risk of adverse outcomes than men. *Journal of Trauma, 53,* 882–888.

Horowitz, M. J. (1989). Posttraumatic stress disorder. In American Psychiatric Association Task Force on Treatments of Psychiatric Disorders (Ed.), *Treatments of psychiatric disorders: A task force report of the American Psychiatric Association* (pp. 2065–2082). American Psychiatric Association.

Hutchison, C. A., & Bressi, S. K. (2018). MDMA-assisted psychotherapy for posttraumatic stress disorder: Implications for social work practice and research. *Clinical Social Work Journal,* 1–10.

Jackson, C., Nissenson, K., & Cloitre, M. (2009). Cognitive–behavioral therapy. In C. A. Courtois (Ed.), *Treating complex traumatic stress disorders: An evidence-based guide* (pp. 243–263). Guilford Press.

Jackson, C., Nissenson, K., & Cloitre, M. (2010). Treatment for complex PTSD. In D. Sookman (Ed.), *Treatment resistant anxiety disorders: Resolving impasses to symptom remission* (pp. 75–104). Routledge/Taylor & Francis Group.

Johnson, J. L. (2004). *Fundamentals of substance abuse practice*. Wadsworth/Brooks Cole.

Johnson, J. L., & Brookhouse, G. (2020). Co-occurring disorders treatment: Best practices. In J. L. Johnson & G. Grant Jr. (eds.), *Substance abuse and mental health practice: A casebook on co-occurring disorders*. Cognella.

Johnson, J. L., & Grant, G. Jr. (2020). A multiple systems approach to practice with co-occurring disorders. In, J. L. Johnson & G. Grant Jr. (Eds.), *Substance abuse and mental health practice: A casebook on co-occurring disorders*. Cognella.

Jones, B. H., & Knapik, J. J. (1999). Physical training and exercise–related injuries. Surveillance, research and injury prevention in military populations. *Sports Medicine, 27*, 111–125.

Kang, H., Dalager, N., Mahan, C., & Ishii, E. (2005). The role of sexual assault on the risk of PTSD among Gulf War veterans. *Annals of Epidemiology, 15*, 191–195.

Kersting, A., Reutemann, M., Gast, U., Ohrmann, P., Suslow, T., Michael, N., & Arolt, V. (2003). Dissociative disorders and traumatic childhood experiences in transsexuals. *Journal of Nervous and Mental Disease, 191*, 182–189.

Kessler, R. C. (2000). Posttraumatic stress disorder: The burden to the individual and to society. *Journal of Clinical Psychiatry, 61* (Supplement 5), 4–12.

Kessler, R. C., Berglund, P., Demler, O., Jin, R., Merikangas, K. R., & Walters, E. E. (2005). Lifetime prevalence and age-of-onset distributions of DSM-IV disorders in the National Comorbidity Survey Replication. *Archives of General Psychiatry, 62*, 593–602.

Kessler, R. C., Sonnega, A., Bromet, E., Hughes, M., & Nelson, C. B. (1995). Posttraumatic stress disorder in the National Comorbidity Survey. *Archives of General Psychiatry, 52*, 1048–1060.

Kessler, R. C., Sonnega, A., Bromet, E., Hughes, M., Nelson, C. B., & Breslau, N. N. (1999). Epidemiological risk factors for trauma and PTSD. In R. Yehuda (Ed.), *Risk Factors for PTSD* (pp. 23–59). American Psychiatric Press.

Kilpatrick, D. G., Acierno, R., Resnick, H. S., Saunders, B. E., & Best, C. L. (1997). A 2-year longitudinal analysis of the relationships between violent assault and substance use in women. *Journal of Consulting and Clinical Psychology, 65*, 834–847.

Leitch, L. (2017). Action steps using ACEs and trauma-informed care: A resilience model. *Health & Justice, 5*(1), 5–10.

Lilly, M. M., & Graham-Bermann, S. A. (2009). Ethnicity and risk for symptoms of posttraumatic stress following intimate partner violence. *Journal of Interpersonal Violence, 24*, 3–19.

Linehan, M. M. (1993). Dialectical behavior therapy for treatment of borderline personality disorder: Implications for the treatment of substance abuse. In L. S. Onken, J. D. Blaine, & J. J. Boren (Eds.), *Behavioral treatments for drug abuse and dependence* (pp. 201–216). National Institute on Drug Abuse.

Lutz, G. M., Kramer, R. E., Gonnerman, M. E., Lantz, G. L., & Downs, W. R. (1995). *Substance abuse and the Iowa flood disaster of 1993: Final report.* University of Northern Iowa.

Marques, L., Robinaugh, D. J., LeBlanc, N. J., & Hinton, D. (2011). Cross-cultural variations in the prevalence and presentation of anxiety disorders. *Expert Review of Neurotherapeutics, 11,* 313–322.

Mayo Clinic. (2018). What Is Post Traumatic Stress Disorder? (PTSD). Retrieved from: https://www.mayoclinic.org/diseases-conditions/post-traumatic-stress-disorder/symptoms-causes/syc-20355967

McCann, L. & Pearlman, L. A. (1990). Vicarious traumatization: A framework for understanding the psychological effects of working with victims. *Journal of Traumatic Stress, 3,* 1.

McCormick, A., Scheyd, K., & Terrazas, S. (2018). Trauma-informed care and LGBTQ youth: Considerations for advancing practice with youth with trauma experiences. *Families in Society: The Journal of Contemporary Social Services, 99*(2), 160–169.

McGovern, M. P., Lambert-Harris, C., Acquilano, S., Xie, H., Alterman, A. I., & Weiss, R. D. (2009). A cognitive behavioral therapy for co-occurring substance use and posttraumatic stress disorders. *Addictive Behaviors, 34*(10), 892–897.

McGovern, M. P., Lambert-Harris, C., Alterman, A. I., Xie, H., & Meier, A. (2011). A randomized controlled trial comparing integrated cognitive behavioral therapy versus individual addiction counseling for co-occurring substance use and posttraumatic stress disorders. *Journal of Dual Diagnosis, 7*(4), 207–227.

McHugo, G. J., Kammerer, N., Jackson, E. W., Markoff, L. S., Gatz, M., Larson, M. J., Mazelis, R., & Hennigan, K. (2005). Women, co-occurring disorders, and violence study: Evaluation design and study population. *Journal of Substance Abuse Treatment, 28*(2), 91–107.

McLean, C. P., & Anderson, E. R. (2009). Brave men and timid women? A review of the gender differences in fear and anxiety. *Clinical Psychology Review, 29,* 496–505.

McLean, C. P., Asnaani, A., Litz, B. T., & Hofmann, S. G. (2011). Gender differences in anxiety disorders: Prevalence, course of illness, comorbidity and burden of illness. *Journal of Psychiatric Research, 45,* 1027–1035.

Menon, S. B., & Jayan, C. (2010). Eye movement desensitization and reprocessing: A conceptual framework. *Indian Journal of Psychological Medicine, 32*(2), 136–140.

Mills, K. L., Teesson, M., Ross, J., & Peters, L. (2006). Trauma, PTSD, and substance use disorders: Findings from the Australian National Survey of Mental Health and Well-Being. *American Journal of Psychiatry, 163,* 652–658.

Monson, C. M., Schnurr, P. P., Resick, P. A., Friedman, M. J., Young-Xu, Y., & Stevens, S. P. (2006). Cognitive processing therapy for veterans with military-related posttraumatic stress disorder. *Journal of Consulting and Clinical Psychology, 74,* 898–907.

Morrissey, J. P., Ellis, A. R., Gatz, M., Amaro, H., Reed, B. G., Savage, A., Finkelstein, N., Mazelis, Ru., Brown, V., Jackson, E. W., & Banks, S. (2005). Outcomes for women with co-occurring disorders and trauma: Program and person-level effects. *Journal of Substance Abuse Treatment, 28*(2), 121–133.

Muskett, C. (2014). Trauma-informed care in inpatient mental health settings: A review of the literature. *International Journal of Mental Health Nursing, 23*(1), 51–59.

Mustanski, B., Andrews, R., & Puckett, J. (2016). The effects of cumulative victimization on mental health among lesbian, gay, bisexual, and transgender adolescents and young adults. *American Journal of Public Health, 106*(3), 527.

Najavits, L. M. (2002). *Seeking safety: A treatment manual for PTSD and substance abuse.* Guilford Press.

Najavits, L. M. (2017). *Recovery from Trauma, Addiction, or Both.* Guilford Press.

Najavits, L. M., Ryngala, D., Back, S. E., Bolton, E., Mueser, K. T., & Brady, K. T. (2009). Treatment of PTSD and comorbid disorders. In E. B. Foa, T. M. Keane, M. J. Friedman, & J. A. Cohen (Eds.), *Effective treatments for PTSD: Practice guidelines from the International Society for Traumatic Stress Studies* (2nd ed., pp. 508–535). Guilford Press.

Najavits, L. M., Weiss, R. D., & Shaw, S. R. (1997). The link between substance abuse and posttraumatic stress disorder in women: A research review. *American Journal on Addictions, 6*(4), 273–283.

National Child Traumatic Stress Network & National Center for PTSD. (2006). *Psychological first aid: Field operations guide.* National Center for PTSD.

Nishith, P., Resick, P. A., & Griffin, M. G. (2002). Pattern of change in prolonged exposure and cognitive–processing therapy for female rape victims with posttraumatic stress disorder. *Journal of Consulting and Clinical Psychology, 70*, 880–886.

O'Donnell, C. & Cook, J. M. (2006). Cognitive–behavioral therapies for psychological trauma and comorbid substance use disorders. In B. Carruth (Ed.), *Psychological trauma and addiction treatment.* Haworth Press.

Office of Applied Studies. (2002). *Results from the 2001 National Household Survey on Drug Abuse: Vol.1. Summary of national findings.* Rep. No. HHS Publication No. (SMA) 02-3758. Substance Abuse and Mental Health Services Administration.

Olff, M., Langeland, W., Draijer, N., & Gersons, B. P. R. (2007). Gender differences in posttraumatic stress disorder. *Psychological Bulletin, 133*, 183–204.

Pietrzak, R. H., Goldstein, R. B., Southwick, S. M., & Grant, B. F. (2011). Personality disorders associated with full and partial posttraumatic stress disorder in the U.S. population: Results from Wave 2 of the National Epidemiologic Survey on Alcohol and Related Conditions. *Journal of Psychiatric Research, 45*, 678–686.

Pratchett, L. C., Pelcovitz, M. R., & Yehuda, R. (2010). Trauma and violence: Are women the weaker sex? *Psychiatric Clinics of North America, 33*, 465–474.

Quello, S. B., Brady, K. T., Sonne, S. C. (2005). Mood disorders and substance use disorders: A complex comorbidity. *Science and Practice Perspectives, 5*(3), 13–24.

Resick, P. A. (2001). Cognitive therapy for posttraumatic stress disorder. *Journal of Cognitive Psychotherapy: An International Quarterly, 15*, 321–329.

Resick, P. A., Galovski, T. E., O'Brien, U. M., Scher, C. D., Clum, G. A., & Young-Xu, Y. (2008). A randomized clinical trial to dismantle components of cognitive processing therapy for posttraumatic stress disorder in female victims of interpersonal violence. *Journal of Consulting and Clinical Psychology, 76,* 243–258.

Resick, P. A., Nishith, P., & Griffin, M. G. (2003). How well does cognitive–behavioral therapy treat symptoms of complex PTSD? An examination of child sexual abuse survivors within a clinical trial. *CNS Spectrums, 8,* 340–355.

Resick, P. A., Nishith, P., Weaver, T. L., Astin, M. C., & Feuer, C. A. (2002). A comparison of cognitive-processing therapy with prolonged exposure and a waiting condition for the treatment of chronic posttraumatic stress disorder in female rape victims. *Journal of Consulting & Clinical Psychology, 70,* 867–879.

Resick, P. A., & Schnicke, M. K. (1992). Cognitive processing therapy for sexual assault victims. *Journal of Consulting and Clinical Psychology, 60,* 748–756.

Resick, P. A., & Schnicke, M. K. (1993). *Cognitive processing therapy for rape victims: A treatment manual.* Sage Publications.

Roberts, A., Rosario, M., Corliss, H., Koenen, K. & Austin, S. (2012). Childhood gender nonconformity: A risk indicator for childhood abuse and posttraumatic stress in youth. *Pediatrics, 129*(3), 410.

Roberts, N. P., Kitchiner, N. J., Kenardy, J., & Bisson, J. I. (2010). Early psychological interventions to treat acute traumatic stress symptoms. *Cochrane Database of Systematic Reviews,* CD007944.

Roberts, A. L., Austin, S. B., Corliss, H. L., Vandermorris, A. K., & Koenen, K. C. (2010). Pervasive trauma exposure among US sexual orientation minority adults and risk of posttraumatic stress disorder. *American Journal of Public Health, 100,* 2433–2441.

Roberts, A. L., Gilman, S. E., Breslau, J., Breslau, N., & Koenen, K. C. (2011). Race/ethnic differences in exposure to traumatic events, development of post-traumatic stress disorder, and treatment-seeking for post-traumatic stress disorder in the United States. *Psychological Medicine: A Journal of Research in Psychiatry and the Allied Sciences, 41,* 71–83.

Rossen, L. M., Pollack, K. M., Canham-Chervak, M., Canada, S., & Baker, S. P. (2011). Motor vehicle crashes among active duty U.S. Army personnel, 1999 to 2006. *Military Medicine, 176,* 1019–1026.

Rothbaum, B. O., Meadows, E. A., Resick, P., & Foy, D. W. (2000). Cognitive–behavioral therapy. In E. B. Foa & T. M. Keane (Eds.), *Effective treatments for PTSD: Practice guidelines from the International Society for Traumatic Stress Studies* (pp. 60–83). Guilford Press.

Sadler, A. G., Booth, B. M., Cook, B. L., & Doebbeling, B. N. (2003). Factors associated with women's risk of rape in the military environment. *American Journal of Industrial Medicine, 43,* 262–273.

Schulz, P. M., Marovic-Johnson, D., & Huber, L. C. (2006). Cognitive–behavioral treatment of rape- and war-related posttraumatic stress disorder with a female, Bosnian refugee. *Clinical Case Studies, 5*, 191–208.

Scott, J. C. (1990). *Domination and the arts of resistance: Hidden transcripts.* Yale University Press.

Segal, Z. V., Williams, J. M. G., & Teasdale, J. D. (2002). Mindfulness-based cognitive therapy for depression: A new approach to preventing relapse. Guilford Press.

Seidler, G. H. & Wagner, F. E. (2006). Comparing the efficacy of EMDR and trauma-focused cognitive-behavioral therapy in the treatment of PTSD: A meta-analytic study. *Psychological Medicine*, 36, 1515–1522.

Shapiro, F. (2001). Eye movement desensitization and reprocessing (EMDR): Basic principles, protocols, and procedures (2nd ed.). Guilford Press.

Skinner, K. M., Kressin, N., Frayne, S., Tripp, T. J., Hankin, C. S., Miller, D. R., & Sullivan, L. M. (2000). The prevalence of military sexual assault among female Veterans' Administration outpatients. *Journal of Interpersonal Violence, 15*, 291–310.

Sommers-Flanagan, J., & Sommers-Flanagan, R. (2015). *Counseling and psychotherapy: Theories in context and practice* (2nd ed.). John Wiley & Sons.

Substance Abuse and Mental Health Services Administration (SAMHSA). (2005). Substance abuse treatment for persons with co-occurring disorders. Treatment Improvement Protocol (TIP) Series 42. U.S. Department of Health and Human Services.

Substance Abuse and Mental Health Services Administration (SAMHSA). (2012). *SAMHSA's working definition of trauma and guidance for trauma-informed approach.* Author.

Substance Abuse and Mental Health Services Administration (SAMHSA). (2014). *Trauma-informed care in behavioral health services.* Treatment Improvement Protocol (TIP) Series 57. HHS Publication No. (SMA) 13-4801. Author.

Substance Abuse and Mental Health Services Administration (SAMHSA). (2015) Trauma-informed approach and trauma-specific interventions. Retrieved from: https://www.samhsa.gov/nctic/trauma-interventions

Suris, A., Lind, L., Kashner, T. M., & Borman, P. D. (2007). Mental health, quality of life, and health functioning in women veterans: Differential outcomes associated with military and civilian sexual assault. *Journal of Interpersonal Violence, 22,* 179–197.

Taylor, S., Thordarson, D. S., Maxfield, L., Fedoroff, I. C., Lovell, K., & Ogrodniczuk, J. (2003). Comparative efficacy, speed, and adverse effects of three PTSD treatments: Exposure therapy, EMDR, and relaxation training. *Journal of Consulting and Clinical Psychology, 71*(2), 330–338.

Terr, L. (1999). Childhood trauma: An outline and overview. *American Journal of Orthopsychiatry, 148*, 10–20.

Turnbull, G. J. (1998). A review of post-traumatic stress disorder; part I: Historical development and classification. *Injury, 29*, 87–91.

U.S. Department of Veterans Affairs, National Center for PTSD. (n.d.). How common is PTSD in veterans? https://www.ptsd.va.gov/understand/common/common_veterans.asp

van der Kolk, B. A., McFarlane, A. C., & Weisaeth, L. (1996). *Traumatic stress: The effects of overwhelming experience on mind, body, and society.* Guilford Press.

Vlahov, D., Galea, S., Ahern, J., Resnick, H., & Kilpatrick, D. (2004). Sustained increased consumption of cigarettes, alcohol, and marijuana Among Manhattan residents after September 11, 2001. *American Journal of Public Health, 94*, 253–254.

Wilkinson, D. M., Blacker, S. D., Richmond, V. L., Horner, F. E., Rayson, M. P., Spiess, A., & Knapik, J. J. (2011). Injuries and injury risk factors among British army infantry soldiers during predeployment training. *Injury Prevention, 17*, 381–387.

Zweig, J. M., Yahner, J., & Rossman, S. B. (2012). Does recent physical and sexual victimization affect further substance use for adult drug-involved offenders? *Journal of Interpersonal Violence, 27*(12), 2348–2372.

ABOUT THE EDITORS

Jerry L. Johnson, PhD, MSW is an associate professor in the School of Social Work at Grand Valley State University in Grand Rapids, Michigan. He received his MSW from Grand Valley State University and his PhD in sociology from Western Michigan University. Johnson has been in the human services field since 1983, serving as a family therapist, clinical supervisor, administrator, consultant, teacher, trainer, and author. He was the recipient of two Fulbright Scholarship awards to Albania in 1998–1999 and 2000–2001. In addition to teaching and writing, Johnson serves in various consulting capacities in countries such as Albania, Armenia, and China.

He is the author of two previous books, *Crossing Borders—Confronting History: Intercultural Adjustment in a Post-Cold War World* (2000, Rowan and Littlefield) and *Fundamentals of Substance Abuse Practice* (2004, Wadsworth Brooks/Cole).

George Grant, Jr., PhD, LMSW is the dean of the College of Community and Public Service and a professor in the School of Social Work at Grand Valley State University in Grand Rapids, Michigan. He received his BSW from Marygrove College, his MSW from Grand Valley State University, and his PhD in sociology from Western Michigan University. Grant is a professor, administrator, evaluator, practitioner, and consultant and is committed to community engagement, primarily in the field of child welfare.

Drs. Johnson and Grant are the editors of a previous eight-volume casebook series, including: *Substance Abuse* (2005), *Mental Health* (2005), *Foster Care* (2005), *Adoption* (2005), *Domestic Violence* (2005), *Community Practice* (2005), *Medical Social Work* (2005), and *Sexual Abuse* (2007).

ABOUT THE AUTHORS

Dianne Green-Smith, PhD, LMSW, ACSW is a professor in the School of Social Work at Grand Valley State University (GVSU) in Grand Rapids, Michigan. In the recent past, at GVSU Green-Smith served as department head and MSW director. Currently, she serves as the lead instructor in clinical diagnosis and treatment planning. Green-Smith received her BA degree in sociology and social work from Xavier University in New Orleans, her MSW from the Tulane University School of Social Work, and her PhD in social work from the Loyola University School of Social Work in Chicago. She is a peer reviewer for *The Journal of HIV/AIDS and Social Services*. She is the founder and director of a community nonprofit, AIDS Inc., providing forums on healthy relationships and self-esteem.

Ash Herald, LLMSW holds a bachelor's degree in biomedical sciences and a master's degree in social work from Grand Valley State University. Herald has served in several community and political advocacy roles. They currently live in Philadelphia with their spouse.

Elizabeth A. Sharda, PhD, LMSW is an assistant professor of social work at Hope College in Holland, Michigan. She completed her MSW at Grand Valley State University and her PhD at Michigan State University's School of Social Work, where her dissertation research focused on social support among foster parents. Elizabeth held a variety of positions in the child welfare field for 13 years prior to entering academia and has been a licensed foster parent since 2008.

Melissa Villarreal, PhD, LMSW is an assistant professor in the School of Social Work at Grand Valley State University. She has over 20 years of experience as a clinical practitioner, teacher, supervisor, and advocate. Villarreal is a research and evaluation consultant for a National Science Foundation grant. Prior to her time at GVSU, Dr. Villarreal was a faculty specialist at Western Michigan University and was the director of field education for Hope College's Bachelor of Social Work Program for over 10 years. Villarreal has worked as a child and family therapist, domestic violence and sexual assault therapist, probation officer for adolescents, child guidance worker for a juvenile home, outreach clinician for status offenders, and as a clinical case manager for teen parents.

Salvador Lopez-Arias, PhD is an associate professor in the School of Social Work at Grand Valley State University. He received a PhD in counseling psychology from Western Michigan University and his MSW from Grand Valley State University. Lopez-Arias has been a practitioner for 28 years with a broad focus. His clinical work has focused on culturally competent practice in co-occurring disorders, trauma, family therapy, and holistic health, with an emphasis in substance use disorders. He is also involved in the areas of community engagement, evaluation, and research.

Glen A. Brookhouse, LLMSW is a graduate of Grand Valley State University. Beginning in 2015, he focused his social work studies in the area of homelessness and substance use disorders. Since that time, he has been employed as a counselor and advocate for homeless individuals. He completed his graduate studies as a recovery management substance abuse therapist at the Family Outreach Center in Grand Rapids Michigan. His position has given him the opportunity to provide substance use disorder services to individuals experiencing poverty and homelessness.

Lightning Source UK Ltd.
Milton Keynes UK
UKHW032005280721
387925UK00008B/1701